Disasters and the Networked Economy

Mainstream quantitative analysis and simulations are fraught with difficulties and are intrinsically unable to deal appropriately with long-term macroeconomic effects of disasters. In this new book, J.M. Albala-Bertrand develops the themes introduced in his book *The Political Economy of Large Natural Disasters* (Clarendon Press, 1993), to show that societal networking and disaster localization constitute part of an essential framework to understand disaster effects and responses.

The author's previous book argued that disasters were a problem *of* development, rather than a problem *for* development. This volume takes the argument forward both in terms of the macroeconomic effects of disaster and development policy, arguing that economy and society are not inert objects, but living organisms. Using a framework based on societal networking, including business networks, and the economic localization of disasters, the author shows that societal functionality (defined as the capacity of a system to survive, reproduce and develop) is unlikely to be impaired by natural disasters.

This book will be of interest to scholars and practitioners involved in disaster analysis and response policy, and will also be relevant to students of development economics.

J.M. Albala-Bertrand is an academic economist at Queen Mary, University of London, UK, specializing in development economics. His research interests include the economics and political economy of disasters, structural change vis-à-vis development strategies, and infrastructure economics.

Routledge studies in development economics

1 **Economic Development in the Middle East**
Rodney Wilson

2 **Monetary and Financial Policies in Developing Countries**
Growth and stabilization
Akhtar Hossain and Anis Chowdhury

3 **New Directions in Development Economics**
Growth, environmental concerns and government in the 1990s
Edited by Mats Lundahl and Benno J. Ndulu

4 **Financial Liberalization and Investment**
Kanhaya L. Gupta and Robert Lensink

5 **Liberalization in the Developing World**
Institutional and economic changes in Latin America, Africa and Asia
Edited by Alex E. Fernández Jilberto and André Mommen

6 **Financial Development and Economic Growth**
Theory and experiences from developing countries
Edited by Niels Hermes and Robert Lensink

7 **The South African Economy**
Macroeconomic prospects for the medium term
Finn Tarp and Peter Brixen

8 **Public Sector Pay and Adjustment**
Lessons from five countries
Edited by Christopher Colclough

9 **Europe and Economic Reform in Africa**
Structural adjustment and economic diplomacy
Obed O. Mailafia

10 **Post-apartheid Southern Africa**
Economic challenges and policies for the future
Edited by Lennart Petersson

11 **Financial Integration and Development**
Liberalization and reform in sub-Saharan Africa
Ernest Aryeetey and Machiko Nissanke

12 **Regionalization and Globalization in the Modern World Economy**
Perspectives on the Third World and transitional economies
Edited by Alex E. Fernández Jilberto and André Mommen

13 **The African Economy**
Policy, institutions and the future
Steve Kayizzi-Mugerwa

14 **Recovery from Armed Conflict in Developing Countries**
Edited by Geoff Harris

15 **Small Enterprises and Economic Development**
The dynamics of micro and small enterprises
Carl Liedholm and Donald C. Mead

16 **The World Bank**
New agendas in a changing world
Michelle Miller-Adams

17 **Development Policy in the Twenty-First Century**
Beyond the post-Washington consensus
Edited by Ben Fine, Costas Lapavitsas and Jonathan Pincus

18 **State-Owned Enterprises in the Middle East and North Africa**
Privatization, performance and reform
Edited by Merih Celasun

19 **Finance and Competitiveness in Developing Countries**
Edited by José María Fanelli and Rohinton Medhora

20 **Contemporary Issues in Development Economics**
Edited by B.N. Ghosh

21 **Mexico Beyond NAFTA**
Edited by Martín Puchet Anyul and Lionello F. Punzo

22 **Economies in Transition**
A guide to China, Cuba, Mongolia, North Korea and Vietnam at the turn of the twenty-first century
Ian Jeffries

23 **Population, Economic Growth and Agriculture in Less Developed Countries**
Nadia Cuffaro

24 **From Crisis to Growth in Africa?**
Edited by Mats Lundal

25 **The Macroeconomics of Monetary Union**
An analysis of the CFA franc zone
David Fielding

26 **Endogenous Development**
Networking, innovation, institutions and cities
Antonio Vasquez-Barquero

27 **Labour Relations in Development**
Edited by Alex E. Fernández Jilberto and Marieke Riethof

28 **Globalization, Marginalization and Development**
Edited by S. Mansoob Murshed

29 **Programme Aid and Development**
Beyond conditionality
Howard White and Geske Dijkstra

30 **Competitiveness Strategy in Developing Countries**
A manual for policy analysis
Edited by Ganeshan Wignaraja

31 **The African Manufacturing Firm**
An analysis based on firm surveys in sub-Saharan Africa
Dipak Mazumdar and Ata Mazaheri

32 **Trade Policy, Growth and Poverty in Asian Developing Countries**
Edited by Kishor Sharma

33 **International Competitiveness, Investment and Finance**
A case study of India
Edited by A. Ganesh Kumar, Kunal Sen and Rajendra R. Vaidya

34 **The Pattern of Aid Giving**
The impact of good governance on development assistance
Eric Neumayer

35 **New International Poverty Reduction Strategies**
Edited by Jean-Pierre Cling, Mireille Razafindrakoto and François Roubaud

36 **Targeting Development**
Critical perspectives on the millennium development goals
Edited by Richard Black and Howard White

37 **Essays on Balance of Payments Constrained Growth**
Theory and evidence
Edited by J.S.L. McCombie and A.P. Thirlwall

38 **The Private Sector After Communism**
New entrepreneurial firms in transition economies
Jan Winiecki, Vladimir Benacek and Mihaly Laki

39 **Information Technology and Development**
A new paradigm for delivering the internet to rural areas in developing countries
Jeffrey James

40 **The Economics of Palestine**
Economic policy and institutional reform for a viable Palestine state
Edited by David Cobham and Nu'man Kanafani

41 **Development Dilemmas**
The methods and political ethics of growth policy
Melvin Ayogu and Don Ross

42 **Rural Livelihoods and Poverty Reduction Policies**
Edited by Frank Ellis and H. Ade Freeman

43 **Beyond Market-Driven Development**
Drawing on the experience of Asia and Latin America
Edited by Makoto Noguchi and Costas Lapavitsas

44 **The Political Economy of Reform Failure**
Edited by Mats Lundahl and Michael L. Wyzan

45 Overcoming Inequality in Latin America
Issues and challenges for the twenty-first century
Edited by Ricardo Gottschalk and Patricia Justino

46 Trade, Growth and Inequality in the Era of Globalization
Edited by Kishor Sharma and Oliver Morrissey

47 Microfinance
Perils and prospects
Edited by Jude L. Fernando

48 The IMF, World Bank and Policy Reform
Edited by Alberto Paloni and Maurizio Zanardi

49 Managing Development
Globalization, economic restructuring and social policy
Edited by Junji Nakagawa

50 Who Gains from Free Trade?
Export-led growth, inequality and poverty in Latin America
Edited by Rob Vos, Enrique Ganuza, Samuel Morley, and Sherman Robinson

51 Evolution of Markets and Institutions
A study of an emerging economy
Murali Patibandla

52 The New Famines
Why famines exist in an era of globalization
Edited by Stephen Devereux

53 Development Ethics at work
Explorations – 1960–2002
Denis Goulet

54 Law Reform in Developing and Transitional States
Edited by Tim Lindsey

55 The Assymetries of Globalization
Edited by Pan A. Yotopoulos and Donato Romano

56 Ideas, Policies and Economic Development in the Americas
Edited by Esteban Pérez-Caldentey and Matias Vernengo

57 European Union Trade Politics and Development
Everything but arms unravelled
Edited by Gerrit Faber and Jan Orbie

58 Membership Based Organizations of the Poor
Edited by Martha Chen, Renana Jhabvala, Ravi Kanbur and Carol Richards

59 The Politics of Aid Selectivity
Good governance criteria in World Bank, U.S. and Dutch development assistance
Wil Hout

60 Economic Development, Education and Transnational Corporations
Mark Hanson

61 Achieving Economic Development in the Era of Globalization
Shalendra Sharma

62 Sustainable Development and Free Trade
Shawkat Alam

63 **The Impact of International Debt Relief**
Geske Dijkstra

64 **Europe's Troubled Region**
Economic development, institutional reform and social welfare in the Western Balkans
William Bartlett

65 **Work, Female Empowerment and Economic Development**
Sara Horrell, Hazel Johnson and Paul Mosley

66 **The Chronically Poor in Rural Bangladesh**
Livelihood constraints and capabilities
Pk. Md. Motiur Rahman, Noriatsu Matsui and Yukio Ikemoto

67 **Public–Private Partnerships in Health Care in India**
Lessons for developing countries
A. Venkat Raman and James Warner Björkman

68 **Rural Poverty and Income Dynamics in Asia and Africa**
Edited by Keijiro Otsuka, Jonna P. Estudillo and Yasuyuki Sawada

69 **Microfinance: A Reader**
David Hulme and Thankom Arun

70 **Aid and International NGOs**
Dirk-Jan Koch

71 **Development Macroeconomics**
Essays in memory of Anita Ghatak
Edited by Subrata Ghatak and Paul Levine

72 **Taxation in a Low Income Economy**
The case of Mozambique
Channing Arndt and Finn Tarp

73 **Labour Markets and Economic Development**
Edited by Ravi Kanbur and Jan Svejnar

74 **Economic Transitions to Neoliberalism in Middle-Income Countries**
Policy dilemmas, crises, mass resistance
Edited by Alfedo Saad-Filho and Galip L. Yalman

75 **Latecomer Development**
Innovation and knowledge for economic growth
Banji Oyelaran-Oyeyinka and Padmashree Gehl Sampath

76 **Trade Relations between the EU and Africa**
Development, challenges and options beyond the Cotonou Agreement
Edited by Yenkong Ngangjoh-Hodu and Francis A.S.T. Matambalya

77 **The Comparative Political Economy of Development**
Africa and South Asia
Edited by Barbara Harriss-White and Judith Heyer

78 **Credit Cooperatives in India**
Past, present and future
Biswa Swarup Misra

79 **Development Economics in Action (2nd edition)**
A study of economic policies in Ghana
Tony Killick

80 The Multinational Enterprise in Developing Countries
Local versus global logic
Edited by Rick Molz, Cătălin Ratiu and Ali Taleb

81 Monetary and Financial Integration in West Africa
Temitope W. Oshikoya

82 Reform and Development in China
What can China offer the developing world
Edited by Ho-Mou Wu and Yang L. Yao

83 Towards New Developmentalism
Market as means rather than master
Edited by Shahrukh Rafi Khan and Jens Christiansen

84 Culture, Institutions, and Development
New insights into an old debate
Edited by Jean-Philippe Platteau and Robert Peccoud

85 Assessing Prospective Trade Policy
Methods applied to EU-ACP economic partnership agreements
Edited by Oliver Morrissey

86 Social Protection for Africa's Children
Edited by Sudhanshu Handa, Stephen Devereux and Douglas Webb

87 Energy, Bio Fuels and Development
Comparing Brazil and the United States
Edited by Edmund Amann, Werner Baer and Don Coes

88 Value Chains, Social Inclusion and Economic Development
Contrasting theories and realities
Edited by A.H.J. (Bert) Helmsing and Sietze Vellema

89 Market Liberalism, Growth, and Economic Development in Latin America
Edited by Gerardo Angeles Castro, Ignacio Perrotini-Hernández and Humberto Ríos-Bolivar

90 South–South Globalization
Challenges and opportunities for development
Edited by S. Mansoob Murshed, Pedro Goulart and Leandro A. Serino

91 Trade Infrastructure and Economic Development
Edited by Olu Ajakaiye and T. Ademola Oyejide

92 Microcredit and International Development
Contexts, achievements and challenges
Edited by Farhad Hossain, Christopher Rees and Tonya Knight-Millar

93 Business Regulation and Non-State Actors
Whose standards? Whose development?
Edited by Darryl Reed and Peter Utting and Ananya Mukherjee Reed

94 Public Expenditures for Agricultural and Rural Development in Africa
Edited by Tewodaj Mogues and Samuel Benin

95 The Global Economic Crisis and the Developing World
Implications and prospects for recovery and growth
Edited by Ashwini Deshpande and Keith Nurse

96 The Microfinance Impact
Ranjula Bali Swain

97 Gendered Insecurities, Health and Development in Africa
Edited by Howard Stein and Amal Hassan Fadlalla

98 Financial Cooperatives and Local Development
Edited by Silvio Goglio and Yiorgos Alexopoulos

99 Digital Interactions in Developing Countries
An economic perspective
Jeffrey James

100 Migration and Inequality
Edited by Tanja Bastia

101 Financing Regional Growth and the Inter-American Development Bank
The case of Argentina
Ernesto Vivares

102 Globalization and Development
Rethinking interventions and governance
Edited by Arne Bigsten

103 Disasters and the Networked Economy
J.M. Albala-Bertrand

Disasters and the Networked Economy

J.M. Albala-Bertrand

Routledge
Taylor & Francis Group
LONDON AND NEW YORK

First published 2013
by Routledge
2 Park Square, Milton Park, Abingdon, Oxon OX14 4RN

Simultaneously published in the USA and Canada
by Routledge
711 Third Avenue, New York, NY 10017

Routledge is an imprint of the Taylor & Francis Group, an informa business

British Library Cataloguing in Publication Data
A catalogue record for this book is available from the British Library

Library of Congress Cataloging in Publication Data
Albala-Bertrand, J.M.
Disasters and the networked economy / J.M. Albala-Bertrand.
pages cm
Includes bibliographical references and index.
1. Disasters–Economic aspects. 2. Economic policy. 3. Social accounting. 4. Macroeconomics–Econometric models. I. Title.
HC79.D45.A4293 2013
363.34–dc23 2012040739

ISBN: 978-0-415-66629-9 (hbk)
ISBN: 978-0-203-40667-0 (ebk)

Typeset in Times New Roman
by Wearset Ltd, Boldon, Tyne and Wear

Contents

Illustrations

Figures

Boxes

Tables

Preface

In a previous work we concluded that, as a rule, natural disasters are a problem of development, but not a problem for development. In the present work, we further support such a conclusion by emphasizing that society is a *living* organism and not an *inert* object. Here, by means of a framework that is set up in terms of societal networking and the economic localization of disasters, we show that societal functionality, defined as the capacity of a system to survive, reproduce and develop, i.e. to be viable, is unlikely to be impaired by natural disasters. This means that institutional resilience and economic resources are, as a rule, always available for recovery. Hence, the main reason why natural disasters don't have longer, let alone cumulative, effects of note on the national economy is because society is a living networked system with permanent functionality and feedbacks, which are associated with inbuilt reactions from horizontal relationships (especially, community and markets) as well as exogenous and endogenized routine responses from vertical linkages (especially public and foreign). Given that this is the context for public policy, then network shifting and reactions, from businesses and people, can in addition be systemically stimulated by public and foreign policy so that the recovery becomes less costly, faster and more developmentally useful, which is what we suggest here.

There are two balances, however, that have to be reasonably secured by the public response to disasters. One is the balance between the local level and the national one, and the other is a complementary one between endogenous reactions and exogenous responses. The former should avoid that the national networking insulates itself at the expense of the affected locality, by bypassing and severing local networks with the wider economy beyond what is systemically necessary. The latter, in turn, should avoid that exogenous public and foreign policy suffocates endogenous reactions in a systemically inconsistent way, which may force an unnecessary aid dependency on the directly affected locality.

Finally we would like to acknowledge those empirical studies carried out by a number of institutions and researchers, such as TEC, ALNAP, ODI, World Bank, and many academics, which are duly credited in our references. We can only look for relevant societal patterns from appropriate empirical studies, whether quantitative or otherwise; so as to enhance some reasonable political-economic theory, and from here derive some useful lessons for the betterment of society.

Acronyms

ALNAP	Active Learning Network for Accountability and Performance
CEPAL	Comisión Económica Para América Latina (ECLAC)
CGE	Computable General Equilibrium
CORFO	Corporación de Fomento de Chile
CRED	Centre for Research on the Epidemiology of Disasters
ECLAC	UN Economic Commission for Latin America and the Caribbean
EM-DAT	Emergency Events Database
EWB-UK	Engineers Without Borders-United Kingdom
FAO	UN Food and Agriculture Organization
GDP	Gross Domestic Product
GFCF	Gross Fixed Capital Formation (Investment)
GO	Gross Output (i.e. Intermediate Output + Final Output)
HDI	Human Development Index
IFRC	International Federation of Red Cross and Red Crescent Societies
INACER	Instituto Nacional de Estadísticas Regionales
INE	Instituto Nacional de Estadísticas de Chile
IO	Input–Output
IRIO	Interregional Input–Output
IRIOS	Interregional Input–Output Software
ITUCC	International Trade Union Confederation
NGO	Non-Governmental Organization
OCHA	Office for the Coordination of Humanitarian Affairs
ODA	Overseas Development Assistance
ODI	Overseas Development Institute
OECD	Organisation for Economic Co-operation and Development
SAM	Social Accounting Matrix
SNA	Social Network Analysis
SOFOFA	Sociedad de Fomento Fabril de Chile
SP	Substitution Potential
TEC	Tsunami Evaluation Committee
TFP	Total Factor Productivity

UN	United Nations
UNEP	UN Development Program
USAID	US Agency for International Development
WFP	UN World Food Program

Introduction

Society is not a collection of inert items, but a living organism made of interrelated parts, which generates societally endogenous reactions to take care of local failures. These societal inbuilt behaviours operate via local and national networks and often with significant connections to international ones. These are bound to produce systemic compensatory adaptations and substitutions, circumventions and shifts, migrations and diversification together with other inbuilt societal feedbacks, altering somehow the dynamics and structure of the affected location and country, at least in the short to medium terms (Albala-Bertrand 1993, 2006a). Longer-term disaster effects on the economy are unlikely to happen if indirect flow effects can be insulated and counteracted at the macro level. In addition, as a rule, public and international responses will normally couple with, or be part of, the above reactions, making the possibility of systemically harmful macroeconomic effects unlikely in the medium term, let alone the long term, and not least making the claim about the existence of significant cumulative economic effects fairly unpersuasive. If this was so, then there would be little foundation to the usual claim that the economy will suffer badly over the long term, especially in the case of large disasters. So there are a few issues that this book should help tackle, which are in the form of questions as follows. How important are long-term and cumulative effects likely to be on a networked macroeconomy? What are the likely networked reactions of economic participants in the face of disasters? Why should there be a policy balance between the local and the national in the aftermath of disasters? Why should there be a policy balance between endogenous reactions and exogenous responses in the aftermath of disasters? How could an appropriate framework help improve response policy in the context of societal networks?

To such an effect, the book proceeds from a critical survey of quantitative studies to the systemic role of business and community networks vis-à-vis public response policy, passing through analytical frameworks and aggregate assessments of potential disaster effects, as follows.

In Chapter 1 we deal with quantitative studies. There has been a plethora of such studies that aim to assess longer-term effects on the economy, mostly via black-box methods (especially, before-after, econometrics and counterfactuals) and simulation methods (especially, input–output, social accounting matrix and computable general equilibrium models). Their conclusions are all over the place, from positive effects to negative effects, passing through inconclusive effects. These approaches all operate on the basis of assumptions over assumptions, which come from three necessary stages of the approaches: the quality of the data, the ability of the technique and the theory behind the interpretation. This necessarily makes for assumption-cascading conclusions. This drawback is present in any study that uses such methods. But the problem compounds when they are applied to analyse disasters, as the three stages are significantly weaker than in usual studies, which makes their results here even more unsatisfactory. And this would then be a pretty weak basis for policy making. Hence, quantitative methods, however well designed, are unlikely to settle the issue about the importance of these effects. They may even contribute to confusion and therefore misguided policy. We suggest that the data quality and technical capability of a model are not the only issues, but also the weakness or lack of a political economy argumentation contextualizing them, as disaster responses represent discontinuities and ensuing societal network shifts.

In Chapter 2, we suggest and set up an analytical framework where disasters should be studied. To such an effect, we start by introducing the concept of societal functionality, i.e. the capacity of a social system to operate in a viable way, and its relation with vulnerability and resilience. We then define the key concept of economic localization, indicating both that the large majority of disasters are economically localized, and that economically localized disasters are unlikely to have significant effects on macro functionality, even in the short run. We also emphasize that development itself makes all countries increase the localization of potential disasters by increasingly and endogenously confining their effects. Policies especially designed for tackling potential disasters can help speed up this process. We then define what we understand by disaster situation, response mechanisms and response aims. This takes us to characterizing societal networking in general and defining communities as a collection of networked individuals via social and economic institutions. We conclude here by showing the dynamic network difference between an isolated and an insulated local economy in the presence of disasters. An integrated local economy to the national one, as in physiology, will first insulate itself from the spread of negative disaster effects and then repair the directly affected area. That is, the basic containment of wider indirect effects would normally occur rapidly via relief and local physical rehabilitation, during which the macroeconomic organism would be already taking care of itself via normal endogenous market and non-market mechanisms. This is normally reinforced by exogenous and endogenized public policy, which is bound to be more effective and faster in a well-developed societal network than in a poorly integrated country.

In Chapter 3 we deal with networked reactions and public policy, especially at the community level. We start by setting this up in terms of the permanent tension between the local and the national and then focus on the key tensions between endogenous reactions and exogenous responses, so that a more appropriate policy approach can be found to secure a functionality balance for such tensions. We then analyse some response policies in terms of their market consistency. We concentrate on cash transfers and in-kind aid, remittances and their infrastructure, shelter provision and migration, insurance and loans, and systemic public policy. We attempt to make salient the importance of response policy that addresses systemic inbuilt responses and institutional networks for securing the recovery of local functionality and in passing development itself.

Chapter 4 focuses on the networked macroeconomy. We start by clearly distinguishing a disaster from a catastrophe, showing that it is highly unlikely that a natural disaster can escalate to a catastrophe level. The latter is a situation in which societal functionality has simply ceased to work, so the system is rendered unviable. In other words, external aid, even if available, cannot re-ignite the system, but only support its now helpless victims. A catastrophe might only happen if a disaster renders economy and society into either inert objects or fully disorganized social entities, which are unlikely propositions, especially in the context of localized disasters. We then proceed to describe and explain why it is unlikely that a country's growth rate can be affected by disasters especially over the medium and longer terms, but often in the short term too, which is what is normally observed. We do this by means of an aggregate economic analytical argument and a derived model, but as this is too aggregate, we move to a more disaggregated argumentation by analytically splitting the economy into supra-, intra- and inter-networks, in the context of disaster localization and macro functionality. In this context, we analyse what behaviours and derived flow effects from capital stock destruction can be expected in a living societal system, showing how endogenous economic reactivity within networks as well as exogenous responses can counteract potential indirect effects and therefore longer-term effects. We also show some examples in boxes throughout the chapter.

In Chapter 5, in the context of the previous chapter, we present the importance of regional and sectoral disaggregation to analyse the potential for negative indirect flow effects and its potential local and national counteraction. We show two empirical examples: one for Indonesia (the 2004 tsunami), where interregional input–output (IRIO) tables and other statistics were available, and another for Chile (the 2010 earthquake), where only national input–output tables and regional national accounts are used, as IRIO tables were not available. Both cases not only did not endure falls in the growth rates of GDP, but also these rates were better than the expectation without the disasters, for reasons indicated there. We derive some lessons from this analysis, showing that the potential effects on the economy can generally be anticipated by analyses of this type.

Finally, in Chapter 6, we move from the aggregate to the networked reactions at local level, via community and businesses, and set up the basis for systemically consistent policy responses. We start the chapter by calling attention to the required balance between endogenous and exogenous responses, especially focusing on inbuilt (endogenous) networked reactions. We then set up the analytical criteria that should prevail in the exogenous response policy to secure systemic consistency. Within the text we present via boxes some examples of actual policy vis-à-vis community reactions on the basis of the analysis of

Chapter 3. We then deal with business reactions in the face of disasters and the importance of their networks. We show here that size, sector, management, pre-disaster environment and government response all matter in anticipating the effects of disasters on businesses. We show here how network shifting via the bypassing of standard supply and demand sources is of common occurrence, when such sources fail after disasters, which helps to explain why the macro-economy does not endure longer-term negative effects, even if the directly affected firms (and households) do. On such basis, we retake the macro model of Chapter 4 and show that, incorporating a parameter for a policy-induced degree of substitution or network shifting, the reconstruction investment required to keep the economy as if there were no disaster can be even smaller than without it. This simply means that if public policy can make the substitutive shifts behind the substitution potential more efficacious, then the cost to bring the system back to normal functionality would likely be lower, achieving general recovery faster than it would be otherwise. Given that studies about this area are scant and normally for developed countries, they should be extended to be a more systematic practice for all countries. In the Appendix, we suggest the use of enhanced surveys that can be carried out in a systematic fashion to learn more about business networks and reactions after disasters so that policy can be designed closer to them.

Therefore the book attempts to help the understanding of potential flow and counter-flow effects coming from both inbuilt societal reactions and exogenous response policy as well as the need to frame the analysis in terms of societal networks and systemic consistent response. In past work, we concluded that, as a rule, disasters are a problem *of* development but not a problem *for* development (Albala-Bertrand 1993). In the present work, we back and complement such a rule by emphasizing that disasters do not happen in a societal vacuum, as society *is* a living organism and *not* a piece of inert matter, which operates via societal networks.

1 The problem with quantitative studies

Introduction

Society is a living organism in which inbuilt feedbacks and reactions take care of societal failures so as to secure systemic functionality. These endogenous behaviours operate at local and national levels, including their connections with international levels. When a disaster strikes, such endogenous responses are meant to produce systemic compensatory adaptations and substitutions, circumventions and shifts, migrations and diversification, altering somewhat the dynamics and structure of the affected location and country, at least in the short to medium terms (Albala-Bertrand 1993, 2006a). In addition, as a rule public and international responses will normally couple with, or be part of, the above reactions, making the possibility of systemically harmful macroeconomic effects unlikely in the medium term, let alone the long term, and not least making the claim about the existence of significant economic cumulative effects fairly unpersuasive. Hence, quantitative methods, however well designed, are unlikely to settle the issue about the importance of these effects. We suggest that the data quality and technical capability of a model are not the only issues, but also the political economy argumentation behind a general framework, as disaster responses represent both discontinuities and qualitative changes. If this was sound, then partial studies, set within a general framework, would probably help advance the understanding of these and other effects with more propriety. To this aim, we focus on the relation between economic *localization* and societal *networking* as regards *societal functionality*, as defined in Chapter 2. This chapter then sets out to explore the potential and actual failures of quantitative studies about disasters.

Three failures of quantitative studies

Any quantitative study has three types of interactive insufficiencies that have to be addressed and hopefully minimized. These are: (i) the quality of basic data. This is invariably constraining, as a good deal of expedient assumptions implicit or otherwise have to be made to make them usable; (ii) the inherent limitations of any quantitative technique, which more often than not are overcome by means of convenient assumptions to secure tractability at the expense of realism; and (iii) the paramount issue of the interpretation of results, which necessarily frames the quantitative results into some kind of existing theoretical model, normally associated with axiomatic principles, adding to the whole exercise even stronger assumptions.

In other words, we end up with final numerical results and derived information on assumptions that cascade over assumptions that cascade over assumptions, i.e. assumption-compound .dependent results. It would then not be unpersuasive to accept that if any of these three insufficiencies is strong, then that would seriously invalidate the results so obtained, let alone if each of them has major difficulties. The final result would not just be in all propriety inconclusive, but it would also be unreliable and therefore largely useless. It would then be dangerously misleading to use it for any real-life purpose, especially as a policy foundation. This is not a call for more use of standard theoretical approaches, which have often proved to be even poor in analysing standard economic issues, but to call attention to the largely insurmountable deficiencies of standard methods, which all too often are ignored for academic and/or political expediency.

The problem with standard quantitative studies of disaster effects is that they are subjected to these three types of insufficiencies almost as a matter of fact. This means that they are largely unable to capture the very essence of a disaster situation, making policy-derived conclusions unreliable if not misleading and unnecessarily costly. These empirical and theoretical incapacities are unlikely to be overcome significantly over time. So a different type of approach would be required: one that may use quantitative analysis in a more focused and bounded manner, implying a shift in perspective or standpoint. So let us have a look in more detail at these three handicaps in the case of disasters.

The source data

We refer here to disaster data, as the other data required for studies would normally come from countries' standard statistical offices whether directly or compiled by international organizations from data supplied by these offices.

There are a number of institutions that keep and compile data sets, but most have variations in definitions, focus, accuracy and consistency within and across sources. Among the best known international databases are EM-DAT from the Centre for Research on the Epidemiology of Disasters (CRED) of the Université Catholique de Louvain, NatCat from Munich Reinsurance Company, Sigma from Swiss Reinsurance Company and a few others (Tschoegl *et al.* 2006). EM-DAT is however more all-embracing, transparent and accessible than the latter ones, which is why most if not all of the well-known empirical studies rely upon this database, especially those dealing with economic effects (e.g. Skidmore and Toya 2002; Rasmussen 2004; Heger *et al.* 2008; Fomby *et al.* 2009; Raddatz 2009; etc.). The question is then how acceptable is this particular data source for the purpose?

First, EM-DAT operationally defines disasters as events in which at least one of the following may happen: (i) ten or more people killed and/or (ii) 100 or more people reported affected and/or (iii) there was a declaration of a state of emergency and/or (iv) there was a call for international assistance. This is a very low threshold, so almost every accident initiated by a natural event will be classified as a disaster. The data show an overwhelming proportion of small or very small so-defined disasters, with highly heterogeneous recorded effects, even for physically similar ones (Cavallo and Noy 2010). Most of them cannot possibly have much impact on the local economy, let alone the national one. So if studies use this series to analyse disaster effects, and show some statistically significant effect on the economy, the most likely outcome is that the effects are only concomitant to them and not caused by them, but black-box methods will rarely be able to discriminate between concomitance and cause. More on this later. Second, EM-DAT reports the following disaster effects: number of killed, number of affected, number of homeless, area affected, total estimated damages (including insured losses when available) and disaster impact on some selected sectors (e.g. on utilities, transport, etc.). The compilers are aware of the difficulties with some numbers, especially those about affected and homeless, but the number of killed is also very variable in the case of a large killing disaster. These variations in estimates may have significant effects in the way economic losses and aid are estimated.

The least tractable problem however is that of estimating economic damages, where standard procedures are lacking. The most elaborate approach is the one proposed by ECLAC (2003), but this is not amenable for fast estimations and not devoid of difficulties itself (e.g. the difficulty of estimating indirect flow economic effects, the need for a regiment of specialist assessors, the need for hardly available or reliable coefficients to discount depreciation or to calculate productivity changes, and some other purely theoretical and fairly intractable considerations). Still, the methodology touches most of the important problems and requirements that a disaster effect assessment should focus upon.

The standard issues are how to value direct losses of stocks (infrastructures, machinery, etc.) and indirect flow effects derived from the former (changes in output, unemployment, prices, etc.). Stock losses should be easier to assess, but the methods about how to fine-tune the extent of damage and its cost are not perfunctory. Are initial observations about losses the same as those that come (if at all) after the mass media dust has settled? What is the difference between destruction, damage and recoverable assets? What is the cost of stock losses: the replacement value at current market prices, some properly depreciated value, or some nonsensical discounted value of capital services?[1] Who carries the stock losses assessment: independent experts or public authorities? And so on and so forth. For indirect flow effects at macro level the problems are significantly worse as they are not very tractable to direct observation, as interruptions of production or supply have to be assessed against substitutions and compensations over a given period, which cannot be done except via strong assumptions and theoretical interpretations, but often a value is produced that cannot possibly be verified.

For example, in the case of the February 2010 Chilean earthquake, at least 25 per cent of an official estimate of total losses of US$30 billion is attributed to indirect effects under the category 'losses of GDP' (Gobierno de Chile 2010), i.e. output that will not be produced because of the productive interruption that comes especially from the destruction and damage of capital. What is lacking in this document is how this value was calculated. This clearly does not take into account substitutions and demand and supply shifts, general network shifting and other endogenous reactions, let alone the counter-effect of exogenous responses themselves. Not surprisingly, the economy grew by more than expected at the end of 2010, at 6.1 per cent, although there were sectors in the affected area that were still below the pre-disaster levels, which is an indication of network shifting or economic bypassing. This is similar to the estimates of the December 2004 Asian tsunami. The TEC (2006) reports that the initial expected losses of income (indirect losses) to total losses were between 21.3 per cent (Sri Lanka) and 76.9 per cent (Thailand). But by the time of the report, July 2006 (one and a half years after the event), it was clear that that was a gross overestimation, as most countries were already showing strong GDP growth rates. So they add:

> This table should be interpreted with caution as it presents initial estimates of loss and damage. Estimates of GDP growth were later revised and the figures for projected losses were probably pessimistic. The economic impacts of disasters are dynamic and complex (Benson and Clay 2004), and the lumping together of damage (the capital cost of rebuilding assets) with losses (expected lost income) is problematic. Estimating the true economic impact of the tsunami will be difficult even with hindsight because of the many confounding factors at the national and international levels.
>
> (TEC 2006: 38 and note E6)

The official figures however are the ones that remain in EM-DAT information and are used without corrections and often without qualification in quantitative work. EM-DAT defines estimated damages as the 'value of all damages and economic losses directly or indirectly related to the disaster' (EM-DAT website). These mix direct (stock) effects with indirect (flow) effects, ignoring substitutions and economic bypassing (Albala-Bertrand 1993). So the normal myth about the importance of indirect effects, or simply the existence of vested interests bent on magnifying them, go unchecked and echoed by mass media and professionals in the field. And these so-called estimates are used sparingly as the basis for policy and academic and other studies, as shown later.

Third, EM-DAT compiles and classifies disaster effects from many sources, such as governments, UN agencies (UNDP, OCHA, WFP and FAO), NGOs, IFRC, research institutions, insurance institutions (Lloyds, Munich Re, Swiss Re) and press agencies, although priority is given to UN agencies. The latter of course, rarely carry their own independent assessments, relying on disaster information from member governments, and normally when there is an explicit request from a government to a UN agency to participate.[2]

Governments usually rely upon rapid assessments carried by the official authorities of the areas affected, but more often than not go along with mass media assessments, which report the first opinion of national emergency officers, NGOs and local authorities in the affected areas. This is hardly an accurate basis for assessment, which is invariably subject to huge overestimations, especially as regards economic costs. Take the case of Chile, which is a fairly transparent country. The estimation of economic losses from the 2010 earthquake was set at US$30bn, but a few months later this was challenged by academics who estimated that it actually was between one-third and half of that (*La Tercera*, 22/3/2010, 20/2/2011). The government however kept its official figure unchanged, which is the one that feeds EM-DAT. It is not difficult to imagine that in less transparent countries the benefit of open challenges like this will be unlikely; the government getting away with any figure it wants to make official (e.g. Haiti assessments). And EM-DAT will record this unreliable figure, which will be used as information for empirical work. But notice that it is not just the economic information which will be suspect, but also information about the number of people killed, let alone that for affected people. The 2010 Haiti earthquake is a good example of this. The official figures were 316,000 deaths, but USAID and others set it out at between 20 per cent and 50 per cent of this (*New York Times*, 31/5/2011).

EM-DAT officers are aware of some of these deficiencies and have tried to incorporate national governments to harmonize the data (e.g. Guha-Sapir and Below 2002; Below *et al.* 2010). Surely, definitions and assessing methods can be standardized, even catering for different social setups, so that estimation discrepancies and errors can be made less significant, making the results hopefully more comparable across countries and over time, e.g. for the killed, the missing, the affected, the homeless. But the problem of assessing economic damage would still persist, as the deficiency here is incorporated from primary sources and compounded by lack of technical expertise, required speed and not least vested interests. So for as long as primary sources are not independent from the government or from disaster-acting institutions like NGOs and mass media, and for as long as standard methods are not technically sound for fast assessment, and for as long as little or no interest is exercised in correcting the initial figures afterwards, economic disaster data will be at best just an order of magnitude and at worse fantasy.

So to use such data for empirical research, without the required caution, will be a misleading way to derive knowledge and not least policy. It is not enough to warn about some of these flaws at the beginning of a study and then go ahead with conclusions and proposed policies as if the flaws were just an afterthought, often making the warning only as a necessary item to have the study published, as many studies do. This is not uncommon in publications in economics, in which mathematical tractability trumps realism and relevance.

The techniques

Indirect, long-term and cumulative effects of disasters are fairly intractable to direct observation, especially at macro level, which is the main reason why they deserve more theoretical and empirical attention. Otherwise, we will keep feeding the disaster industry with uncheckable and unfalsifiable statements about them (Albala-Bertrand 1993). There have been many studies dealing with this issue, whether directly or otherwise, like Albala-Bertrand (1993), Charvériat (2000), Horwich (2000), Skidmore and Toya (2002), Auffret (2003), Benson and Clay (2004), Briguglio (2004), Okuyama *et al.* (2004), Rasmussen (2004), Cuaresma *et al.* (2008), Noy (2009), Cavallo *et al.* (2010), and others. For each study that shows some long-term effects, there are others that show none at all or, more often than not, are inconclusive. As known, the values of macroeconomic variables contain pre-disaster societal features and post-disaster effects, which would likely make a quantitative study of even a single case country inconclusive in any case, except in the most simple of environments.

There are two main approaches to empirical studies of economic effects of disaster: (i) black-box methods (notably before-after, econometrics) and (ii) simulation methods (notably input–output, social accounting and computable general equilibrium). The former relates disaster variables to some standard (normally macro) economic variables in a socio-economic institutional vacuum, so it requires strong interpretations of results based usually on existing theoretical mainstream economic models. In turn, the latter assumes a theoretical reality or model with given parameters, behavioural functions, basic equilibrium conditions and the like from the outset. Then disaster data are used to feed the parts of the model that can assumedly be affected by a disaster so as to observe the numerical results that the model throws out after an assumption-ridden iterative convergence has been achieved.

Of these two sets of techniques only black-box methods are meant for the assessment of *actual* (as distinct from theoretical or hypothetical) effects of disasters on the economy, especially growth rates. In turn, simulation methods are meant to assess the *possible* effects, especially derived from an interactive, or networked world, of economic participants (firms, industries, regions, consumers and the like). There is here no pretension of dealing with real short-, medium- or long-term effects, but only with assumption-forced final equilibrium results, serving as the basis for analysis of possible policies. Both types of methods are somehow valuable, if only to call attention about certain aspects of the disaster phenomenon. But both types of methods are either insufficient or unreliable, and therefore misleading for policy purposes, as we show below.

The issue of interpretation: a necessary caution

It seems necessary to clarify what follows from the very outset. Economic explanations are normally done via models, i.e. thought constructs to argue about a real issue, e.g. inflation, unemployment, growth, taxation, etc. Without necessary cautions a model can become a fetish to 'explain' or worse justify almost anything and everything. This cautionary effort is either fully ignored or done perfunctorarily in economic studies, especially theoretical ones, let alone in standard textbooks.

Analytical and simulation models are not representations of reality, but only interpretations of it. At best a model is a simplified representation of a simplified interpretation of reality via assumptions and axiomatic principles or stylized facts. Except for trivial observation, societal reality, as a meaningful whole, cannot be known directly, but only subjectively interpreted. An *interpretation* is necessarily a stylized and abstract opinion about certain facts from what we normally call 'reality'. Opinions are subjective assertions about the seemingly chaotic facts and behaviours that happen 'out there'. Contrary to religion, opinions in social disciplines are about these chaotic facts and behaviours, the aim of which is to make logical sense of them via hypotheses carried through descriptive and/or explanatory theories and models. But opinions are founded on values that shape the inner preferences of an individual. Emotions, passions and obsessions are never far away from them, nor are a sense of acquired duty, morality and ethics. His values are created via socialization, beliefs and living experiences, not necessarily independent from each other (i.e. cultural and religious allegiances, peer habits and behaviour, formal education and occupation, social rewards and punishments). This is the stuff that leads an individual to take an institutional position as regards events (political, economic, cultural and religious) and share a conception of the world or an ideological persuasion, consciously or not. Unsurprisingly, this actual *social* being seems very different from the axiomatic *homo economicus*, i.e. the social-less 'rational' maximizing individual of neoclassical economics.

Not unheard of, a simplified interpretation of a phenomena can also come close to pure ideology (as distinct from science), ideology being a dogmatic belief, i.e. a belief without evidence, or at best a false perception of real facts, coming from political, economic, cultural or especially religious institutional quarters, e.g. Creationism as opposed to Evolutionary Biology. Hence, a model is not a 'representation of reality', as often careless textbooks and not least practicing economists have it. Societal reality can only be subjectively interpreted. As Theil (1971: iv) put it: 'It does require maturity to realize that models are to be used, but not to be believed.' That is, intellectual maturity is required to deal with real phenomena via models. They should not be believed, but more importantly they should not be used as a plank to justify ideological agendas. It is a pity that such a wise caution is ignored so often, especially in economics and economics-based political agendas. As a complementary caution, it is also necessary to clarify that the mathematical wrapping of an opinion does not make the opinion any more valid. We have no quarrels with mathematics, but we have a great deal of them with both its use[3] and with investing mathematical models with scientific validity by the mere fact of being set up mathematically. Spanish countries have a wise motto: 'A monkey dressed in silk is still a monkey.' A poor theory dressed in elegant mathematics is still a poor theory.[4]

Black-box techniques and interpretation

Black-box techniques refers to the fact that all that is often known is the data that go into the box and that which come out of the box as a result. *Before-after exercises* have the particularity of expressing the data and results openly via descriptive statistics, mostly avoiding the use of more elaborated techniques and therefore assumptions, i.e. probabilistic statistics and the like, so it is regarded as an unsophisticated approach. But as such, it does not require a minimum number of observations to generalize, as it is more in search of stylized facts than of statistical validity, which in itself is a worthwhile platform for further research. Contrary to econometrics, however, it usually analyses each included country (or other level) with a view to secure some direct knowledge within the box. This inside-the-box knowledge would minimize excess theorizing through axioms and often uncheckable assumptions about the results. As a first approach it is not a bad way to spend time in analysis, as often new ideas and hypotheses turn up this way. Still, the conclusions cannot be considered strong enough for generalization without clear qualifications (Albala-Bertrand 1993, 2004/1993).

Econometrics techniques are what empirical economists use more widely. The aim of them is to relate, normally linearly, one or more (supposedly independent) variables to one single (supposedly dependent) variable by means of estimable parameters and an error term. The latter is one of the main focuses of the technique, which looks for methods that can estimate the parameters while minimizing the error term (e.g. via ordinary least squares estimators, maximum likelihood estimators and the like). The independent variables are supposed to 'explain' the behaviour of the dependent variable within a stochastic or probabilistic range, given the error term. The strength of this relationship is then submitted to a number of alternative specifications and tests to determine whether the relationship is statistically significant. For these tests to be statistically acceptable a large number of observations and not least assumptions are required, so the technique is necessarily both data and assumption intensive. What the technique does not do is to explain *how* the independent variables impact on the dependent one, so outside theory is brought to bear to explain the channels by which this could happen.

Theoretical economists as a matter of fact attempt to test their theories by resorting to econometric methods. But as is well known, all that can be tested is a derived proposition or relationship from the model, e.g. between the money supply and inflation or fast GDP growth and balance of payments or GDP growth and taxation, etc. The problem is that the same proposition or relationship can be derived from alternative models that do not encompass or are not encompassed by the initial model, so the testable proposition becomes disembodied, i.e. not belonging to any particular model. In other words, theories cannot be tested by quantitative methods, as only a hanging-in-the air proposition can be the subject of this type of testing. And in passing a model cannot be *directly* tested against reality, as the latter is the result of complex and varied concomitants of societal factors that go well beyond a few economic variables. Of course, the normal weight of evidence should indeed be taken into account, but still with significant caution about interpretation. And full-blooded reality checks, like the Great Recession of 2008 and beyond, should indeed be taken into account when analysing the theories and policies that were behind it. This simply means that models and theories may go some way towards explaining something of reality, but not normally much for complacency, let alone in definite ways. That is why social disciplines, whether wrapped in mathematics or otherwise, are definitely not hard science, and should be taken on their own merits with extreme methodological caution, which is rarely done by academic practitioners, let alone by vested policy makers (Hausman 1992; Keen 2011).

But the fact that only theoretically disembodied quantitative relationships can be subject to testing does not put an end to the many methodological problems. There is the serious problem of assessing causality, e.g. is the money supply that leads to inflation or is inflation that put pressure on money availability to rise? Is it higher foreign trade that leads to higher GDP growth rates or is it the latter that leads to higher foreign trade? And so on. Tests for causality are not very strong, except in very simple cases, so it is theory and therefore interpretation that will pick one or other direction of causality. In addition, there is the question of omitted variables, i.e. the strength of a relationship may appear larger than it actually is because essential explanatory variables are not present, which makes the value of the relationship, however well tested, spurious and therefore misleading. Furthermore, given that the verbal theoretical concept does not always have a quantitative value, then there is the need to look for quantitative proxies that are supposed to be somehow correlated with the qualitative concept, so that the statistical relationship can be submitted to testing, e.g. human capital estimated by the expenditure on secondary education or on health. And of course there are many other moments in which a relationship can be spurious, unspecified or unstable, e.g. autocorrelation, multicollinearity, stationarity, etc., for which there are a number of probabilistic tests to check and hopefully improve the relationship, but this also means the introduction of yet more assumptions. And not least, it is the technical and ethical question of the use and abuse of polynomials, i.e. the crutch of adding more and more variables until the econometric equation happens to fit the data and pass the necessary tests. This would make interpretation of the final equation strenuous, and that of the initial one largely irrelevant. But this is mostly ignored as a matter of expediency, because if the initial econometric model did not fit the data then it would be less likely to be published (see Hendry 2000; Freedman 2005; Bergman 2007; Kennedy 2008; Wooldridge 2010; Zaman 2010, 2012).

In addition, when carrying panel data studies, many countries are regressed with the same testable relationship, which necessarily pools together countries with very different histories, cultural traits, societal idiosyncrasies, development stages, social dynamics, economic structures and policy traditions, but very rarely do the studies go into the country realities themselves, preferring to homogenize them in terms of conventionally uncomplicated summary numbers (e.g. GDP, GFCF, population and the like), which themselves are founded in implicit assumptions rarely spelled out. This is a thoroughly unwarranted way to derive sound knowledge, let alone clear-cut conclusions, but there is not much effort to differentiate countries according to important societal traits. That is, content is sacrificed for the sake of tractable appearance. Finally, the issue of long-term effects is necessarily a time-series one, associated with a given reality (one single country over time), so to try to capture them via a cross-section study is no more solid than trying to justify the Kuznets inverted-U hypothesis via cross-sectional analysis, which badly fails to do the job.[5]

In the case of disasters, econometric testing goes the other way round. First, an isolated relationship to estimate is proposed, e.g. disasters have a long-term effect on economy growth. This can be estimated in many ways, e.g. GDP growth regressed on disaster stock losses or panel data GDP growth regressed on pre-disaster trends, or the like. And second, the regression parameters are tested for statistical significance, and then, especially if the regression coefficients are significant, a theoretical interpretation is brought to bear. Just as with theories that cannot be reliably tested by estimating isolated econometric relationships, isolated econometric relationships can hardly produce a reliable theoretical explanation either, as they would not be unique, let alone bi-univocal.

As regards causality, in the case of disasters it is easy to assume that whatever happens after the impact is primarily considered as effect, so causality in this sense is less of a problem, but the disaster itself might not necessarily be the cause of macro effects, as independent and dependent variables can be fundamentally affected by the traits, trends and discontinuities of the ongoing economy and society. This means that the regressions will normally carry a plethora of other influences not necessarily captured by explicit 'explanatory' variables. Econometrics is extremely weak in dealing with sudden, short-term, shocks to a system, as most disasters are. This means that the technique reports in its parameters the total disaster effects, which would include the direct ones, so whatever effect that seems to be found will actually be mostly confined to the first year, which is hardly a basis to assess longer-term disaster effects on the economy (Okuyama 2009). So apart from the weakness of econometrics to meaningfully estimate a system subject to discontinuities, there may also be serious problems in distinguishing between explanatory variables that appear to explain the dependent variable and both omitted and/or ignored concomitant factors, especially qualitative ones, that may be the genuine cause for the apparent effect. The latter are partly incorporated via (quantifiable) proxies, which are often forced into the task, and partly simply ignored.

In addition, when analysing longer-term effects, there is the need to extrapolate trends from before the disaster to compare before-trend with after-trend, which is always unsound, or create theoretical counterfactuals, which is strong-assumption dependent and not particularly reliable, or simply use similar disaster-unaffected countries to that affected by a disaster so as to hopefully recreate what would have been the GDP growth rates in the aftermath had the disaster not happened, which is also full of pitfalls, as we show later. Extrapolation falls, of course, in forecasting analysis, which in normal cases is pretty unreliable, let alone in abnormal situations.[6] The case of disasters appears to bring all these problems to the fore, which makes extrapolations, however well logically set up, pretty unreliable. Then it is hardly surprising that for each study that shows some (normally moderate) negative disaster effects in the longer run, there will be another study that shows no effect at all and another that shows positive effects, and of course a plethora of inconclusive ones in between (World Bank 2010). In turn, the use of built-up counterfactuals falls into the realm of puzzles, i.e. how to build a system that more or less replicates the observed one from empirical pieces and theoretical expectations so as to assess what would have happened, especially to GDP growth rates, had the disaster not occurred. This is bound to gloss over inconsistencies, making the result suspect. So these types of studies cannot but be taken with extreme caution, especially when used for policy purposes.

Some typical econometric studies and their interpretation of results

For a collection of inconclusive and contradictory results in the medium and long term, see the survey by Cavallo and Noy (2010). This survey itself, however, is not devoid of summary conclusions that don't appear to be backed by the surveyed studies, e.g. 'the emerging consensus in the literature is that natural disasters have, on average, a negative impact on short-term economic growth [two to three years]' (ibid.: 17). As there is no counterfactual in most models and the single one where there was one is hardly definite, this summary seems hasty (Hochrainer 2009). In addition, all the studies carry no control group and, not least important, the first impact year carryforward, which may make the effect even more confined if at all. This does not mean that at the local level the disaster may not have some significant negative effects, but this is less warranted at macro level, especially in the case of economically localized disasters. More on the concept of economic localization later.

There is no point of repeating in this chapter the results from competent surveys about econometrics studies of longer-term effects of disasters (e.g. Okuyama 2009; Cavallo and Noy 2010). But it is useful to show some of these studies to pinpoint typical types of failing. As expected, medium-term econometrics analysis (two to three years after the impact) carries the direct, first year, loss into this longer term. So it normally shows that there are some statistically significant, but moderate, medium-term effects in the case of large (direct) disaster losses. This has to be differentiated by the type of natural disaster, as some are more likely to have a positive effect, such as earthquakes, and not the least by the economic localization and development level of the country affected, which is rarely done.

A study by Jaramillo (2007) takes over a hundred disaster cases from EM-DAT over the period 1960–1996 and appears to find some small long-term effect, this depending on the type of disaster. He is aware of some of the problems and biases coming from the data, although he seems to hope for the best. As said, in cross-section econometric analysis, there are normally serious problems with the quality of data, with the proxies used as disaster measurement and not least with the heterogeneous aggregation of both different countries and different historical backgrounds. But, in addition, there are also problems with the chosen regression equations, their interpretation and error margins. For example, his regressions carry the direct loss forward and not least there is no control sample to compare with. And of course the small effect may have been fully confined to the first year, but econometrics cannot differentiate. Therefore, his conclusion and interpretation are not fully warranted.

Another study, by Loayza *et al.* (2009), uses a panel approach for 90 countries over 1960–2000. They conclude that while small disasters have on average positive economic effects, large ones have always insignificant or negative ones in the immediate aftermaths. Apart from size, the effects differ according to disaster type vis-à-vis the affected sector. This is based on a collection of strong assumptions and axiomatic models, which in addition does not carry the benefit of a control sample. Assuming that the econometric assumptions were solid, the results could be interpreted in many more realistic ways than a standard Solow-Swan growth model, which is used here for the purpose. This model not only is founded on strong assumptions (closed economy, saving identical to investment, speed of light adjustment, full factor substitutability and the like), but it is meant for the very long run, which clearly excludes most disasters. To determine the size of the disaster, this study relies heavily on data from EM-DAT, in particular the number of affected people, as the one for economic damage is deemed incomplete or unreliable. But the number of affected people is actually the second worse recorded variable in this data set, as indicated above. So again, even if the technique were solid in abstract, which it might be, even if the technique were meant for this type of sudden event, which it is not, and even if it were properly applied, which it may have been, the original sin would still be in the data and would also be compounded by the interpretation.

A report by the World Bank (2010), based upon a number of background papers, does not fare better by concluding that:

> Disasters always reduce well-being of those affected, but may or may not have a negative impact on output growth in the medium term (5 years), which depends, in part, on the severity and type of hazard and level of economic development. Storms and droughts seem to have systematic negative impacts on medium-term growth; not so for floods and earthquakes. But severe disasters (10 percent of all disasters) have adverse effects regardless of their type.
>
> (Ibid.: 57)

If the impact on GDP growth depends on the level of economic development, how can it be concluded that ‘severe disasters (10 percent of all disasters) have adverse effects regardless of their type’? Clearly this does not refer to GDP, but to local effects, as it would be easy to show a good number of counter-examples, which cannot be considered as exceptional, where medium-term effects did not arise, e.g. Guatemala 1976, Mexico 1984, Malawi 1994, Bangladesh 1998, Dominica 1998, Indonesia 2004, the Maldives 2004, Chile 2010, etc. In other words, their conclusions are not clearly borne by the studies they are supposed to summarize.

Notice that if a disaster does not appear to have short-, let alone medium-term, effects then it is highly unlikely that it will have long-term ones. Long-term econometric studies are mired with the same insufficiencies as medium-term ones. For example, Raddatz (2009) uses panel autoregressive distributed lags (PARDL) and panel vector autoregression (PVAR) applied to the EM-DAT database for climatic disasters and concludes that in the long run *per-capita* GDP is 0.6 per cent lower on average as a result of climatic disasters, but over 80 per cent of it is confined to the first disaster year. That is, GDP was estimated to be around 0.5 percentage points lower on average in the first year, so only 0.1 per cent is attributed to the long term. This simply confirms once more that econometric studies invariably carry the first disaster year (especially direct effects) into the long term. So even assuming that the variables are accurate and the analysis impeccable, there appears to be no significant long-term effect. As such, a small remnant beyond the first disaster year may well fall within the confidential interval.[7] In addition, this study is again mounted on a series of strong assumptions that make the results conditional on them. True, they are of normal use among econometricians, but this does not give them a status of soundness, rather one of tractability, which is not the same. Furthermore, Raddatz considers disasters as exogenous, confusing the natural event with the disaster. Given that he seems to believe that global warming induced by human activity is behind a good deal of the increase in climatic natural events, then not even the event itself could be devoid of endogeneity. Apart from showing the results, there is no attempt at interpreting them in any meaningful way.

In turn, Cuaresma (2009), using data from EM-DAT, attempts to analyse via a well-applied Bayesian approach the effect of disasters on human capital. Like other studies, he proxies human capital via secondary school enrolment. He concludes that there is some statistically significant negative (dropout) effect on such a variable, in his words: 'Exposure to natural disaster risk is a robust determinant of differences in secondary school enrolment between countries, but not necessarily within countries' (p. 1). Setting aside the fact that the most relevant focus for policy purposes would be within a country, rather than a panel cross-section, there is something missing. Dropouts do not disappear from a system, but are entrants somewhere else. What he doesn't do is to include vocational training enrolment among the observed variables. First, it is hardly clear that secondary education has a higher impact on human capital than vocational training, as the other way round seems to be more likely. Second, if it could be shown that secondary school enrolment falls over time simply because a vocational one is preferred as a matter of culture and policy, then the disaster will be incidental to the former (i.e. happening side by side but unrelated to it). This will be magnified by the fact that the EM-DAT database classifies as a disaster almost any negative shock, so disasters and other normal variables would move hand-in-hand, but be highly likely unrelated to each other.[8] So again, this is a case of omitted variables that should have been included and proxies that might not actually represent well a qualitative concept such as human capital.[9]

As regards forecasting counterfactuals, Hochrainer (2009) uses time-series GDP forecasting by means of an autoregressive integrated moving average model (ARIMA). He is careful about the reliability of data and the use of the method, which are necessarily assumption driven, but that does not deter him from producing a number of conclusions where his own qualification is ignored. He concludes that large natural disasters on average lead to significant negative effects on GDP in the medium term (five years on), capital stock losses being the main predictor of such results. Disaster data (monetary loss, GDP loss and capital stock loss) come mostly from EM-DAT and Munich Re (as compiled by Okuyama 2009). The counterfactual, which attempts to estimate what would have been the GPD level in the next five years after the impact if there was no disaster, is however as weak as any forecasting based on past data. This would be problematic for a single country, let alone when 225 disasters occurring over 1960–2005 (the number of countries is not given) are used.[10] There is neither an attempt to differentiate the first post-disaster year from the other ones nor an attempt at interpretation.

Cavallo *et al.* (2010), also using EM-DAT data for the direct disaster effects, implement a counterfactual approach based on comparative countries. The counterfactuals are not constructed by extrapolating pre-event trends from the affected countries, but by building a control sample of unaffected countries that, optimally weighted, may estimate the counterfactual of interest. They don't find any significant disaster effect in the long run, whatever their size. This method is not devoid of criticism, but at least incorporates foreign shocks affecting control countries where disasters have not happened. Domestically initiated policy shocks are not quite allowed for. The method is based on equating the unaffected country group with the affected country sample by weighting stages of development and policies via some convenient coefficients, which require strong assumptions. This approach may be likely to produce more reliable results if each single disaster-affected country is analysed independently against a hopefully similar country or composite of countries, rather than relying upon averages of disparate countries. The study has the additional sensible approach of investigating the outliers, which happen to be all cases where political upheaval and revolutions negatively affected longer-term economic performance, which had little or nothing to do with the natural disasters, so they were wisely excluded. Again there is no attempt at explaining why their results happen that way.

Then given all the insufficiencies shown above, it is not surprising that some studies show positive effects (e.g. Skidmore and Toya 2002), no significant effects (e.g. Raddatz 2009) and negative effects (e.g. Noy and Nualsri 2007), or are simply inconclusive, using pretty similar data, but different econometric approaches and therefore implicit and explicit assumptions (Cavallo and Noy 2010).[11] As can be seen, most results are not explained and sometimes only generally interpreted, which is the main purpose of this book, i.e. how to explain why disasters sometimes have or do not have longer-term effects of note.

Simulation techniques

Contrary to black-box techniques, a simulation model by definition contains a clear-cut interpretation of how the economy behaves and operates, i.e. it is meant to *simulate* a national economy by means of production and demand functions, imposed parameters and the like, coming from socially wide interactive sectors and parts. Contrary to standard analytical models, like the Solow–Swan model or the Mundell-Fleming model (Dornbusch *et al.* 2008) simulation techniques are quantitative models, the complexity of which are not amenable to analytical solutions, but only numerical ones. Simulation models, contrary to analytical ones, go well beyond three-sector models, allowing focus on the productive interconnectedness of real economies, i.e. between many producers of intermediate goods, between these and many demanders of final goods, between domestic and foreign markets, and so on. They are not meant to assess actual long-term effects of disasters, but to enquire what would happen, through this web of complex interactions, to the numerical value of key variables when some exogenous variables undergo changes via policy, via shocks or simply as a result of long-term structural change. This raises two serious problems: (i) how close the model is to 'reality' and (ii) what channels could explain the numerical results.[12]

Some simulation models, like input–output (IO) and social accounting matrix models (SAM), by being empirically and quantitatively mounted, are partly but not fully devoid of deducing 'reality' from strong assumptions (Bulmer-Thomas 1982; Ciaschini 1988; Alarcon *et al.* 1990). Others, like computable general equilibrium models (CGE), contrary to input–output ones (IO), are normally strongly associated with deriving reality from axiomatic principles. They are based on maximizing exercises, well-behaved production functions (i.e. decreasing returns), equilibrium economics and other theoretical or purely expedient traits imposed to secure tractability rather than realism. Tractability in this context simply means how to secure convergence so that a unique numerical solution can be produced. So the name of the game is to secure *internal consistency* (i.e. no logical contradictions) and a unique numerical convergence (i.e. one set of equilibrium solutions).[13] As such, the numerical solutions (their direction and general levels) are often a foregone conclusion from the technical choices imposed by the practitioners. So the actual solution numbers and the qualitative interpretation, derived from the already incorporated choice of equations, functions, ad hoc parameters, calibration,[14] closures rules, assumptions and axioms, can only be taken with a good deal of caution if not scepticism about their relation with 'reality'. Furthermore, even when the equilibrium numbers after convergence are made available, it is not easy to interpret which included factors contributed more to it, as interactive simultaneity prevents clear-cut transmission channels. What is the use of results that show a negative GDP from some initial affected variable, if we cannot ascertain how that happened within the conceit of the model? Then more theory and assumptions are brought to bear for the purpose (Dervis *et al.* 1982; Shoven and Whalley 1992; Greenaway *et al.*

1993; Mitra-Khan 2008). For example, 'if a tariff on trade is increased by x percent, then GDP will fall by y percent, so a tariff policy should be this and that'. This conclusion can only be for the built-up simulation, via all this plethora of imposed traits, rather than for 'reality'. That is, the so-called *external consistency* (i.e. between the model and reality) is very much another supposition, or worse a truism, rather than the result of some proper methodological testing. To assess how robust the model is when changing some endogenous parameters slightly is hardly a proof of realism, but mostly one of stability.[15] Unfortunately, the way they are normally reported is by either glossing over all these creative features or simply ignoring them after presenting some of them explicitly at the beginning of a paper.

Simulation structure and solution numbers

Setting aside that most coefficients are set up from standard statistics, which may be subject to standard data quality, and that residual calibration in CGE models is simply forced to secure an accounting rather than economic equilibrium, solutions numbers are not easily interpreted. These come after several direct (first round) and indirect interactions (second and further rounds) until the interactive process converges to a unique numerical set, being its equilibrium solution. It is not easy to interpret analytically how this would actually happen, in which moment and where there could have been an amplification or, vice versa, what kind of behavioural actions and reactions primarily account for this or that result, so again a good deal of alternative explanations might do, which is another reason why simple tractable neoclassical functions and traits are preferred.

In the case of input–output (IO) models, this is simplified via empirical fixed coefficients and by implicitly assuming that in any round participants behave exactly in the same way given basic assumptions (e.g. linear structure, existence of idle capacity, no demand price changes, no use of buffers or other substitutions, elastic expectations, etc.), which may be reasonable in the short term for a stable economy, or as an accounting mechanism for comparing structural change between two periods (Albala-Bertrand 1999, 2006b). This may not be the case for an economy under the effects of a large disaster. Social Accounting Matrix (SAM) models are an extension of IO models that, by explicitly endogenizing variables and introducing some institutional disaggregation, may allow assessment of distributional and financial issues, but the bases are the same as the IO model. IO and SAM models have few behavioural traits incorporated, which makes them more mechanical than societal. But as long as such insufficiencies are properly recognized, its focus on economic interconnectedness is highly valuable for assessing possible transmissions of exogenous shocks or changes throughout the economy (Alarcon *et al.* 1990; Raa 2005).

In turn, CGE models, apart from the large amount of data they require and the fact that they also base a good deal of their structure on a SAM, are far too flexible as they are meant for the very long term the moment they use standard well-behaved functions.[16] So they are able to accommodate substitutions, and endogenize and respond to price changes as well as capacity constraints in a non-linear fashion (Okuyama 2009). But the way this is done is iterative, parsimonious and continuous and the result of standard optimized behaviour. In addition, by construction CGE models assume that the economy will operate with the same functional structure (production function, demand function, etc.) now and in the future, which is unwarranted (see our reference to forecasting economics above). This approach would exclude any discontinuity due to development traits, let alone a shock like a disaster.[17] So although these techniques offer some knowledge, this has to be taken at a long arm's length and qualified outside the model, especially via institutional and cultural traits, to serve any useful purpose, particularly in the case of disasters. It has been said that IO models overestimate the effects of a disaster, as there are no substitutions, while CGEs underestimate them, as substitutions happen at the speed of light (ibid.), but again this should be taken with caution, as IO models are necessarily short-term models, while CGE models are very long-term ones, so they are hardly comparable in what they simulate. As with the previous section, there is no point in doing a survey, as there are pretty competent surveys or edited collections available, such as Kunreuther and Rose (2004) and Okuyama (2007, 2009). Let's just see a few examples of what has been done via IO and CGE by their practitioners and the difficulties that they have encountered, whether they are aware of them or not.

Some simulation studies about disasters

I INPUT–OUTPUT (IO) AND SOCIAL ACCOUNTING MATRIX (SAM) MODELS

Some IO and SAM models have been applied to disasters to pinpoint the type of indirect (flow) effects that a disaster may have so as to assess the policy options that can be used to minimize such effects. Okuyama and Sahin (2009) resort to basic data on disaster loss from EM-DAT and refer to 184 disasters occurring between 1960 and 2007, attempting an ambitious enquiry in two parts.[18]

First, they attempt to know what would be the indirect effects of a loss of income from the direct effects on the capital stock working through an IO-SAM model. And second, they apply econometrics to the total effects so as to assess whether the inverted U-hypothesis actually holds, i.e. the total disaster effects on income losses will be lower in simple basic economies and in sophisticated richer economies, but higher in middle of the road economies, as proposed by Benson and Clay (2004). As regards the former, it can be used to learn how and where *potential* indirect effects could happen, and their strength, but it can also be used to show the weaknesses of the approach for anything that goes beyond identifying the sectors with higher normal multipliers. The second attempt about the inverted U, however, appears to hold little or no water, as I show below.

Setting aside the quality of the original data, as we have mentioned above, the study has several assumptions that should be spelled out. First, the authors are fully aware that they are assuming no disaster response whatsoever, as if the affected system was inert and lifeless. They justify this by saying that 'without knowing how the ... economy ... is crushed, the relief efforts may become inefficient and ineffective and the pace of recovery may turn out to be slower' (Okuyama and Sahin 2009: 2). This is hardly persuasive, as by proceeding this way they ignore the reality of inbuilt societal reactions. We would of course encourage the identification of *how* a direct effect may work its way out throughout the wider economy, but we see no point in assessing *how strong* these effects would be in a lifeless economy. What is the point of analysing how strong the bouncing of a ball would be if immediately after its first bouncing gravity is assumed to disappear! What matters is what endogenous response mechanisms are available and how effective they are, i.e. inbuilt resilience, and then where exogenous public and foreign support would be required. In other words, once the backward and forward linkages as well as the importance of sectoral and regional effects are known, it would then be possible to assess which of the affected sectors or regions have a higher pull and push power over the wider economy. It would be less relevant to learn what would be the strength of potential indirect effects in a lifeless system than to learn what are the substitution potential and inbuilt systemic trends and counteractions, as the same assumed unopposed strength is bound to have very different results, according to affected community and society. This is like the difference between earthquake magnitude and its social severity. The 2010 earthquake in Chile had a magnitude 63 times stronger than that of Haiti's in the same year.[19] But Haiti ended up on its knees, while Chile just suffered minor consequences (i.e. less than 500 deaths in Chile as compared to over 100,000 in Haiti, and so on). To include levels of development and resilience is a very different type of enquiry than that which seeks to know what would be the indirect (spreading) disaster effects in an inert system. Unsurprisingly they get large indirect losses of gross output, i.e. those ones that work through sectoral interdependence after a direct income loss occurs. But their system may also be inconsistent in other ways.

An IO model (and similarly a SAM) works by accounting all the intermediate demands (and corresponding supplies) that a system of interacting industries have to exercise so as to satisfy the production of a given amount of final demand output (aggregate demand or GDP). As is expected, one unit of final demand output would require more than one unit of gross output (i.e. intermediates plus final output), as the industry that receives the direct demand (e.g. shirts) will have to buy intermediate from other industries to satisfy it (e.g. cloth, sewing machines), and these other industries would have to demand intermediates from other industries to do the same (e.g. cotton and iron), and so on. That is, this is the sum of direct and indirect demands. Then, what an IO model can show is what amount of gross output one unit of final demand would require. So the starting point is a change in demand and the consequence of this is a final change in total (or gross) output. The inverse, or Leontief matrix, is a matrix of parameters that shows what this total effect will be (after first and later rounds), which is then also a matrix of total intermediate multipliers. In simple terms, it is the ratio of total gross output per unit of final demand. The fact that the models require a change in final demand (or income) to operate is the first serious problem, as disasters directly affect capital assets and very secondarily income. So how capital losses can be transformed into income losses without time and economic inconsistencies becomes a thorny issue.

The standard IO assumptions do not favour a situation like disaster either, as the authors are fully aware. As in short-term models, IO assumes that the capital stock is given and that it operates with idle capacity so that prices are also fixed to changes in final demand. Technical coefficients and therefore multipliers are assumed constant, i.e. whatever happens to the economy, the intermediate input requirements will be the same. It implicitly assumes that any change in final demand will be permanent, so producers will not modify their plans in any way whatsoever and will simply accept the effect of that initial change on their own intermediate demands. It also assumes linearity, so whatever the level of final demand, the total gross output requirement will keep the same proportion, so the implicit production function will relate primary inputs (capital and labour) in the same linear way. The IO model is then a transformer of final demand into gross output in an interdependent multi-sectoral system. This may work well for a stable economy in the short term (two to three years), but is very unlikely to in the case of abnormal exogenous shocks, like disasters, especially when their effects are considered transitory in nature (Albala-Bertrand 1993). That is to say, a negative change in final demand cannot possibly keep agents unmoved. They will try to weather the situation for as long as it lasts with a view to re-establishing their positions once normality returns. And this is the interesting and useful enquiry, which is the main thrust we attempt to address in this work.

The authors however assume that the system is inert and this leads to some technical problems. They transform direct stock losses (direct disaster effects) into final income losses so that the latter can be used as the starting point of the IO system mechanics. They use the capital–output ratio for the purpose, but then there are two snags here. First, this ratio is calculated from official statistics, which come in yearly terms. So by applying the ratio to get a number for the potential effect on income, they are implicitly assuming that one year has already elapsed and no response whatsoever has occurred. The second snag is that not only is this value unlikely to happen, as shown by Albala-Bertrand (2004/1993), but in addition they are also implicitly assuming that the capital-output ratio transforms capital into gross output rather than final demand. Capital-output ratios are always capital-to-GDP ratios, as the authors seem aware of but find inconsequential. So we already have the inert impact on final demand (i.e. GDP) from capital losses, but they further transform this into 'final income' by using the multiplier matrix. This makes no sense, as GDP is already final income.

In addition there is a conceptual inconsistency, which if put right the whole imaginary economy is likely to collapse. If the system is inert, then it is inert everywhere. This means that capital losses cannot be replaced or substituted. So the economy has to operate with less capital than it started with, but they implicitly assume that the starting capital is the same as before the disaster, which is inconsistent unless the capital destroyed was only from the one that was idle in the first place, as substitutions are not permitted. But if that was the case, then it cannot possibly have any effect on income.[20] All this simply shows that the standard IO and SAM models are not equipped to deal with disasters without serious inconsistencies. The disaster capital loss and its transformation into income are only warranted in a completely inert and lifeless system. For an actual disaster, it would be enough to know which sectors or industries or regions have the stronger normal backward and forward linkages, and how important these units are for the national economy and how strongly these happened to be directly affected by a disaster. That is, what matters is to learn about both the economic localization of the damage and the wider linkages of the damaged sectors. And from here to assess what is their substitution potential (see Chapter 2), their endogenous resilience and how they can be exogenously supported, if need be.

The study then goes into an attempt to assess the validity of the inverted-U hypothesis. Once the study has arrived at the total disaster impact on gross output in the way described above, this is used as an independent variable (i.e. total impact divided by GDP) to assess via an econometric model whether the inverted-U hypothesis holds. They find that it does not. Countries with higher development levels (GDP *per capita* is used for this) have a lower share of total indirect effects in GDP in a rather linear way, without the bump for countries in middle development levels. But the data used cannot possibly warrant such results, as their total impact numbers are the ones coming from an inert system, not a living one. In other words, what was meant to be *potential* (i.e. the result of an inert system) is openly used as if it was *actual* (i.e. the result of a living system) so as to assess empirically a theoretical proposition. Hence the model does not use comparable data. But there is also a further conceptual inconsistency. The data of gross output loss, which feed the econometric model, come from a system that does not acknowledge levels of development, i.e. the inert system. These data are now used against actual GDP *per capita*, which comes some way to differentiating development levels, at least those associated with activity levels and development potential.[21] Technically, all this is interesting, but not particularly relevant to assess disaster in real societies.

Other models use the same inert approach to deal with more focused potential problems, but on the whole the approach carries similar insufficiencies to the above. For example, Yamano *et al.* (2007) aim at identifying hotspots. That is, the economic importance of districts (units of 500^2 meters) and their regional potential indirect effects from a direct disaster impact via IO coefficients and input relationships (trade flows and distances) especially associated with transport networks. The economic loss is defined as (gross) output loss based on the IO framework, explicitly ignoring any exogenous counteraction (public, foreign, etc.) and implicitly ignoring any endogenous reactions (from insurance to communal responses, passing through network shifts and others). The main aim of the simulation is actually to measure the economic importance of each district by means of its inert total gross output impact. The main assumption is that capacity cannot be recovered in the short run (implicitly assuming that network shifting at national level is nonexistent). In addition, they come up with a final demand loss without explaining how they arrive at it. In other words, they implicitly assume that a good deal of time has passed (probably a year) before the system operates via losses of demand, which is the same problem described above. Simulations are carried out for this purely hypothetical set-up to assess the potential output effect of each district, assuming that economic activities are suspended for 12 months. Then they produce another simulation for electricity disruptions (economic loss from power outages), again assuming 12 months' interruption, despite the fact that they are fully aware that this type of disruption is sorted out in a few days, if not hours. And a third simulation refers to actual material damages coming from the 1995 Hanshin Awaji Great Earthquake. Under the assumption of a lifeless system, it is not surprising that they estimate that indirect effects are significantly higher than the (equally) estimated direct loss.[22] Why did they not produce an *actual* overall GDP loss (if there was any) and compare it with their estimated ones? Beyond assessing the linkage importance of the said districts, which only require the calculation of backward and forward linkages, this exercise is of little policy consequence.

Other models have attempted to correct for the said inertia, with moderate success. For example, Anderson *et al.* (2007) use an 'inoperability IO model' or IIM (i.e. an IO model with normalized production losses by reducing production plan levels in virtue of disaster damage), to assess the indirect effects of an actual three-day blackout in the 2003 US North-East, within the electrical power grid system. This ignores both endogenous and exogenous reaction, during and especially after the blackout when full work resumed. Notice that no capital or labour was lost, neither was production. Production got delayed not lost. And no doubt intensification of work over the following weeks, plus increased production coming from other non-affected areas and states recovered the lot and more. So again this is an academic exercise that compares the official and other loss estimates (from the same authors) with the ones coming from the IIM model, and they are not very different. The interesting thing would have been to compare with what actually happened after the disaster. This analysis might be OK for very specific firms rather than an industry, as macro-level recovery is very different from a micro one. Again, simple backward and forward linkage associations with the source of the blackout and its economic localization plus the sophistication (potential endogenous reactions) of the areas (firms and communities) affected would have come a good way towards assessing risk and therefore exogenous response. Policy options without reference to inbuilt reactions (local, regional and national) are little more than an academic exercise.

A different kind of approach is found in a study by Donaghy *et al.* (2007). The main aim of this model is to assess disaster effects in shorter periods, as most of the disaster effects are actually concentrated on the impact and its immediate aftermath, which cannot be captured in models based on annual data. Of course, a question can emerge right away: what is the point in capturing these shorter effects if they will fade away soon afterwards? Anyway, they use quarterly data and the attention is directed to the estimation and adjustment of IO coefficients to this shorter period via REIM (regional econometric IO model). So a set of econometrically calculated parameters are to modify the standard IO coefficients. A SIM (sequential industry model) is then applied on quarterly data, which may still be too long to capture short-term effects. This is applied in continuous time and somehow in a non-linear fashion. Non-linearity is OK, but is not a parsimonious type, as stops and goes are clearly the real thing. Differential equations are hardly a feature of reality, but of tractable models. And finally, the use of econometrics as an implicit forecasting of continuous time IO coefficients is just as unreliable as standard econometric forecasting. But it has also issues related to data and forced ad hoc features (see Okuyama *et al.* 2004). In addition, by construction, it lacks actual responsiveness within sectors, i.e. the type that does not necessarily affect the IO coefficient by representing shifts within the sectoral network. Furthermore, shifts across sectors and borders may affect coefficients in very different ways to the SIM.

The authors claim that industrial fragmentation via outsourcing and disaggregation of activities is a source of serious problems when the network where this operates gets disrupted. This is unpersuasive. First, a disaster in an old fully vertically integrated industry/firm has the capacity to exert significantly more damage than in the alternative case. It can cripple the industry at source and in addition it can sever it from input and output markets via destruction of transport infrastructures. A disaggregated one, on the other hand, will have the benefit of leaving significant portions unscathed, and therefore can react via network shifting within the sector, between sectors and across borders, apart from standard inventory counteractions and the like (see Albala-Bertrand 1993). So again we have here a study that focuses on convenient but unrealistic targets. All we actually require is the standard normal pre-disaster backward and forward linkages, economic localization and normal industrial behaviour as a setup.

II COMPUTABLE GENERAL EQUILIBRIUM (CGE) MODELS

In turn, CGE models have, as said, the problem of excess flexibility and a plethora of unrealistic traits to make them tractable. This technique is carried out via multi-market simulation models based on the simultaneous optimizing behaviour of categories of consumers and firms, as if they were single individuals, subject to economic account balances and resource constraints. Although CGE models are non-linear and therefore seemingly closer to aspects of real economies, such as economies of scale and the like, optimizing individualistic behaviour is hardly a trait of reality, and even less at the macro and social levels. Treating a sector, let alone the whole economy, as if it were a single 'rational' individual is methodological nonsense (Kirman 1992). Setting aside the insurmountable problems of information and its processing, optimizing behaviour operates only via the market in response to relative prices, and these from supply-demand imbalances, which is already a strain in normal times, as interaction of utilities and inertia, like herd behaviour, cooperative behaviour, goodwill and other societal non-market behaviour, are ignored (Kirman 2010, 2011), i.e. socially networked individuals are ignored.

The response in disasters is hardly in the general direction of individualistic optimizing behaviour. It mostly operates outside the market via non-price information and both endogenous and exogenous responses, which go well beyond relative prices. What an impacted community seeks is not to maximize a so-called utility function or a profit function, but to re-establish basic pre-disaster conditions at communal and individual levels, which has little or nothing to do with maximizing behaviour. So as an academic exercise, CGEs are interesting, but marred by the implicit interpretation associated with the mathematically tractable behavioural functions and the other mentioned insufficiencies.

For example, Tsuchiya *et al.* (2007) use Spatial CGE to assess the impact of a hypothetical earthquake on transport in 14 zones of Japan. This is part of similar studies about disruption of main utilities from disasters (e.g. electricity grids, water supply and the like). The model is set up, as are most CGE models, under the strong assumption of equilibrium from individuals' optimizing behaviour, well-behaved production functions, convenient expenditure functions, imposed closure rules and not least a forced calibration process to establish an initial quantitative equilibrium. Once this is done, different scenarios are imposed with and without exogenous countermeasures. The problem is not just that the earthquakes are hypothetical, but also that the simulated 'reality' is. In many ways this is still, like standard IOs, a societally lifeless and mechanical model. In addition, this CGE model (implicitly) translates capital losses into final demand ones (transport losses into output and final demand losses), which is unwarranted, as shown earlier for IO.

Actual inbuilt reactions are not just those resulting from supply-demand disequilibrium in the market, but more importantly those resulting from institutional, communal and national reactions, operating outside the market, but reinforcing the market mechanisms at global levels. It is easy to show that if indirect effects are stopped in their tracks, then it is highly unlikely that there will be important effects at national level or at all. The fact is that normally containment does actually happen at regional and national levels so as to secure macro functionality, even at the expense of the directly impacted areas (see Chapters 4 and 5).

Finally, Rose and Liao (2005) develop an ambitious CGE to analyse the consequences of water disruptions following a disaster in the USA. They add some variations in the calculation of parameters for shorter-term effects and also some theoretical decomposition to separate direct from indirect effects. Although more properly what they do is to separate first round income (flow) effects from later flow rounds. Direct effects are always stock effects, which can only be transformed into flow effects under strong, timeless and pretty unrealistic assumptions, as criticized above. They link CES production function parameters to various types of producer adaptations and responses in emergencies, meaning that the closure is necessarily neoclassical with fully optimizing behaviour. Still, there is here an attempt to make equilibrium less easy and speedy than normal unrestricted neoclassical CGE models. They also develop algorithms for recalibrating the parameters of production functions to empirical or simulation data via optimizing mathematical exercises and also decomposing partial and general equilibrium responses. This is certainly a more elaborated and academically interesting CGE model than standard types. According to them, it has the advantages of theoretical formality and consistency. They are however aware of most of the insufficiencies of the methodology.

But for all the trait-realism they attempt to incorporate, this is still a pretty theoretical exercise based on neoclassical tractable functions, albeit with certain modifications. For example, they attempt to modify the elasticity of substitution between factors and/or total factor productivity (TFP) to allow for possible changes in the disaster aftermath. But the functions they use do not allow for resource idleness, so the only way to modify neoclassical elasticities is under the assumption that a new equally efficient technology is available. That is why these functions are meant for the long term, as there is no expectation that alternative efficient combinations of factors could happen in the short term, as that would necessarily imply an alternative efficient combining technology. On the other hand, changes in TFP can be more acceptable, as it is known that in the aftermath of disasters responses via labour and community resilience, operating on productive factors from outside, are intensified over normal times. So given a basic resource availability, the process can become more productive in the short to medium run, but probably more costly, so not necessarily more efficient. This may be represented by a short-run jump in the TFP parameter, but this will still be done over the same pre-disaster production function, which may still be unwarranted. Finally, this CGE is regional and mostly self-contained (for the Portland Metro Area in 2000), which mostly excludes responses from outside the area, which is again unrealistic in real disaster cases.

So, following Okuyama (2009), IO models overestimate disaster effects, while CGE models underestimate them. But the two approaches are clearly unrealistic in general, let alone for the case of disasters, and don't measure the same things, so they are hardly comparable. However, the issue about interconnectedness, benchmark linkages and counteractive behaviours at firm, industrial, sectoral and national levels, both economic and extra-economic, are paramount to understanding the importance of indirect effects and therefore long-term and cumulative effects. These techniques however are not nearly appropriate enough for the task. The IO framework, rather than the model, is however a good starting point.

Conclusion

We started this chapter by claiming that any quantitative study produces results that are assumption ridden. Assumptions on data sources enter assumptions on quantitative techniques, the results of which (black-box techniques) or the construction of which (simulation methods) are then interpreted with assumption- and axiom-dominated theoretical models. We then showed that in the case of quantitative methods applied to disasters, the assumption-cascade-dependent numerical results were more unreliable than in normal studies for a number of reasons associated with the quality of data, the ability of techniques and the theoretical interpretation of reality and, in passing, that of the results. So the conclusions that come from them have to be taken with a good deal of caution and scepticism, especially when analysing longer-term effects of disasters on the economy and not least for policy design.

Quantitative methods, however well designed, are unlikely to settle the issue about the importance of these effects. On the one hand, black-box methods are not strong enough to capture sudden shocks like disasters, let alone if the shock fades away soon after the impact, as they carry the first year effect forward. This in addition has the problem of a realistic interpretation, which more often than not is relegated to axiomatic theory with its plethora of convenient assumptions. On the other hand, simulation methods create models that already contain the interpretation of reality via mathematical features of standard economic theory, which are mounted on a bed of axioms and assumptions that depart from reality as a matter of mathematical tractability fact. These simulation models especially fail to deal with sudden shocks, while in addition the tracing of numerical results, especially in CGEs, is not a foregone conclusion, given the complex interactions and endogeneity of most of the process of numerical convergence.

Some simulation models attempt to capture some of these sudden disaster features via ad hoc manipulation of parameters, which is welcome, as ad hoc solutions (i.e. exogenous modifications of model traits), should not be relegated to a secondary place, given that disaster impacts and responses are more likely to represent *discontinuities* and network shifts than smooth processes. Assuming that economics is a science, then it is definitely not a hard science like physics, so attempts at capturing changing societal behavioural characteristics (parameters, functional forms, specifications and the like) with features endogenous to a mathematical model are at best academically interesting, but largely devoid of societal reality, and therefore not very useful for both understanding and policy. What these models lack and are unable to incorporate is a proper political economy framework of institutional stylized facts of observed societal reality under stress.

So given that disasters represent discontinuities, qualitative changes and fast substitutions, a political economy argumentation behind a general framework may better advance knowledge and policy. If this was sound, then partial quantitative studies, set within this general political economy framework, would help advance the understanding of these and other effects with more propriety. We then focus on the relationships between economic localization and societal networking, so there is no intention to justify observations on the back of statistics, but only to illustrate some issues in relation to societal functionality.

2 A political economy framework

Functionality, localization and networks

Introduction

In a political economy context, we want to show how concepts of societal functionality, disaster localization and societal networking can have an important bearing on the importance of national macroeconomic effects, including long-term and cumulative effects, which we define below. Macroeconomic effects, whether short, medium or longer term, should be referred and analysed in the context of macro functionality and development. Even if the national macroeconomy is not functionally affected, and therefore can re-establish its activity levels soon after the shock, which is normally the case with sudden disasters, directly affected people, businesses and localities may lose significant degrees of functionality at least in the immediate aftermath. But we first focus on the national macroeconomy and society as a unit. In later chapters we focus on affected people's and business's endogenous response mechanisms vis-à-vis systemic traits in connection to some *ex-ante* and *ex-post* public and foreign policies.

Functionality

This book is about the issue of functionality of an economy and society in the aftermath of a disaster impact. Stock losses and direct income losses (direct effects) could potentially affect macroeconomic functionality only via flow effects (indirect effects).[1] We define *societal functionality* as the capacity of a system to operate in a *viable* way. In the term 'societal' we group the network of social, political, economic and cultural institutions and their behaviours, whether formal or otherwise, which makes up the social system. By *system viability* we mean a system that can *endogenously* survive (self-repair), reproduce (stably expand) and develop (evolve and improve). Longer-term functionality can be assessed by means of an appropriate analytical framework, which is what we intend here. We do not attempt a quantitative analysis, as criticized in Chapter 1, nor do we focus on trivial long-term effects. For example, the disaster loss of a bridge, or for that matter of a single bean, if not replaced, will carry as a loss forever. But if it does not cause problems of macro functionality, then it is not a long-term problem for the national economy. On the other hand, if it is replaced, the replacement cost will carry as an accounting loss forever, but again functionality will now not be impaired. In other words, losses of labour, capital stock, direct losses of consumption and investment goods, and direct losses of money and income, may only make macroeconomic sense, i.e. avoiding the fallacy of composition, if they are assessed in terms of their effects on the workings of the economy as a whole. Otherwise, we will be treading on triviality, i.e. any loss item to a disaster has a long-term accounting effect in itself. That is, a direct loss of say the equivalent of 5 per cent of GDP will, just like the loss of a single bean, carry forever. But if it does not affect macroeconomy functionality, i.e. the economy re-establishes its capacity and dynamics, then in this conception it is unlikely to have long-term macro effects of significance or at all.

Systemic functionality and local/national tension

If economy and society can endogenously absorb and/or react to a disaster shock as well as give endogenous use to exogenous response flows, then this economy has systemic functionality. Notice that in this definition if the exogenous response (domestic and foreign) only establishes a parallel structure that bypasses the ongoing system either because the latter is unable to absorb such a response or because the exogenous response is badly designed and competes with the system, then functionality will be either precarious or impaired, respectively, as has sometimes been reported (Lateef 1982). This is related to the issues of vulnerability and resilience that we discuss later.

Disasters are overwhelmingly localized, as properly defined later, so they affect a segment of a national system, which is normally integrated to the national and international economies at many levels and strengths. The local and the national levels are however tightly linked, as there is a permanent systemic tension between the national interest at country level and the local interest at community level, e.g. groups, towns, cities, regions within a country, which is even more present in the case of disasters. A proper balance between the national and the local should be the way to tackle disasters, but normal endogenous and exogenous responses, wittingly or otherwise, tend to sequence a response favouring first national functionality and then that of the directly affected areas.

From a systemic outlook, the above would be functionally consistent. That is, systemic actions from private and public reactive behaviours, which seek to divert and create resources in favour of the disaster area, should be generally considered as a consistent response. But it would also be systemically consistent if these response actions initially and partially insulate the national economy from the disaster area at the expense of such an area so as to secure macro functionality. The latter however may have negative consequences for the integrated autonomy of the affected locality. In an extreme theoretical case, supplies and demands can be fully compensated outside the affected locality so that the national economy does not undergo significant differences. But the local economy would then be fully bypassed, impairing its national and foreign economic insertion and therefore its development. Most sudden disasters do not have serious consequences on the macroeconomy, even if the directly affected locality is badly affected and still trying to recover a few years after the impact. This may be an indication of functionality bypassing and probably lack of political will to help the affected locality to re-establish its full functionality. Here is an area where public response policy, via direct and indirect stimulus and actions, both *ex ante* and *ex post*, can and do play a fundamental role in securing a minimal balance.

Vulnerability, resilience and functionality

The vulnerability and resilience of a system are two sides of the same coin. Vulnerability is associated with the degree of exposure of society's frameworks, social groups and individuals to extreme events, while resilience is associated with the specific processes and items that characterize such exposures and therefore with the mechanisms and policies that can be resorted to to recover the affected system. Authors have referred to them, whether using the terms or not, from the very beginning of the analysis of society under stress, especially in the case of disasters (e.g. Prince 1920; Sorokin 1942; Dynes 1970; Quarantelli 1978).

We may simply call vulnerability the risk of potential destruction and damage to a given societal unit from the direct impact of a disaster. So it refers to the state of things as they are just before a disaster strikes. Resilience, in turn, refers to the capacity and ability of such a societal unit, and the ones that can be indirectly affected, to react and recover after such an impact has happened. Both are clearly related, as units that are less vulnerable because they have a quality of resources that can withstand a good deal of the impact and have better and diverse network connections will normally be more resilient. This is what some authors call inherent resilience, i.e. the resilience associated with the inner and outer architecture and conditions enjoyed by the societal unit in focus. They differentiate this type of resilience with one that they term adaptive resilience (Mileti 1999; Perrings 2001; Rose and Liao 2005), which refers to the ability to adapt and innovate, usefully exploiting the new environment and conditions for the sake of survival, continuity and development, i.e. functionality. Again, a good deal of this adaptive reaction comes from conditions that were in place before the disaster, such as management ability and flexibility, precaution and preparedness, motivation and ingenuity, existing and new networks and the like. So a unit may be vulnerable, but may still have a high degree of resilience.

However, to put concepts in a consistent framework with our approach to a disaster situation (Albala-Bertrand 1993), it would be more useful to differentiate between endogenous and exogenous responses and speak of endogenous resilience and exogenous resilience. Inherent resilience would then correspond to the endogenous capability to bounce back, given the structure, dynamics and ethos of an affected social and/or economic unit and its societal links with other units within and outside the disaster zone. This type of resilience does not require especial changes to face disasters, but only to extend and deploy its existing protocols and routines. It is endogenous because it is inbuilt as part of the standard self-regulatory mechanisms to tackle normal changes in the social and economic environment. As such, it mostly operates from below. In turn, adaptive resilience would correspond to the exogenous abilities and availabilities that can be resorted to to bring the unit back to functionality, i.e. survival, continuity and development. This type does require significant changes in objectives and therefore policies, as expectations suddenly change in virtue of the sudden ambience changes. This then goes well beyond the standard self-regulatory mechanisms associated with formal and informal response following the feedbacks from a normal societal environment. It is exogenous because it mostly operates from above and acts via ad hoc changes in ingenuity, policy and decision making.

An analytical framework

An important issue then is the extension, strength and quality of interconnectedness between the local and the national. In the context of droughts in sub-Saharan Africa, Benson and Clay (1998) proposed that the countries that are more vulnerable to disasters are those in an intermediate stadium of development, while simple economies (made mostly of isolated local economies) and complex economies (made of a more integrated and diversified national whole) are less vulnerable. That made for a Kuznets type of inverted U, with vulnerability on the vertical axis and development level on the horizontal one (Kuznets 1955).[2] This is, generally, a useful way of thinking also about societal networks and their associated vulnerability and resilience. It should be noticed that most of the intermediate countries studied by the authors recovered functionality levels within a year or so, which means that while they were potentially more vulnerable and less resilient in the immediate short term, they were not equally so in the medium term, which included external support. Associated with endogenous reactions, this seems to depend more on the type of disaster and how confined its economic effects were than only on the country's development complexity, which takes us to the issue of localization.

Economic localization

In most studies, the use of the word *localization* usually refers to the geographic extent of either the event or the disaster impact itself. This type of extent does not appear to mean much in the absence of the type of economy that is within the affected area, so we define a disaster as *localized* if it affects a confined area of economic activity. This implies that a geographically widespread disaster can be economically localized (e.g. a drought in a diversified country), or widespread (e.g. a drought in an agriculturally undiversified least developed country, like a Sahelian country). In what follows, the term '*disaster zone or area*' is used for any collection of stock items affected by the initial impact, whether this is located within a given geographic area or not.

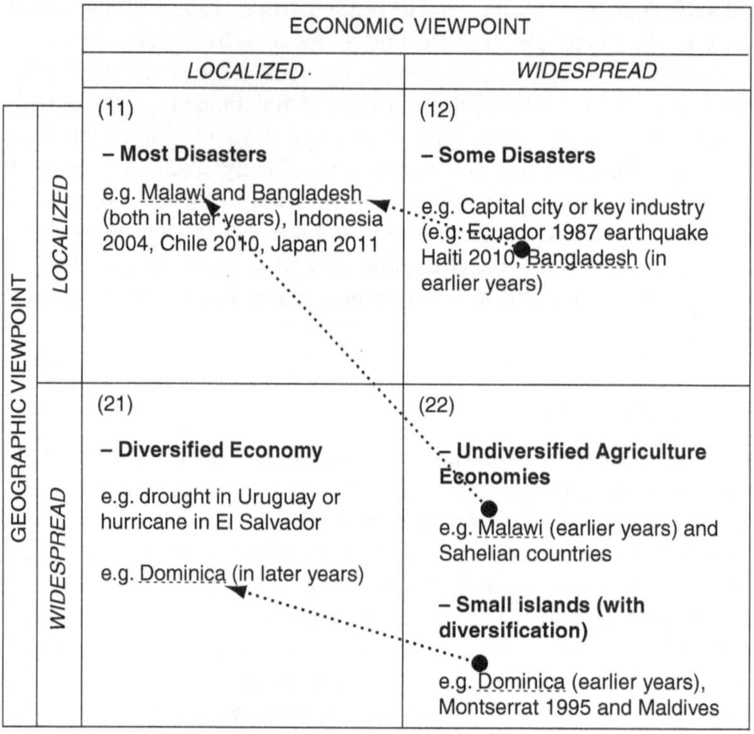

Figure 2.1 The issue of localization.*

Note
* This classification refers only to direct disaster effects (stock effects). Notice also that some countries are underlined when they appear in two different cells at different times. This shows that similar disasters are likely to become more localized over time, as countries both generally develop and specifically protect against hazards.

Our concept of localization corresponds to the first column of Figure 2.1, i.e. *economic localization*: cells (11) and (21). This shows that a disaster can be economically localized, whether it is geographically localized or widespread. Cell (11) shows the most common case, as it is likely that the majority of geographically localized disasters are also economically localized. As examples, we can focus on Bangladesh (especially floods and cyclones) and Malawi (droughts). Since the 1990s these countries have undergone geographically localized disasters, which had severe impacts in the affected areas, but did not translate into significant losses for the functioning of the economy as a whole in the medium term (Clay *et al.* 2003; Benson and Clay 2004). The initial impacts were short-lived and more than compensated for within a year or so. This is also the case of the 2004 tsunami in Indonesia, which would have been localized even without the overgenerous aid committed by the rest of the world (Cosgrave 2007). The same was the case with the very high magnitude earthquakes of Chile in 2010 and Japan in 2011 (Richter 8.8 and 9.0, respectively). Cell (12) shows that some geographically localized disasters can also be economically widespread if they strike a key industry or staple (normally an exporting one, like oil or bananas) or a main industrial/political city (normally the capital city). For example, in 1987, an earthquake in Ecuador damaged the main oil pipe for this export. This is however a rare event, as even when major earthquakes strike a capital city (e.g. Managua 1972, Guatemala City 1976, Mexico City 1985) they do not translate into widespread economic effects, so this is more possibility than necessity (Albala-Bertrand 2004/1993). Haiti's earthquake in 2010 may qualify for this cell as well, but mainly because the country was in serious and almost permanent difficulties, which the disaster worsened. Another possibility would be the cyclone and floods in Bangladesh (then East Pakistan) contributing to the separatist momentum and civil war of independence in the early 1970s. The disasters appear to have acted as triggers of a growing institutional conflict with West Pakistan (Albala-Bertrand 1993). But the above disasters were geographically localized, which in normal times would be unlikely to create significant widespread effects on the polity, let alone the macroeconomy.

Cell (21) shows that geographically widespread disasters can also be economically localized. This is the case when a geographically widespread disaster strikes a diversified economy, mainly affecting one economic sector, normally the agricultural sector, e.g. droughts in Latin America or even widespread hurricanes in diversified islands like Dominica since the 1980s. It would be unusual that this unleashes important longer-term macroeconomic effects, unless the affected sector was pivotal for the rest of the economy, which is less likely in diversified open economies. Notice also that even when one sector or industry undergoes the brunt of damage from a sudden disaster, like a flood or earthquake or hurricane, this sector would be unlikely to be fully impaired, as disaster impact effects are never homogeneous. Finally, cell (22) represents the case of geographically widespread disasters that also have an economically widespread impact. This normally refers to a geographically widespread disaster that strikes an undiversified agricultural economy (e.g. droughts in Sahelian countries) or a small semi-diversified island (e.g. hurricanes in small Caribbean islands, like St Lucia and Dominica in the late 1970s – fishing, agriculture and tourism might suffer badly). It also includes rare events like Montserrat's volcano in 1995. The latter would have been widespread however diversified the economy was at the time, as all sectors would have suffered total or partial impairment, which might be expected to cause structural change (Benson and Clay 2004). Significant structural change in the wake of this disaster would be an indicator of its catastrophic nature, as was the case in Montserrat. In most cases of widespread disaster, however, the persistence of the macroeconomic effects, whether positive or negative, would be confined to around two to three years after the disaster impact, except in slowly developing disasters, like some droughts (Albala-Bertrand 1993; Benson and Clay 2004). So only cases in cell (22), and to a lesser extent in cell (21), might satisfy the basic conditions required for a disaster to become a catastrophe, as defined in Chapter 4. But even here this is highly unlikely, as explained later.

The dotted arrows in Figure 2.1 show that some disaster-prone countries, which were located in cells (12) and (22) in early years, reappear in cell (11) or (21) in later years, i.e. the countries undergo more localized disasters from similar natural events over time. For example, Malawi moves from (22) to (11), while Dominica moves from (22) to (21) and Bangladesh from (12) to (21). This is an indication that for disaster-prone countries, as a rule, development can be conceived as a process that transforms all types of disaster into economically localized ones, i.e. towards cells (11) and (21). This appears to have been the case of the three countries mentioned above (Benson and Clay 2004). This is then also an indication that development is likely to reduce macroeconomic vulnerability to disasters, while increasing societal resilience to withstand them. This process would be reinforced and sped up by disaster policies that explicitly seek such an outcome, but such policies are more likely to come up in the aftermath of large natural disasters than in normal times.

Therefore, development itself appears to be a process whereby all disasters become more economically localized. That is, 'disasters are primarily a problem *of* development, but essentially not a problem *for* development' (Albala-Bertrand 1993: 202, original emphasis). Thus, any policy process contributing to a diversified, integrative and sustainable development must incidentally contribute to reducing economic and social vulnerability to disasters, and therefore increasing resilience, as in developed countries. That is, given that development is a process that increases the complexity of a societal setting via all-embracing networks that widen and deepen society's interconnectedness, then societal networking is of paramount importance in analysing functionality and therefore the duration and intensity of disaster effects.

Localization and substitution potential

The more economically confined the direct disaster effects, the more the potential for substitution from unaffected economic units. Once we know what the geographical spread of the disaster is, it would be possible to assess its economic importance in terms of sectoral, regional and national dimensions, focusing especially on production, exports, domestic demand, capital and employment. These can come from standard national income accounts, hopefully divided into appropriate regions. Assuming that there are appropriate statistics, then it would be useful to count with the importance of the pull and push factor on the rest of the economy via the pre-disaster backward and forward linkages.

At a more disaggregated level, the information is normally scattered and hardly consistent, but if possible information about how many and which type of firms and households were directly affected would be of great use to circumscribe the effective localization of the disaster. In the same vein, what type of infrastructures, especially transport and communications, were affected. The latter, together with housing, is normally the one for which there is more information, especially in the case of vital infrastructures. Then information about the expected duration of the hindrance, especially in the case of physical

Box 2.1 The case of the Maldives' hidden economic localization

The Maldives is an archipelagic small country with some 300,000 people, currently enjoying a lower-middle GDP *per capita* of US$4,900 (in ppp) and generally good social indicators. Its main economic sector is tourism, accounting for 28 per cent of GDP, most of employment and more than 60 per cent of the Maldives' foreign exchange receipts. Over 90 per cent of government tax revenue comes from import duties and tourism-related taxes. Some 80 per cent of the country area is one metre or less above sea level, which sets worries about sea erosion and sea levels from global warming in the long term. Fishing is the second leading sector, and agriculture and manufacturing play only a secondary role.

The 2004 tsunami caused some 100 casualties and 12,000 displaced people. It initially affected only two of the main islands in a widespread way and significantly so all the other islands. Initial estimates of loss and damage, which should be taken with caution (Telford and Cosgrave 2006), claim to represent some two-thirds of GDP. The fact is that GDP fell by 5.1 per cent in 2005, but recovered swiftly after that, by means of a fast recovery in tourism, helped by disaster reconstruction and the development of new resorts, among other positive response policies. The growth rate reached over 20 per cent in 2006 and around 7 per cent in 2007. Here is the case of a widespread impact which seems to have affected housing, infrastructures and productive sectors but does not translate into economic functionality consequences. This is mostly due to the fact that in 2005 GDP did not fall mainly because of constraints in tourism's physical capacity to receive normal levels of guests, but to both significant falls in new tourists and a strong level of cancellations due to misplaced disaster fear. By mid-2005 nearly 100 per cent of tourist capacity seems to have recovered (World Bank-ADB-UN 2005), but some half of existing room capacity remained empty. It recovered fully the following year, however. So, setting aside the likely overestimation of losses (especially on the expectation of significant foreign aid), public reaction plus insurance and foreign funding helped repair and rehabilitate affected infrastructures, associated with the service tourist industry, which seemed to recover more easily than other sectors. This is especially true as the standards of international tourism, associated with building structures and conditions, were basically unscathed once the sea withdrew. Most of the response was concentrated in the clearance of streets and landscape as well as the repair and clean-up of hotel basements, ground and first floors (IMF 2005; TEC 2006).

Although it is still too early to judge, it seems that there is no indication of negative longer-term disaster effects on the functionality of the macroeconomy. This is actually the case of a geographically widespread disaster with deceptively widespread economic direct effect. The direct effects of the tsunami on the built-up environment (of tourism especially) were mostly superficial, meaning that the disaster was actually a localized one, which thanks to the foreign aid (acting on tourist linkages) recovered significantly faster than expected.

network infrastructures, would also be useful in generally assessing the potential flow effect of the directly affected area in question alone, which of course is not the same as the indirect flow effects on the economy as a whole, as we have clarified and will more specifically clarify later.

The potential for substitution comes from the existence of available alternative supply/demand sources, from alternative transport infrastructures available, and from how reactive private endogenous reactions and public exogenous responses are. Of course, a good deal of this cannot be known from existing statistics and data, which is why we propose specific surveys in our Appendix to make it easier to anticipate firms' behaviour and reactions and therefore to make more effective the public and foreign responses. The surveys would help the learning about how many economic units depend on the affected supplies and/or demand of directly affected firms, as this will be both the source of indirect effects as well as the stimuli of frustrated economic units for compensatory network shifting.

Meanwhile, we can anticipate the importance of potential effects on macro functionality via the calculation of economic substitution potential, assuming that the emergency is over and some infrastructure rehabilitation is under way (i.e. via existing alternative and makeshift infrastructures), which normally happens in the first few weeks. Then we can produce indexes of substitution potential (SP) by simply inverting the ratio of the actually affected sector-to-total sector, actually affected regional economy-to-total regional economy and these two to the national economy. This gives rise to two main types of substitution potential: (i) at general level, e.g. if 5 per cent of the economy has been directly affected, then the national SP would be 20 times (100/5) and (ii) at sectoral level, e.g. if 10 per cent of a sector had been directly affected, then the sectoral SP would be 10 times (100/10). So the SP is the number of times that the rest of the economy could substitute the potential losses of output coming from both the directly affected sectors and the local economy. This would be done via increases in output, reduction of inventories, imports and the like in a networked economic context of linkage shifts and other substitutions, which we deal with in the next chapters.

Disaster situation

A disaster situation can be analytically divided into the impact side, the response side and the institutionally interfering effects coming from both (Albala-Bertrand 1993). A disaster impact is normally the result of a physically or societally uncompensated tension, which translates into death, damage, destruction and the disarticulation of societal frameworks. In the case of natural disasters the uncompensated tension is due to the physical weakness of structures and societal processes that fail to compensate for extreme natural events, such as earthquakes, hurricanes, floods and the like. As such, even if the natural event were fully exogenous to society, the physical resistance to geophysical phenomenon would not be. It depends on both disaster-proof technology and organization, and sociopolitical access to it, which mostly respond to endogenous societal processes.[3]

Once a disaster impact has occurred, three main types of effects ensue: direct (or stock) effects, indirect (or flow) effects and societal interfering (or institutional) effects. The latter are more clearly associated with the response, as shown below. Direct effects have an impact on the quality and levels of human populations (injury and deaths) as well as on the quality and levels of physical and animal stocks (damage and destruction). In turn, indirect effects derive from the disarticulations caused by the direct effects, affecting the interrelations between physical structures and between people, which may translate into flow or functionality failures in the economy, public activities, household conditions and the states of health and nutrition (ibid.).

For the economic system, direct effects mostly represent losses to the capital stock and labour, while indirect effects are a consequence of the disarticulation of productive units and distributional channels wrought by direct effects. These represent losses to functioning flows and activity, in terms of foregone production and income, savings and investment, productivity and efficiency and the like, which if not counteracted may be represented in out-of-trend variations of end-year macro variables such as GDP growth, investment ratio, unemployment rate and the like, especially in the short term, which are extremely difficult to isolate from other non-disaster perturbations, as was shown in Chapter 1.

Disaster response, on the other hand, is motivated by the disaster impact and can be defined as a wide array of endogenous and exogenous reactions, measures and policies that are aimed at mitigating, counteracting and preventing disaster impacts and effects. The response side of a disaster situation can be articulated as follows. Once a disaster impact has arisen, the impact effects themselves stimulate both the unfolding of systemically inbuilt mechanisms of response, i.e. endogenous response, and the creation of especially designed response measures, i.e. exogenous response. These two sets of responses aim at compensation via emergency activities that temporarily counteract functioning flow losses (i.e. emergency relief and emergency rehabilitation) and at reconstruction activities that tend permanently to redress the consequences of stock losses and institutional insufficiencies. The impact effects and the derived compensatory responses also stimulate an anticipatory response aimed at prevention and mitigation of future potential disasters. This then generates three not independent main areas of attention, which makes up the response side of a disaster situation: response mechanisms, compensatory response and anticipatory response (Albala-Bertrand 1993, 2006a).

Given that the above impacts and responses happen in an ongoing system, there will also be societal side effects that can come from both the disaster impact effects and the response to them, which are mostly unintended but potentially predictable. These translate into changes in the timing and speed of social dynamics, changing the pattern of standard opportunities, and generally upsetting societal trends. This could happen via the redirection and rationalization of resources and/or the substitution and circumvention of private activities and/or the reallocation and postponement of public projects, which may affect overall institutional patterns. This may translate into short-term changes in private savings and stocks, in the shifting of supply and demand sources, in the shifting of investment opportunities and credit sources, in public and trade deficits, in changes in inflation and relative prices, in changes in capital flows and remittances, in changes in the patterns of employment and participation rates. In other words, there will be a generalized pattern of network shifting and a more specific one associated with market network shifts. Some of these may have developmental overtones (technical change, demographic shifts, disaster-induced political change), others may be short-lived (new formal market opportunities, new initiatives, solidarity), others can be counterproductive (aid dependency, aid politicization, social fragmentation, indebtedness, speculation) and others may accelerate existing trends in economic and political dynamics, e.g. East Pakistan 1971 (secession), Ethiopia 1974 (monarchy demise) and Indonesia 2004 (Aceh's end of civil war) (Albala-Bertrand 1993; Blanco *et al.* 2008).

Responses that are primarily non-economic, like those on household conditions, on nutrition and health and on some public activities, are likely to have a variable bearing on economic responses. Setting aside financial and resource usage and the fact that most people's disaster reactions will not be clearly reflected in any statistics, they may impinge on economic responses in positive or negative ways. In addition, especially in the type of response associated with NGOs, there normally is some implicit intention of activities that go beyond disaster recovery towards some kind of contribution to development. But, on the one hand, development from above may act in opposition to established institutions and endogenous patterns, affecting systemic processes in various ways (Cosgrave 2007). And on the other hand, the empowerment of grass-root activities, although welcome in principle, may produce longer-term systemic inconsistencies. Development from above or grass-root empowerment should not be at cross-purpose with existing endogenous patterns of activity, unless these can be identified as a clear obstacle to economic and social progress in the wake of disaster, which is not an easy task, as it strongly tallies with entrenched political structures. In other words, this is hardly a set of decisions that can be properly taken in the short window of opportunity that a disaster aftermath normally provides, especially when funding is available and NGOs coordination is lacking, notably the 2004 tsunami. There is then an important role for *ex-ante* international and public policy on this score (Telford and Cosgrave 2006).

Disaster response mechanisms

Response mechanisms refer to endogenous and exogenous processes of response. Endogenous mechanisms, normally associated with primary relationships (or bonding capital), but generally also with secondary ones (or bridging capital), are those channelled through society's inbuilt institutional processes. In socio-political jargon, these behaviours and activities come *from below*. These processes represent a series of formal and informal feedback mechanisms, which are part of the existing self-regulatory social organism, e.g. 'communities' represented in institutional subsystems like the family, the informal sector, formal markets, political parties, trade unions, religious institutions, social clubs, cultural institutions and administrative frameworks, and network structures therein, with its norms and customs, psychological attitudes and habits, legislation and rational preferences. These involve a wide array of activities that range from highly automatic to non-automatic inbuilt responses. For example, family and extended family solidarity represents a highly automatic endogenous reaction, while the use of the hazard-reserve item of the public budget is mostly a non-automatic inbuilt response. Likewise, market reactions and emergent organizations and coalitions appear to lie somewhere in between. A good deal of these processes may act as an informal insurance mechanism, associated with social cooperation and solidarity as well as individual reciprocity and altruism, both being societally founded processes, which can be resorted to in times of distress (Dynes 1970; Hirschleifer 1987; Albala-Bertrand 1993; Rodriguez *et al.* 2006).

Exogenous mechanisms, more generally associated with hierarchical relations (or linking capital), in turn, are those channelled via ad hoc, irregular processes that are not patterned or guaranteed. In socio-political jargon, these are decisions and activities that come *from above*. These are expressed in action, measures and policies that may formally fill gaps left by inbuilt responses, by-pass endogenous channels, shift initiatives away from regular actors or superimpose alternative structures. This normally implies private and public interventions that go beyond inbuilt actions, like the setting-up of newly specialized NGOs or the private lobbying for discretionary legislation or political/familial organizations trying to replace some normal public roles, e.g. Camorra in the case of the 1976 Fruily earthquake, as shown by Geipel (1982), or the public design of specific response policies. Exogenous responses will also include international assistance and aid that go beyond existing guarantees. In the long run, however, these two response types might not be necessarily independent. The endogenization of societally useful exogenous initiatives and behaviours via social institutions, e.g. via general socialization and education, organizational and technical change and the like, is the normal way in which society strengthens and develops, even if it often carries by tradition and/or vested interests the baggage of some attributes that have become socially useless, if not counterproductive, over time (Prince 1920; Sorokin 1942; Barton 1970; Dynes 1970; White 1974; Davis 1978; Quarantelli 1978; Cuny 1983; Albala-Bertrand 1993; Rodriguez *et al.* 2006).

The main difference between an exogenous mechanism and an endogenous mechanism is that the former is both carried by formal institutions and is intermediated by a well-defined stage of assessment and decision making. This means that the potential exogenous response may not happen, e.g. disbursement of aid commitments, NGOs' official permit to enter a country and the like. These two sets of response mechanisms are normally initiated and/or channelled via domestic or international institutional 'communities'. Community is normally a collection of interacting subsystems, with varying degrees of tension and competition within and between them. It is not the idyllic and harmonious unity of purpose that the word conveys. This means that some level of fragmentation and conflict, especially at local level, is normally observed in disaster aftermaths (Kendra and Wachtendorf 2006), which is part of what we called societal interference above, and something that the exogenous public response normally considers by design or default.

Response characterization

Many vulnerability reducing or resilience increasing factors are incidental to the development process, globalization being part and parcel of it. Development is ideally supposed to increase *per-capita* income, societal access, diversification and mobility, while reducing poverty levels, inequalities and societal disenfranchising (Todaro and Smith 2006; Thirlwall 2011). These should take care of a good deal of disaster effects on individuals and groups. But in practice, it is a messy, discontinuous, uncertain and unbalanced process, which may fail to cater for vulnerable local communities, disenfranchising them and being too slow to reintegrate them usefully, in a seemingly endless transition towards an ideal higher social stadium. Traditional communities, especially if seen as a collection of networks of individuals and institutions, are a form of endogenous social insurance in moments of distress, such as disasters, but these networks can be badly eroded by unconcerned development policies, notably socially unconcerned globalization, i.e. integration to both international trade and finance at the expense of societal checks and balances (Chang 2002; Stiglitz 2002, 2006; Serra and Stiglitz 2008). This simply means that to speed up disaster safety, normal development processes might not be enough. Therefore, direct policy on disaster vulnerability and resilience should take higher prominence and be usefully consistent with development dynamics. In other words, public policy on disaster should ride on, and stimulate, useful endogenous development processes, seeking to increase resilience in general and disaster resilience in particular.

Endogenous and exogenous responses can be classified according to their purpose both in prevention and in the wake of recovery after a disaster impact has occurred. Hence, four main analytical areas of attention should be considered: actions on *the event* (anticipatory);[4] actions on *the boundary* (anticipatory);[5] actions on *the social system* (mostly anticipatory);[6] and responses on *the effects* (mostly compensatory or counteracting).[7] These are not fully independent, as many anticipatory measures and policies, acting on the boundary and/or the social system, may become pivotal for the after-the-event response, e.g. insurance, warning system reaction, disaster training, etc. In addition, most anticipatory actions are part and parcel of the development process, which are not necessarily motivated by past or impending disasters, e.g. improvement of materials and design, education and social protection, increases of *per-capita* income and choice, poverty reduction and integration, etc. That is, as a rule, development itself seems to be the best reducer of disaster vulnerability, or increaser of resilience, especially at the macroeconomic level, but it may take too long for current generations, so specific responses and development policies associated with them should be aims in themselves.

Therefore, endogenous and exogenous response types may have significant interference with the normal working of society, the more so the larger and more economically widespread the direct effects. Their aim is a double-fold difficult balance: on the one hand, to re-establish impaired local livelihoods and, on the other, to insulate the national system from its local failure. These two are not necessarily complementary; the latter normally takes precedence over the former, whether by design or default (via market reactions and some public response). That is, output restitution at national levels can result in affected local activities being substituted for activities in other locations, which might be permanent. The role of public activities here would not necessarily be to prevent such a substitution, but to create conditions for failed local business and activities to adapt to the changed economic environment in a sustainable systemic fashion. A discussion of all possible responses is beyond the scope of this book. Therefore, only a few of these reactions/responses will be discussed later to illustrate endogenous reactions and public policy. Most of these items respond to institutionally induced patterns and activities, like market reactions, code enforcement, remittances or migration. There is however the need to refrain from analysing them in a vacuum, so we turn to the foundations of relationships and linkages associated with societal institutional networks.

Societal networking

Societal networking is the interconnectedness of interdependent societal units or agents at local, national and international levels. The better and more stable the physical networking (roads, utilities, communications), the more effective the societal (institutional) networking (organized individual, groups and other agents). The conception of society and nature as collections of interrelated parts can be traced back to the writing of the ancient Greeks or before. There is no single thoughtful essay about society that did not imagine it as a system of interacting and interdependent parts or components integrating, whether unwittingly or not, into a purposeful whole, such as those from Plato, Aristotle, Machiavelli, Marx, Hayek, etc. (Bottomore and Nisbet 1979; Russell 1991; McClelland 1996). The perception of the natural world from early researchers to ecologists, with less or more elaboration, has been equally conceived and interpreted. From Copernicus to Newton through Galileo, heavenly bodies have been implicitly or otherwise observed as a system of interrelated parts. Similarly, the physical world has been interpreted and verified as a system of atoms and atoms as a system of particles and the like. And of course biology has been the discipline that has developed the concept of system, its structured interrelated parts and its regulating feedbacks in a more detailed and thoroughly elaborated approach, from Da Vinci to Crick and Watson and beyond. That is, from the structure of the body as an organized set of organs to the structure of the cell to the structure of the DNA to the sequencing and mapping of the human genome and beyond (Serafini 2001; Dawkins 2008).

More to the point, in the social sciences the concept of system and structure has been a permanent feature. Structure is the more or less stable pattern in which the interdependent acting parts of a system are related. It is this organized set of relationships as part of the encompassing whole that gives viability to the system, i.e. it can survive and self-repair, reproduce and continue, adapt and reform, and develop and change. The system approach has been a staple of especially anthropology, as the study of cultural relationships (e.g. Levi-Strauss 1963), sociology, as the study of social groups and their inner and inter-relationships (Lukes 1982) and history (e.g. Pyrenne 1958; Hobsbawm 1997). Marx is attributed as the first social thinker who explicitly approached the study of society and its evolution from a structural viewpoint by means of his historical materialism, i.e. history has always been the history of opposing and conflicting interdependent and interacting fundamental social groups engaged in the process of production and distribution of commodities or, in his terms, the history of class struggle (Marx 1976). Most sociologists and political thinkers have then used the concept of social structure as the main organizing paradigm of their studies (e.g. Weber, Durkheim, Merton, Parsons, Althusser, Poulantzas, Giddens). And a few neoclassical economists did also venture into a systemic or structural approach to market relationships, whether using the term or not (e.g. Walras and Pareto). And in a Keynesian quantitative line, Leontief (1953) developed his input–output approach, which in turn had precedents in Marx's schema of reproduction and Walras's general equilibrium model, from Marx's *Capital* (1976: Vol. III) and Walras's *Elements of Pure Economics* (Walras 2003/1954). And of course, common streams or schools of thought and enquiry have appeared explicitly named under the key concepts, such as the Systems School, Structuralist School, Complexity School, Social Network School and the like.

A direct precedent of social networks analysis, with its focus on individual links, can be found in the sociology of Durkheim, Tonnies and Simmel around the 1900s (Simmel 1971; Lukes 1982). But the first systematic mapping and analysis of small groups is attributed to the psychiatrist J.L. Moreno in the 1930s, who also coined the term sociometry to denote a method and approach to measure and study confined social relationships (Hare and Hare 1997). Since then, a collection of professionals, especially anthropologists, psychologists and sociologists, but also mathematicians, working in the theory of graphs, and game theorists, analysing maximizing rational choice within networks, developed the approach further. And in turn, in the theory of organizations, which can be traced to the late eighteenth century or before, networks have been a permanent feature from organizational charts to more elaborated hierarchical and horizontal links within an organization and between them, e.g. the network structure of empire, that of the army and that of the Church. But it was not until the inception of the World Wide Web took hold, especially via internet social networks, such as Facebook and Twitter, that the use of computerized network simulations and network software took a technical leap and the term penetrated common jargon and imagination. The ancient term 'through the grapevine' encapsulates its general characteristics and use. It is particularly appropriate for the study of the spread of information, ideas, innovation, epidemics and many other areas where the transmission and access within and across networks may matter for policy design and decisions, e.g. rumours, fashion, publicity, ideology, goods, money.

Given such a wealth of precedents, it is surprising that every time you read any of the very many contemporary books and other writing on networks, they normally pay little attention to anything that happened before in the social sciences (Hanneman and Riddle 2005; Goyal 2007; Jackson 2008; Wasserman and Faust 2009, and many others). This is also one of the main weaknesses of what comes today to be called social network analysis or simply SNA.

What is particular to SNA is the empirically detailed mapping of existing social networks, which more often than not refers to individuals (natural persons) rather than agents representing organizations and institutional behaviour. An arsenal of varieties of social networks according to the structure of nodes relationships, e.g. complete, star, line, empty, core-periphery, and working concepts such as centrality, clustering, cliques, equivalence, homophily, structural holes with some measuring methods thereof, have been put forward and used to describe empirical networks. Description is the more interesting and useful part of the approach so far. The explanation about how and why social networks form and develop is however poor. This is mostly based on axiomatic applications of game theory and variants to pair-wise individuals operating under instrumental and substantive maximizing rationality. That is, this is based on individuals maximizing some preference function under rules of mutual and normally transparent knowledge in the context of methodological individualism, i.e. reductionism of the whole to one of its parts. But as the individual in question is either an already networked individual or one who wants to negotiate a contact with a networked individual, then the insufficiencies of standard game theory to deal with the real world are multiplied. The main problem is that, whether the individuals are networked or not, the games and explanations happen in an institutional vacuum. It is yet again two self-serving individuals operating outside real societal norms, like most of the artificial experiments of game theory, which ignore the rich literature on systems and structure and therefore the societally (institutionally) based condition of individuals. Not surprisingly, most of the axiomatic results do not coincide with the empirical evidence of networks (see Goyal 2007; Jackson 2008). So the axiomatic approach, framed on methodological individualism and the maximizing rational agent, runs the risk of becoming rigid, unrealistic and just as largely irrelevant as a good deal of the disciplines based on it.[8] Lastly, internet networks by their very nature operate in an institutional vacuum, as all individuals have the same initial access and individual decisions to accept or reject invitations carry little or no consequential risk or reward, let alone commitment. In addition, as a sense of social belonging, the internet social networks are pretty shallow and mostly irrelevant. Their main social role would be to make it easier to put together individuals who are part of the same groups of interest and probably social strata, for information, protestation, etc.

A social network is then a social structure made of nodes or actors or agents (individuals, organizations, groups, countries, etc.), which are linked (connected or tied) by given types of interdependence, such as basic relationships (friendship, kinship, sexual, prestige), belief links (political, religious, ideological), economic links (trade, finance, production, markets), common interest (clubs, associations, schools, firms, grass-root movements and other types of formal and informal relationships) and of course antagonistic ties (dislike, enmity, competition). Most of these are just the result of socialization into norms and beliefs that translate into common and predictable behaviour and as such appear as spontaneous (cultural and religious beliefs, national and regional identity, and general habits and customs). That is, we are born into them and as such are bearers, carriers and reproducers of structures with little or no individualistic autonomy to change them significantly at any one time. Others are the result of semi-conscious decisions (i.e. to join a political party or club) and others are semi-obliged adaptive decisions if you want to participate and benefit from a particular arrangement (i.e. if you want to become a producer of something you will have to join existing networks of suppliers and markets and cannot just create them). And there are also some emotional links that are more properly but not fully the result of individual decisions such as sexual encounters, marriage, friendship and the like. Some links can be physical (e.g. communication grids, transport routes, utility webs) and others non-physical (e.g. friendship, kinship, primordial ties). Physical links normally respond to socio-economic links and needs, the latter being the motivator. What flows along these links are either information (like data, knowledge, emotional signals) via verbal, written or other visual communication, or physical items (like people, goods and services) via transports, utility networks and the like. Some links are formal and legally binding (e.g. market transactions), others are universal and informal (e.g. use of streets), others are informal and personal (e.g. friendship) and others are informal and ephemeral (e.g. casual encounters). So the same nodes are normally connected via many types of links, for many types of purposes, and with many levels of strength, most of the time. Consciously, networked individuals or agents can call upon nodes of existing or new networks in accordance with their needs, but more often than not, networks facilitate and satisfy needs unconsciously. The old saying 'a man is known for the company he keeps' is a clear case of shifting the attributes of a person to the network where he belongs. So the focus is no longer on the individual, but on his networked circumstances. This brings up the old debate about structure versus agency or objective versus subjective or determinism versus free will or voluntarism (Marx, Althusser, Hayek, Popper, Giddens, etc.).[9]

To simplify, we will simply assume that individual actions and practices, whether from well-positioned individuals or not, are the bearers of structures and institutions and as such have only a narrow autonomy to act outside, let alone against, such structures at any one time. Structures can change not as much by the will or acts of a single individual, but by their failure to accommodate and satisfy their participants. This can be due either to external shocks that change the internal dynamics or to growing endogenous insufficiencies to tackle slow, but unchecked, socio-environmental changes until an institutional or major behavioural breakage arises. When this happens, disaffected groups challenge existing institutions, transmitting and spreading their dissatisfaction via social networks, involving more and more individuals until a critical mass is reached, creating either reforms within the structure or major structural change or revolution. So individuals as social agents are both creatures of structures and, in so far as networked beings, modifiers of structures. A single individual may not make much of a difference, however well positioned, but networked individuals, clustered into some identity group, may and often do, especially when social institutions fail to accommodate competing identity groupings, i.e. the breeding ground of complex emergencies (Albala-Bertrand 2000a, 2000b).

It must then be clear that network analysis requires the existence of network mapping to understand the type of structure of the focus network and the implications that that might have for particular situations and emergencies. Therefore, who is linked with whom (direct nodes), what type of link (flow types), how does it operate (transmission mechanism), where does it happen (geographic place and nearness), when does it happen (timing and persistence) and why does it happen (explanation and prediction) are extremely time consuming and costly endeavours, except for very simple networks. Once this primary information has been gathered, normally for very narrow networks, the hope is that computer software will do the work of generating the required mapping. The rest, based on experience and some logic, will be to analyse the potentialities of the given network and how they can be made more effective for particular processes. So the mapping is the first drawback, but the analysis of how and why networks form and ensuing predictions, especially carried via substantive rationality, does not fare a lot better. The former is costly, time consuming and necessarily confined, while the latter is poor, unreliable and generally irrelevant, as most of the analysis is centred on rational decisions devoid of institutional context. Notice that social networks do not necessarily constitute self-contained systems, but parts or fragments of systems. So there is the need to analyse such fragments as part of the system that contains them, which is rarely done. The encompassing system should matter more than the particular network and probably informs most of the network behaviour and potentials.

We intend to use networks here in a contextual political economy way to assess, via the input–output network and the network of business behaviour under stress, how endogenous and exogenous reactions and behaviours can be visualized and hopefully tapped to enhance functionality and therefore recovery from disaster. So the aim is to analytically contextualize societal network, but not to create descriptive mappings and/or giving axiomatic explanations about them.

Community and networks

Community can be simply defined as an interacting collection of economic and non-economic purposeful subsystems and individuals, which exhibit varying

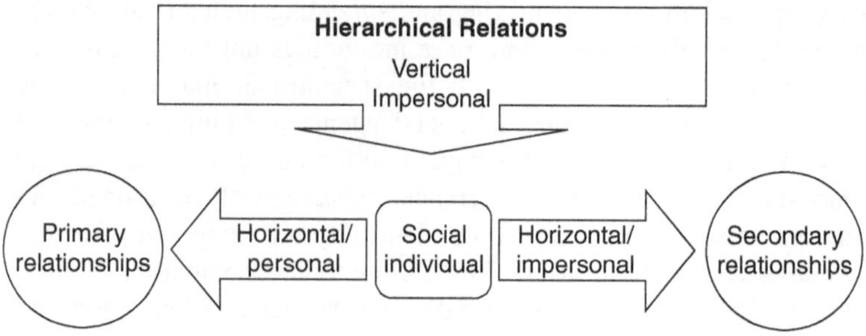

Figure 2.2 Endogenous and exogenous relationships.

degrees of tension, cooperation and competition. In normal times, a community comes across as a relatively balanced societal segment (e.g. local community), which is part of a wider societal whole (e.g. regional and national). The levels of integration of communities, within themselves and with the social whole, depend on political, economic and cultural variables (Nakagawa and Shaw 2004a, 2004b). To this effect we can analytically characterize social (institutionally networked) individuals by means of three main types of informal and formal institutional linkages and ties with their communities and the wider national (and foreign) whole: horizontal linkages and vertical linkages, which give rise to three kinds of relationships: primary, secondary and hierarchical. These can more or less correspond to the concept of social capital and its classification into bonding capital, bridging capital and linking capital (Putnam 2000; Szreter and Woolcock 2004).[10] The diagram below, focusing on a single social individual, helps visualize such relationships.

Primary relationships refers to family, extended family, friends, neighbours, and race, ethnic, religious and other kinship or primordial groupings, implying a closer bond and allegiance. These relationships *within* groups of very similar individuals, also termed 'homophily' by social network theory, represent a net of *horizontal linkages* that constitute the very base of directly endogenous disaster reactions (e.g. remittances, victims' hosting and general informal insurance). This is what is sometimes called 'bonding social capital' that characterizes its members as exhibiting high levels of trust, participation, solidarity and reciprocity. From the viewpoint of disaster response, let's call it primary or personal-endogenous reactions.

For example, following the 1995 Kobe earthquake in Japan, some neighbourhoods organized the setting-up of cooperative housing while other areas waited for external aid, which much depended on the strong links that had developed before the disaster (Aldrich 2011). One of the most important social resources when communities are under distress is that of informal insurance. This is associated with primary links that give financial and physical support to affected people, from family remittances to community support passing through tribal cooperation. It is however also true that if in a social set-up a dominant tribe or religion or ideology prevails, then this dominant network is likely to monopolize aid and support at the expense of the minorities, meaning that strong links are not always socially beneficial. Inequality of support and aid distribution after disasters is a common feature, from extreme cases in undemocratic traditional setting to more developed ones, the latter ones normally associated with corruption by the people in charge of distribution (Albala-Bertrand 1993; Rodriguez *et al.* 2006). As regards the former, after the Asian tsunami, some coastal districts of south-east India were badly hit, where Dalit families, outcaste and non-member victims were eligible for relief, but did not receive it in part, or at all, due to discrimination by the dominant caste. When two Dalit families in one village sought to stand in line to receive assistance, they were beaten and driven away (Tata 2005, 2007).

Secondary relationships are especially *between* groupings, linking individuals across groups and cleavages by means of social, political, economic and cultural associations, e.g. formal and informal markets, school interactions, broad political parties, public employees, private workforces, consumers' associations and other social, political and economic organizations. So diversity rather than similarity, pluralism rather than monism, heterogeneity rather than homogeneity are the main features of these relationships, which whether formalized or otherwise, are also part of the societal fabric of *horizontal linkages*. They mostly operate as interrelationships between heterogeneous primary groupings or outside their confines. As such they are mostly impersonal connections in the sense that no endemic personal bond is required to achieve it, although some occupational or other status traits might be required to qualify for formal or informal access and membership, implying some levels of trust, expected behaviour or collateral. But trust and participation are normally either legally enforced or ethically/morally motivated and sanctioned. A great deal of endogenous reactions are carried out via these relationships, especially via the economic networks provided by the market or associated with it via formal organizations (e.g. trade unions and employers' associations), but also via naturally born coping networks, like emergent organizations. This type of inter-relation is sometimes called 'bridging social capital', i.e. it sets 'bridges' between otherwise unconnected diverse groupings and social beings. Strong affinities can also be observed in relation to organization objectives, but these are more of choice than inbuilt, e.g. political party or sports club membership. Contrary to the primary endogenous reactions above, these are more societally endogenized than primordially endogenous. By endogenized we mean that they have a good deal of choice vis-à-vis institutional pressure. So from the viewpoint of disaster response, let's call them secondary or impersonal-endogenized reactions.[11]

For example, inter-ethnic trade unions, political parties, sports clubs and other organizations bring together Hindus and Muslims in India and dampen social conflict between them. In times of distress such links can moderate strong bonding tendencies. In the USA parent-teacher associations bring together individuals of various ethnic backgrounds and religions, as do public schools, so where bonding social capital reinforces primary affinities, bridging social capital can usefully connect diverse individuals (Varshney 2001).

Hierarchical relations refers to state institutions (executive, legislative and judicial offices), private institutions (firms, banks, etc.) and international institutions (UN, World Bank, NGOs, etc.). These are *ranked* relationships and are part of the network of *vertical linkages* between individuals or groupings and formal authority. Most of the exogenous response is associated with these hierarchical links. *Ex-post* response without *ex-ante* endogenization is what we call *proper exogenous response*. Then there is also *ex-post* response with *ex-ante* endogenization, i.e. institutions, procedures, routines and funds to deal with potential disasters. Vertical *endogenized* responses are therefore less automatic than those related to horizontal linkages, as they require both societal incorporation (socialization) and enforcement, but in time they can become endogenous (e.g. primary education or respect for norms). They are more all-embracing and normally better resourced than horizontal relations, operating at supra-individual and supra-grouping levels, as the official administration of the country is always involved. They can then be more politically controversial. This type of interrelation is sometimes called 'linking social capital'. Contrary to bridging social capital that links individuals of about similar social status, i.e. horizontal level, linking social capital relates individuals of various status levels, providing them with access to influence and power via decision makers and leaders who hold positions of authority and control political and economic resources. So from the viewpoint of disaster response, let's call the collection of both exogenous and vertically endogenized responses simply general policy response.[12]

For example, after the 2004 tsunami some caste councils developed direct connections to outside aid agencies, international NGOs and civil servants within the Indian government. It has been shown that in India and abroad, disaster victims who are able to access such higher authority personnel had better recovery patterns than those without such extended networks (Beggs *et al.* 1996; Wetterberg 2004). Of course, this can be and normally is a breeding ground for ideological-political prioritization, discrimination and/or direct corruption in the distribution of aid and general recovery support.

Therefore, individuals are born into a variety of societal systems (family, tribe, creed, ideology, race, culture, idiosyncrasies, nation, etc.). These whole societal systems then constitute a collection of interdependent parts or subsystems, which makes their social individuals interact within and between them, whether horizontally or vertically, via formal and informal but patterned behaviours, making up a societal network structure. Hence, people are bearers, carriers and reproducers of structures from their very inception into life. It should then be understood that even if a particular network was originally formed by individuals that started to prefer a particular behavioural pattern over others, for whatever reason, the fact is that once the pattern has been endogenized it will becomes internal or 'natural' to even the individuals that pioneered it, let alone to the ones that were born into it. In other words, the pattern becomes institutionalized and individuals are now embedded and carriers of such patterns with little or no say about it. Individuals are empowered by the institutional networks they belong to and by their status in them. But they are also constrained by them, so they have only a relative autonomy to choose systemically the one they would like to belong to (Kilduff and Tsai 2003).[13]

Economic networks, especially market relationships, appear less constrained, but individuals hardly behave in an individualistic optimizing fashion. They behave in clusters that are determined outside the market (e.g. publicity motivated behaviour, financial herd behaviour, social group preferences and the like). In our disaster context, the choice that matters is that of the access to alternative networks that disaster frustrated participants can have to continue their plans, which has little to do with maximization of self-serving opportunities. It has to do with survival and stability of individuals and that of the surrounding community. We will come back to this later. So now we turn to the networking of the economic system to complete our political economy context.

Formal economic networking

As shown in Chapter 1, in economics there is a rich and useful tradition on networks from especially the input–output approach, as we will see later. For the formal economic system, networking can be represented diagrammatically as follows:

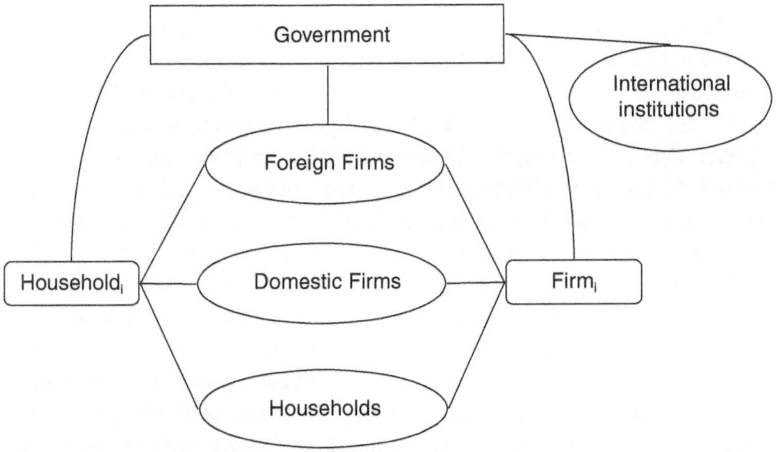

G: Taxation and subsidies
FF: Trade and financial (some transfers)
F: Real and financial, private and public (producers and intermediaries)
H: Demand, labour, savings, transfers (including foreign remittances)
IN: Bilateral and multilateral (credit and transfers, including NGOs)

Figure 2.3 Economic networking (formal economy).

So each firm ($Firm_i$) or household ($Household_i$) can be actually linked to, and potentially face, a collection of networks, belonging to domestic and foreign quarters. Productive and income interrelations in an economy can be *theoretically* affected by the physical and/or organizational failure of any single productive unit (e.g. steel-production plant) or any single distribution channel (e.g. industrial motorway) to deliver, indirectly affecting the whole economic circuit and associated non-economic activities. The magnitude and spread of such effects depends simultaneously on the economic importance of the production involved (i.e. how strongly and how many economic units depend on the affected production or supply), the alternative supply sources available (i.e. how many alternative sources, from local, national and foreign suppliers are available, and how easily can they be accessed) and infrastructures available (i.e. rehabilitated and/or alternative ones). Not least, it also depends on the duration of the hindrance, affecting the range of possible adjustments (i.e. from weathering the problem to significant structural change). The greater the severity, extent and duration of effects, other things being equal, the more likely the consequences for the economic circuit as a whole. But then the more localized and better integrated the local system to national societal networks, the more unlikely the spreading of effects towards the macroeconomy as a whole, especially in the medium and long terms.

Globalization, in turn, may strengthen endogenous (inbuilt) and exogenous (policy decision) channels of response. Foreign trade benefits a country by delinking the domestic structure of production from that of demand and vice versa. This diversifies the sources and markets of inputs, outputs and finance. This is bound to increase the localization of a disaster, as the output and capital losses as well as the ensuing demand losses in the disaster zone can now be more easily made up with alternative domestic and foreign markets. This may not only reduce even more effectively the potential for widespread effects on the macroeconomy, but also change the structure of supplies and demands towards more stable markets. This may promptly shelter and compensate the macroeconomy from unwanted indirect flow effects, but it may also put out of business a number of affected economic activities in the disaster zone. So while the disaster becomes even more economically localized than before, it might also worsen the plight of affected communities by passing them over.[14] But if the functionality and activity levels of the macroeconomy are not affected, then there will be resources and available networks in the affected country, making it more expedite and less onerous to counter the effects in the disaster zone. But that would depend more on domestic politics and political will than on the mere fact of resource and network availability. Lower vulnerability and higher resilience of the national macroeconomy are perfectly compatible with higher vulnerability and lower resilience of the local economy. As we mentioned earlier, there is here a permanent tension and as such an important role for *ex-ante* and *ex-post* public and international policy.

Isolation and insulation

An isolated, autarkic, local economy cannot by definition have spreading effects towards the national economy. If it happened to be affected by a disaster, however large its direct or stock effects, the indirect effects would be contained within its boundaries, which may make the total local effects more intense. Without outside aid and endogenous macro integrative reactions from a national encompassing economy, the recovery would likely be more trying, as it would have to be met with resources and reactions within the local economy alone. From the viewpoint of the national macroeconomy, the disaster would be localized and unintrusive. Contrariwise, if the local economy is integrated to the national economy via mutual demands and supplies of factors, goods and finance, then the disaster can remain local only in so far as the indirect spreading effects can be contained within the disaster zone boundary and/or counteracted outside it. From a national standpoint, the disaster would be localized if the macroeconomy could insulate itself from the indirect effects that originate in the disaster zone. For this to happen, the national economy has to compensate with inbuilt economic and other societal reactions, which in addition are likely to be reinforced by exogenous domestic and foreign responses. This would initially insulate the disaster effects, confining it to the affected locality, and later help recover the disaster zone itself. The basic containment of wider indirect effects would normally occur rapidly via relief and local physical rehabilitation, during which the macroeconomic organism would already be taking care of itself via normal endogenous market and non-market mechanisms.

By analogy, this is like physiological reactions that first insulate a wound, preventing the spread of infection, and then start a healing process that fully re-establishes biological functions. Once the macroeconomy has managed to insulate itself from local failure and therefore functions almost normally, appropriate policies and not least political will are likely to be required to do the same with the affected locality. Nation building and its development imply the integration of otherwise isolated, or autarkic, localities into a common centre of loyalties and decision making, which necessarily implies a process of political, social and economic enfranchising via institutional and physical networks. Nation building represents societal incorporation, which develops via more and more all-embracing and sophisticated interconnectedness. This is the original globalization, i.e. all-embracing societal networks within country administrative boundaries.

We then expect that a more developed country will be more economically diversified and more internally and externally articulated. That is, its societal networking will make both its inter-sectoral and income linkages more all-embracing and dynamic, less dependent on given domestic or foreign sources, and not least its people will more likely be institutionally integrated to a more responsive centre of allegiance or state. This means that a disaster might have the possibility of spreading via linkages to the wider economy, through indirect or flow effects, which would not happen from an autarkic location, as shown above. But at the same time the interlinked system is likely to generate market endogenous reactions via buffer stocks, substitutions, circumventions, new supply/demand opportunities and other network shifts that would work in the direction of damping down negative effects. In addition, other inbuilt or institutional mechanisms (political, cultural or economic) plus the standard exogenous ones (public and foreign) would likely respond in the same direction, mutually reinforcing each other. The tension between national requirements and local recovery may have some negative implications for the latter, but the former would likely remain fairly unscathed especially in the medium run and beyond.

In this conception, both indirect effects and long-term effects from localized disasters are likely to be unimportant for the macroeconomy. In highly diversified developed economies they would be rapidly compensated and outweighed, even in the disaster zone itself. So the *direct* disaster stock loss, which is associated with residential, infrastructure, business and inventory capital, plus current production and labour, might represent almost all of the total loss. In sudden, localized, disasters this is unlikely to have major effects on the macroeconomy even in the short term, especially after relief and rehabilitation are under way, as argued below. In addition, globalization via trade integration, financial development and speedy communications is bound to support and foster the general requirements for enhanced localization and resilience, despite its current shortcomings. This is likely to be reinforced by exogenous and endogenized public policy, which would be more speedy and effective in a well-developed societal network than in a poorly integrated country.

Conclusion

We started by defining societal functionality as the capacity of a system to operate in a viable way. We then related this to the issues of vulnerability and resilience, arguing that these are implicit parts of any definition of functionality. They however allow for more specific focus when analysing societies under stress, more particularly in the case of disasters, which is what we are interested in in this work. To this effect, we then introduced the concept of economic localization, showing that this is a key tool to understand and analyse economic substitution potential and hence functionality. In the context of socio-economic networks, this becomes an essential approach to assess the economic importance of longer-term and cumulative effects from disasters. After we defined our concepts associated with a disaster situation, we introduced and contextualized our political economy approach by means of social and economic networks. Here we distinguish the main types of societal links that are potentially available to networked individuals as well as the main economic networks that are potentially available for firms and households in the process of production and reproduction of societal life. By means of distinguishing between isolation and insulation of disaster affected social settings, we argued that societies that enjoy a more all-embracing level and a better access to social and economic networks, domestic and foreign, are in better endogenous and exogenous conditions to damp down potential indirect effects and hence long-term effects from disasters. That is, they would be in better condition to gain back and secure stable functionality after disasters. If this is correct, then the question is to answer by which means and channels this can be done. We now turn in the next chapter to the macro-economic network possibilities and arguments.

3 Networked reactions and public policy

Introduction

There is a dynamic tension between the local and the national as part of the normal development process, which by means of a socially wide network integration brings societal change at a higher stadium of economic and social functionality. But this also leaves a trail of destruction of previous forms of economic and social organizations, marginalizing those who are unable to join the development highway: development is as such a process of societal acculturation. The policy point is how to reduce the cost of the transition from the old forms to the new ones, reducing both the quantity and depth of victimization. Often the new forms are at best assumed and their transitional side effects ideologically ignored, which makes the whole process even more messy, discontinuous and unnecessarily harsh than it otherwise would have been. The vested and socially unconcerned push for globalization in the last few decades is a clear witness to this, i.e. a push for worldwide economic networking with little or no concern for its social victimization (Chang 2002; Stiglitz 2002, 2010).

In this general context, after disasters have destroyed and/or damaged the capital stock and income directly, there will then be frustrated participants on the supply and demand sides, whether within or outside the geographic and/or economic disaster zone. Here is an important role for public response, via facilitating the contact between such frustrated economic participants and new sources/destination of demand and supply, including foreign ones, and via speeding up recovery of affected participants so that they do not lose their regular connections with demanders/suppliers and not least with their community networks. Public response can support endogenous reactions via appropriate information and via incentives and disincentives associated with subsidies, taxation, supply of shortage goods to firms, cash transfers to keep demand, as well as create and/or reinforce marketing (network) infrastructures and the like. Public activity should aim at a twofold systemic balance. On the one hand, it should seek to prevent the macroeconomy from undergoing unnecessary negative indirect effects that may translate into losses of functionality and therefore future GDP; and on the other, it should prevent that directly affected localities are fully bypassed by macro considerations, rendering them less effective in re-establishing their positions after recovery is well under way. This of course represents also the requirement of *ex-ante* public activity in arrangements leading to collating and disseminating information and given access to funding so as to facilitate network diversification.

The aim of this chapter is first to advance some general contextual issues about the required balance between policy responses and general inbuilt networked reactions, advancing some elements for securing systemic consistency, which we will revisit in Chapter 6. We illustrate the consistency issues via some well-known disaster response needs and policies.

Endogenous and exogenous response balance[1]

The role of endogenous (inbuilt) reactions/responses cannot be overstated enough. International and public disaster responses can become both more effective by harnessing useful endogenous mechanisms and less harmful by avoiding trampling on and/or suffocating them. In other words, supra-networks have to be consistent with existing and/or potential subordinated networks, i.e. intra- and inter-economic networks plus other societal ones. This is close to, but not fully part of, the perennial debate about what the right balance between the market and the state is. More generally, about what the appropriate economic role of the public sector vis-à-vis the private one should be. This is of course a debate with strong ideological undertones and tallies with the political preferences and vested interests of main actors and existing institutions. On the one hand, we know that in a market economy, an excessive state role and intervention may stifle profit-seeking private initiatives and competition, which may translate into lower technical progress, growth and choice. But at the same time it may secure a stronger economic and social stability, with a minimum safety net for especially the poorest strata of society (e.g. Chile or Mexico under import substitution). On the other hand, an excessively unregulated private sector may lead to higher technical progress, growth and choice during stable periods, but build up deep inequalities and unsurmountable disequilibria leading to periods of deep economic instability, capital flights and recession (e.g. Mexico 1994, East Asia 1997, Russia 1998, Argentina 2001, and not least the 2008 Great Recession), undoing much of the better times and creating political and social instability in their wake (Krugman 2008; Minski 2008; Cassidy 2009; Saleh 2010). So there is an important role for both sectors and this is precisely the debate that has reinitiated once more on the back of the current world crisis.

The functions of public and private sectors in the case of disasters are however less ideological, as the role of the state is fundamental for *ex-ante* preparedness, including preventive and anticipatory policies, as well as *ex-post* responses and policy implementation with its administrative framework and legal enforcement. The point here is to look for ways to make public responses more effective by their acknowledging and complementing inbuilt (endogenous) private behaviours and reactions, but not just at market behaviour level. For example, at least in the early relief, it has been suggested that exogenous response may not reach a number of affected social segments and individuals, e.g. the illiterate, small agricultural producers, street children in main cities, squatters, banana plantation workers, female-headed households and indigenous populations or that the amount of in-kind relief may be independent of need (World Bank 2001; Morris and Wodon 2003) or that the exogenous replacement of small business capital goods (e.g. boats and equipment) may be inappropriate to the climate requirements (Telford and Cosgrave 2006; TEC 2007). These are other reasons to incorporate endogenous responses into *ex-ante* and *ex-post* public disaster policy in a more systematic way.

We assume that the aim of any disaster response, beyond purely short-term relief requirements, is to re-establish damaged macro functionality and help recover lost local livelihoods in a sustainable manner. The only possible way to achieve this is by economically securing the autonomy of gainful activities, at least in the medium to long term after a disaster impact, both via the market system directly and via necessary and sustainable public activities and employment. We expect the latter to affect indirectly the market system and directly societal integration. The market is, of course, subject to perverse or antisocial dynamics (i.e. monopolization, negative externalities, herd behaviour, inequalities and the like), but it is the main endogenous mechanism that can help sustain livelihoods autonomously, within institutionally established rules. Ignoring private endogenous initiatives and activities may lead to unnecessary dependency from subsidies, let alone handouts, delaying the incorporation of disaster affected people and activities into the regular economic system.

Public activities (e.g. on infrastructures, social services and public administration) take the shape of legislative decisions and legal enforcement in response to potential and/or actual disasters. *Ex-ante* public disaster response is mostly aimed at formally (legally) endogenizing regular behaviours and procedures that can in a more or less automatic way unfold in the wake of disasters. This normally requires time to create roots and not least enforcement to secure them. On this score, *ex-ante* policy should seek to tap useful existing endogenous behaviours so that already rooted dynamics can be reinforced and developed, which would likely be more efficient, requiring less exogenous enforcement than it might otherwise need. Exogenous responses are meant to be a complement to inbuilt reactions; hence, the question is how to make exogenous public response *systemically* compatible with endogenous reactions, so as to increase the effectiveness and efficiency of the recovery, in relation to both societal functionality and long-term development.

Inbuilt networked reactions

In any society, there are social sectors that are marginalized from stable jobs, whether because of lack of employment, lack of skills, lack of access, i.e. the poor and the destitute, which are normally also politically uninfluential. Public disaster response can and has partly helped incorporate such sectors into gainful employment, especially via reconstruction work, food-for-work schemes and micro finance, at least in the medium term. This may help open systemic opportunities and expand and create economic linkages so that social sectors and communities can integrate into sustainable business and employment in the longer term. Society and individuals are part of a dynamic inbuilt setup, which is the way disaster response has to be understood. The social system is not an inert thing but a living organism. Like any viable living organism, society and economy are endowed with reactive feedbacks that aim at self-preservation by keeping needed balances and counteracting functionality failures in sustainable fashion. Local failures are then primarily tackled via endogenous (inbuilt) compensations, substitutions and circumventions aimed at rehabilitating impaired productive and distributional functions, which should be identified before a pervasive exogenous response comes about.

Exogenous public actions are of course also part of this feedback, but they are intermediated by assessment, planning and ad hoc formal decision making, with normally synoptic outsiders' mindsets and political urgencies. Exogenous responses are meant to speed up the recovery process by bringing in personnel, materials, finance and technical know-how to the affected (economic and/or geographic) area. From a systemic viewpoint, they are not meant to frustrate existing inbuilt dynamics, creating unnecessary dependencies and resource wastage, but to tap, reinforce and complement endogenous reactions and initiatives. But sometimes the former is unavoidable. Inadequate responses from exogenous sources may affect the ways in which affected systems are meant to work in normal times, by negatively affecting local initiatives, bypassing local markets, making local institutions irrelevant, creating wrong incentives and hence making disaster recovery inconsistent with normal socio-economic functionality (Cosgrave 2007; TEC 2007). As with the social body as a whole, most individuals, households and businesses do not respond to disasters just to palliate adversity, let alone to maximize normal objectives, but to preserve both their livelihood and social status. They seek to preserve their community and domestic linkages as well as their relationships and institutional mobility, which may partly explain why communities' endogenous reactions and response activities are so pervasive and massive in the aftermath of disasters (Bruneau *et al.* 2003; Skoufias 2003; Rodriguez *et al.* 2006; Telford and Cosgrave 2006). But just as with the contribution of household or other unpaid work to value added, which is excluded from GDP accounting, endogenous reactions are fairly intractable to measure. They however can always be accounted for, at least indirectly, in a qualitative fashion.

If we use a biological analogy, at an individual level, a disease or accident (like flu or injuries) can be dealt with by the body's natural response mechanisms, i.e. antibodies and healing processes, which are endogenous homeostatic mechanisms. If the body response is not enough and/or the recovery is to be sped up, then available medical responses and special treatments may be required (drugs, hospitalization, diet, exercise, lifestyle, etc.), which are exogenous recovery sources. Like a vaccine, which is an *ex-ante* preventive response, exogenous responses are meant to stimulate endogenous reactions, rather than creating unnecessary dependencies and unwelcome side effects by bypassing them (e.g. medical drug addiction). Sometimes, of course, the body mechanism is so impaired that dependency of single individuals on drugs and other medical treatments is the only way to keep the body (i.e. the system) with a minimum of viability. However, for a heterogeneous group of people taken as a system in its own right, even under the worse cases of mass infestation, like the last century's avian flu, endogenous biological responses tend to create their own physiological defences, reducing over time vulnerability to similar diseases, but this might be a slow process that takes a high human and economic toll in the interim. This is where usable and efficient exogenous responses can make an important difference, i.e. by reinforcing natural endogenous process (e.g. vaccine, diet) and/or by helping endogenize useful traits (e.g. hygiene, lifestyle, condoms), as in the case of AIDS.

Market consistency and some response mechanisms

Given the experience of communities and firms in the face of disasters, there are a number of response mechanisms that should be evaluated in terms of its systemic consistency with institutional networks, especially via the market, for longer-term sustainability and development, i.e. for systemic functionality. We focus here on some important types of response: cash transfers and in-kind aid, remittances and its infrastructure, shelter provision and migration, and insurance and loans. These all have a good deal of interaction between them, as shown below.

Cash transfers and in-kind aid

Cash transfers (including vouchers) can often be the appropriate form of assistance not only for emergency relief and rehabilitation, but also for reconstruction activities, e.g. owner-driven reconstruction (Özerdem and Jacoby 2006). At the level of the individual, this allows affected people themselves to decide about their needs. At the systemic level, this also enables them to engage directly in local markets and indirectly in the economy as a whole. To assess whether in-kind aid or cash transfers are more appropriate a balance has to be struck between local needs and the states of both the local and the national markets. For example, an excessive food aid in Malawi forced the government to use scarce financial resources to buy the same food from local producers so as to keep local markets afloat (Clay *et al.* 2003) or in one location in India after the 2004 tsunami, both the proliferation of uncoordinated NGOs and donations created 'oversupply, depressing both the market for trained labour and products' (Alexander 2006: 33) or inappropriate aid piled up, using up storage and personnel wastefully (Indonesia Relief 2005) and so on and so forth. But it should be also understood that they are not necessarily substitutes, as both can coexist at different levels and for different people. What should also be understood is that cash transfers should not be ruled out without a proper assessment. Contrary to customary in-kind aid, cash transfers may always have some important systemic contribution, which if well assessed and implemented can positively feed back into recovery speed and quality, i.e. by endogenizing cash transfers and aid, vis-à-vis accessible credit systems, into potentially stable livelihoods. As cash transfers may be more likely to aim at smoothing consumption than re-igniting productive investment, micro credit and other soft loans may be used to support the latter, so cash transfers can be part of a comprehensive financial response.

Cash transfers have been recognized in recent years as an appropriate form of assistance, against traditional practice that was normally based on incomplete information. Governments in Thailand, India, Sri Lanka and Indonesia provided cash assistance in response to the 2004 Asian tsunami. Some feasibility studies for both conditional (on some socially beneficial behaviour, e.g. children going to school) and unconditional cash transfers, as part of a complementary response toolkit, have been carried out for some aid agencies that have lately included cash as an alternative to food aid, like Save the Children Fund in Sri Lanka or Oxfam in Malawi (Savage and Umar 2006; Schubert 2006). In turn, the Pakistan government also provided substantial cash support in response to the Kashmir earthquake of 2005. There have also been positive pilot schemes in Niger and Lesotho (Bailey 2008; Slater and Mphale 2008), e.g. cash to support families hosting displaced people, as an alternative to temporary shelter in camps, and large-scale cash-for-work projects. They have also piloted cash grants as an alternative to food to enable people to rebuild livelihoods, e.g. Zambia and Malawi. This was also the case in the USA, after the Katrina and Rita hurricanes, in which the government provided billions of dollars in cash assistance, despite the response failures in the former case. And there currently is a good deal of actual and academic interest in studying the possible role of cash transfers in the process of chronic poverty reduction and food vulnerability, which is likely to reduce significantly food aid bureaucracy, e.g. Kenya and Ethiopia. It is to be noticed that in conflict-affected countries, like Somalia and Afghanistan, cash-for-work investment projects have proved to be highly successful too (Hofmann 2005; Ratha 2005; Adams and Winahyu 2006; Harvey 2007; Raschky 2008).

Cash transfers and the market

Cash transfer policies have to be necessarily assessed against in-kind programmes via various economic and non-economic considerations, i.e. from a purely economic cost-effectiveness (and market impact) to security issues, passing through issues of dignity, gender and criminality. For example, cash programmes have lower transport and logistical costs than material ones, although they require more specialized staff and active local markets, and some financial infrastructures. They may also be more secure than transporting in-kind assistance, as they are less visible. But they may increase corruption, especially in corruption leaning settings. Cash can be diverted to anti-social uses, just as in-kind aid, so the use of vouchers, which forces voucher holders to buy specific goods from a given variety of suppliers, might be more appropriate in certain cases. There might also be some gender issues, either empowering women via direct cash transfers to them (which may reduce anti-social use), or in detriment of women when distributed to the household, as they may have less say about how they are spent and distributed among household members.

Cash provides greater choice via its use in the market, allowing less scope for undignifying begging-like goods collection (cash can be collected from banks rather than handed directly to people in a queue). Private remittance companies can and have provided their existing networks as a relatively secure way for cash transfer flows. This naturally couples (endogenous) remittances with (exogenous) public cash transfers, not only by using the same infrastructures, but also by usefully pairing them in terms of remittance stimuli, e.g. by topping up the former with the latter, both income sources being systemically endogenized via the market.

Cash transfers also have to be assessed against both in-kind aid and the state of local and regional markets so as to make sure that the new effective demand can be satisfied. To be sure, in-kind aid also requires analysis of the local market so as to prevent the extra-market supplies competing with, let alone suffocating, local markets and businesses, as indicated earlier. The consideration of endogenous multiplying effects from cash transfers for both livelihood recovery and possible negative side effects is also necessary. If the latter are important, e.g. inflation, then public policy should look for ways to supplement supplies via the market, rather than substituting the market and local business with in-kind aid. In the urgency of an emergency the latter is often unavoidable, but it should not be made so by policy default at the first sign of complication, as in-kind aid cannot be more than a palliative if longer-term dependency affecting local markets is to be avoided (Harvey and Lind 2005). Whether public support is in-kind or cash transfers, the analysis of transparency and accountability of distribution channels, registration and targeting of recipients and not least the monitoring and disciplining of market conditions and reactions (i.e. controlling inflation or otherwise) will constitute an essential part of the process. A good deal of it corresponds to pre-disaster routines, such as training and assessment tools for relief operators and local staff as well as staff involved in supra-local coordination and general control (Harvey 2007). No doubt there is here an important role for *ex-ante* public response.

Cash transfers and development opportunity

In developing countries markets and business are normally poorly integrated into the national economy, let alone foreign markets. And there normally is a good level of underemployment and unstable informality. Except for the immediate aftermath assessment, public policy design should not only consider how to bring back the locality to pre-disaster conditions, but more importantly how to recover employment and activity levels by increasing the domestic and foreign integration of affected localities, and in passing increasing productivity and reducing informality. Surely, this is a tall order that goes beyond the emergency relief effort toward reconstruction and development, which should not be imposed from above if further instability and long-term dependency is to be reduced. It has to appeal to participants via endogenous channels, by providing know-how, training, technology, information, marketing infrastructures as well as some investment subsidies, soft micro loans and standard credit. A large destructive disaster is therefore also an opportunity, as part of the recovery, to introduce and seed the type of development traits that might have been resisted otherwise, helping dislodge regressive institutions and practices. This is the role of incentives and disincentives, acting within endogenous structures and dynamics, associated with the general market, local businesses and public and private institutions, so again there is here an important role for *ex-ante* public policy, at least in terms of facilitating information and access.

There is no need to go into detailed examples of positive results from cash transfers, and/or difficulties with in-kind aid, as they are well documented in our and other sources, so we refer the reader to them. These studies also give indications about how to assess policy alternatives both qualitatively and quantitatively. A general measure would probably be the speed of recovery of otherwise self-sufficient activities. Suffice it to say that cash transfers have a number of systemic advantages that in-kind aid lacks, but this is not equivalent to saying that the latter should be scrapped. Response programmes cannot rely on a single response tool, as it is highly unlikely that it would positively cater for all cases and situations. So a response programme should consider and incorporate all useful policy tools and mechanisms to deal with given heterogeneous conditions (Savage and Umar 2006). This should give prominence to those policies that are consistent with societal systemic traits, as these may prove to facilitate both the recovery of affected people and accelerate their inclusion into endogenous networks, and not least be cheaper as dependency might be shorter lived (see also Box 6.1 for illustration).

Remittances, remittance infrastructure and the market

Remittances are the most prominent form of flows at the level of horizontal relationships, especially primary ones (see Chapter 2). Remittances are cash or in-kind transfers from a migrant worker to close members of his original community, i.e. family, friends or neighbours. These can be made of domestic flows, i.e. between regions of a country or, more importantly, international flows, i.e. from the country of emigration to that of origin. The levels and rates of remittances depend on migration policies and behaviour as well as on economic conditions of countries receiving migrants. Labour migration, especially to bordering countries, has always been a fact of economic life, becoming more prominent as information, communications and transport become more accessible and cheap. But in situations of economic slowdown, especially associated with domestic politics, labour migration, whether legal or otherwise, seems to be the first casualty towards unemployment, significantly reducing implied remittances, e.g. Mexican ones from the USA, affected by the Great Recession (*The Economist*, 13/12/08).

Despite this, migration and outsourcing are likely to keep increasing at a higher rate than now. Outsourcing (from OECD countries to developing countries, especially) is in some ways a counterpart to migration, but it implies structural change, as labour joins new productive activities that cater for foreign demands, away from traditional ones. This implies the dislodging of traditional communities, but for as long as this happens gradually so as to give time and resources to re-adapt and develop, migration and outsourcing should be considered as positive traits of domestic integration to international networks, enhancing in passing domestic networking and institutions.

We however concentrate on cash remittances, as they will directly enter the economic circuit and therefore systemic networks. Remittances are normally massive amounts of cash, representing more than all Overseas Development Assistance (ODA) flows put together, but are difficult to measure, as a good deal of them is carried by hand or outside formal financial institutions. Even when carried through formal channels, there normally is no official centralization of this kind of flow, so the quantitative estimates are built up via scattered information and guesswork. Still, as an illustration of this type of estimate, the recorded remittances to developing countries in 2007 was some US$250 billion. This figure more than doubled in five years, representing around twice that of ODA flows. It has also been said that an important proportion of that figure is carried outside formal financial institutions, with a gross estimated total of US$380bn (Savage and Harvey 2007), but the exact proportion of informal remittances is clearly unverifiable. In addition, in-kind remittances may also represent a significant dollar amount, but their estimates are even less reliable than informal cash remittances. Likewise, an unknown amount of remittances may represent some kind of money laundry (World Bank 2006; Savage and Harvey 2007; Ratha *et al.* 2008).[2]

We know that remittances, especially international ones, tend to be more significant in low-income countries and are less volatile than other international flows. In many developing countries, the majority of poor households have at least one male member working abroad, and therefore sending remittances to their families, e.g. Sahelian countries. We also know that remittances come from numerous migrants in more or less regular periods (e.g. monthly or quarterly), normally in small quantities, say between US$10 and US$200 with a more typical amount of US$100. These may represent some 40 per cent of average income in receiving families, e.g. Niger, Somalia, Pakistan, Haiti or Guatemala (Savage and Harvey 2007), and are mostly spent on food, housing, transport, health and education, but also on some small investment projects (e.g. livestock or tools). We also know that most recipients are women or older men who are not the poorest in the receiving communities, given substantial migration costs. It also seems that the more stable the remittance flow to given households, the more likely they would be prepared to take some risk in terms of investment projects, as their stability provides some informal kind of insurance (Miller and Paulson 2007).[3] So some kind of protected risk taking should be a fertile ground for public policy, whether *ex ante* or *ex post*. This can be done by a mix of stabilizing and stimulating remittances as well as using levelling cash transfers for poorer strata. For example, remittances can be topped up via conditional cash transfers, as in Mexico (CEPAL 2000; Harvey 2007). And conditional cash transfers as well as in-kind aid can go some way to support the poorest strata and help integrate them into economic networks.

Formal remittances also represent an important contributor to a country's international reserves, relaxing foreign exchange constraints somewhat, if the latter are present. They may also contribute to exchange rate appreciation or domestic price pressures, but not necessarily so. We also know that for a given receiving country most of it comes from migrants in bordering countries and also that in times of distress disasters remittances to the affected country increase significantly after an initial disruption (Savage and Harvey 2007). This also means that if disasters or economic downturns affect bordering countries, these transfers may get reduced. An international economic downturn may affect bordering countries in similar fashion, i.e. the downturn might be synchronic for at least some regions, increasing instability and unemployment, and therefore reducing potential (normal) remittances, let alone disaster-induced ones (Albala-Bertrand 2006a). Given the normal lack of formal centralization, a way to have an idea of transfer variations would be to concentrate only in the most popular transfer companies, say Western Union, MoneyGram and Thomas Cook, but also, with significantly less reliability, via surveys of recipients well after the disaster aftermath.

The motivations for these transfers can be heterogeneous, mixed and changeable, so whether they are due to altruistic considerations (e.g. selfless philanthropy) or reciprocity (e.g. implicit insurance) or sense of communal duty (e.g. socialized responsibility) is less important than knowing how they are supplied by donors, and how they are distributed among recipients and used by them. So, except for the trivial, like appealing to people's compassion, attempts at designing public policy with the aim of increasing remittance flows by exploiting a specific motivation type may be unwarranted, as they may vary from time to time and situation to situation, providing no clear-cut pattern, e.g. the massive cash transfer from private citizens to the victims of the 2004 Asian tsunami might be unique, given its timing (Boxing Day) and the fact that many OECD tourists were among its victims. However, improving the supply of infrastructures for channelling remittances and helping orientate their use in an economically systemic way should be an important concern for public policy. We assume that remittances are beneficial to the person receiving them and to the economic system through which they are channelled. This means that public policy attempts at maximizing both the amount and the good use of remittances, while minimizing possible side effects (inflation, appreciation, criminality and the like), are to be sought and stimulated.

Remittance infrastructures and mechanisms

Disasters tend to disrupt standard remittance flows, so the fast and effective re-establishment of these flows must be an important priority of public response policy. That is, helping the rehabilitation of basic financial infrastructures, telecommunications and family identification should be high on the list. For example, remittances towards the affected countries and areas were prominent in the 2004 tsunami, which for Sri Lanka alone was reported to be US$125 million by early 2006 (Flint and Goyder 2006). On the supply side, it would be desirable to provide accessible and cheap infrastructures to motivate donors. This implies the need to reduce or subsidize the cost (direct fee and exchange rate spread) of remitting and collecting remittances and to secure the timing of these donations in the case of disasters. This can be done by getting agreements with foreign specialized institutions, facilitating the entrance to this market, setting banks abroad or even using consulates for the purpose, and increasing telecommunications via agreements, and the use and distribution of mobile phones (Solimano 2003; World Bank 2006; *The Economist* 6/9/2008).

Numerous migrants return to their affected families in disaster situations, risking their employment and status in the countries of emigration. Ways are to be devised to secure their employment in the country of emigration, securing this way the flow of remittances, via international agreements, subsidizing the transport cost and not least drawing on the capacities of more skilful and educated migrants. On the receiving end, remittances can be channelled via national banks or other formal institutions for which both donors and recipients have some trust, like religious institutions or local trade unions, when trust on them is significant. It is known that identity documentation is an important casualty in disasters, so some way to both trace family members and indentify the remittance recipient is required, which again may give some prominence to trusted institutions. Mobile phone distribution can be of great use in such situations. Informal remittances in turn can also be stimulated by resorting to *hawalla* or other informal institutions during a disaster aftermath (Harvey 2007).

The main drawback of remittances is that they may not reach the poorest affected people. Allowing for this fact, public policy can top up each remitting dollar with a percentage in domestic money to a mix of the recipient and a common fund (e.g. for each dollar to a recipient the government tops it up with another dollar: half for the same recipient and half for a common fund), which may then help support the needs of the poorest affected people, if need be. In addition, the topping-up and the cash transfers can be conditioned on useful societal traits. For example, they can be conditioned on children going to school or women learning a trade, let alone learning to read. Surely, this will not work in the immediate disaster aftermath, but can be a useful policy to consider over disaster recovery (Skoufias 2003; Baez and Santos 2007; Santos 2008). It can also be conditional on spending the money in, say, food supplied by local business (i.e. via vouchers rather than cash), which the government can support in terms of food supplies (from domestic sources and/or imports) to prevent inflation, let alone speculation.

There are some good examples of this type of public policy, normally called Bilateral Remittance Corridors. For example, the UK government has developed initiatives that aim at assisting immigrants with improving access and information, reducing costs and encouraging competition in this area. This support of remittance flows is carried by developing partnerships and agreements with both private business in the UK and receiving countries, e.g. Nigeria, Bangladesh, Ghana (UK Remittance Working Group/DFID 2005; Hernández-Coss and Bun 2007). This requires proper monitoring and disciplining to prevent diversion of remittance funds to controversial or illegal causes (see also Box 6.3 for illustration).

Shelter provision, migration and cash transfers

For affected individuals who have lost their living quarters vis-à-vis livelihood there are a few narrow options for temporary sheltering: (i) be accommodated with unaffected family or friends in the same disaster area (when affected livelihood is not badly impaired and is expected to be a short-term problem); (ii) with family or friends outside the disaster area, including outright (voluntary) emigration (when livelihood is badly impaired and expected to be a longer-term problem); and (iii) emergency camps or (involuntary) migration, i.e. forced resettlements (whether livelihood is badly affected or not, but alternatives (i) and (ii) are not available) (Peacock *et al.* 2006). The first two options exploit horizontal linkages (or social bonding and bridging capital) associated with intra- and interrelationships and are as such mostly endogenous. In turn, the third option exploits vertical linkages (or linking social capital) via hierarchical formal authority and relationships.

The question is to assess which of the three alternatives above is more systemically useful, and therefore should command higher support from public policy, assuming that this is possible. What we know from empirical studies is that people accommodated with family or friends recover faster by keeping their original occupation or trades (if in the area) or find work faster (if outside the disaster area) than those in refugee camps. Refugee camps, when they are likely to become more of a permanent feature, can also be made more systemically integrated via public policy seeking to remove restrictions of both movement and interconnections with the outside economy (Werker 2007).

Refugee camps

Refugee camps vary significantly as regards organization and economics. This is especially true as to whether these are the result of complex emergencies or natural disasters. The former is normally a long-term type of camp, e.g. Kyangwali Refugee Settlement in Uganda (ibid.). The latter, with the exception of some famine induced droughts in Africa, is expected to be temporary and downgraded as soon as rehabilitation of basic housing and infrastructures is well under way, e.g. Hurricane Mitch refugees in some Central American countries (Carter 2007; Ferris 2008). At any rate, given that natural disaster refugees are normally devoid of direct political cause or implication, it is normally easier to deal with them than in the case of politically induced disasters, but they may also become a longer-term 'temporary' solution. The main reason why refugee camps are the worse systemic alternative is because these are set up in locations that are extricated from a regular town's physical networks and institutional structures. In conflict-generated camps, their members are often prevented from free movements and free market connections for reasons of security and/or ideology. It has been said that when camps are too close to local populations there may be a risk of damaging relations between the latter and the former, while building camps too close to a border could destabilize a whole region. In addition, poorly planned camps also run the risk of fire spreading, soil erosion, landslides and flooding (Rowley 2008).[4] Longer-term refugee camps normally become a town in their own right, i.e. with producers and traders, sellers and buyers, educational and training institutions, policing and security institutions, as part of endogenous initiatives normally supported by remittances and own savings and/or endogenized by resources from refugee camp setters (NGOs, government and international experts). But dependency on handouts is likely to become more of a trait in temporary camps, as this will by definition have less time to create economic networks both inside and outside the camps.

In addition, the artificiality of a refugee camp and its image as a forced relocation, given both its provisional condition and alien environment, especially for traditional communities, is never far away. In the case of resettlements, the integration of transplanted people into alien environments, whether in existing towns or not, require that they fulfil an economically gainful role, e.g. large construction works or agricultural projects, and some fast institutional incorporation, respecting their original traditions, which is a major endeavour, often with strong political undertones and therefore not always successful, e.g. Ethiopia drought resettlements (Jacobsen 2005; Werker 2007; Hammond 2008). The easy or free provision of mobile phones has proved to be business enhancing in many parts of the most underdeveloped world, especially Africa, so their provision in camps and/or disaster affected localities, where the signal is or can be made available, has been seen to help fast recovery by facilitating the contact with friends and family (including shelter and remittances) as well as potential business adaptations or creation (*The Economist* 6/9/2008; Crowe 2012).

Trade/skill transfer

In the case of refugee camps, there is no guarantee that refugees can transfer their new trades and/or skills to regular towns. A useful public policy here is the reintegration of activities into regular town networks, but this is not straightforward. Will a (camp) business be as successful as in a regular (market) competition environment? And if this is done gradually, will the extrication of some of these successful (camp) businesses affect other (camp) dependent businesses and therefore part of the fragile (camp) network, creating new problems and dependencies? Clearly systemic decisions about camps are always tricky. Education and training are the most important transferable skills, as they can feed regular employment centres (coordinated with camp organisers). Micro finance can also play a role in creating and transferring permanent business from camps to regular markets (Werker 2007). Again, long-term systemic solutions should be preferred to palliative ones, but then this will depend more on the particular situation than on theoretical recommendation.

Family/friends provisional relocation

Host families actually provided the majority of the accommodation for internally displaced persons in Indonesia in the first six months after the 2004 tsunami, but this was mostly done endogenously without public or NGO support or facilitation (Telford and Cosgrave 2006). Here is where the use of public cash support and transfers can play another important role. Where possible, public policy should financially back family and friends that take up affected individuals, and even support some levels of migration (Harvey 2007). The advantage is that refugee guests are likely to (endogenously) trust the hosts and be embraced by the latter's regular societal networks. These networks correspond to horizontal linkages associated with primary intra-relationships and secondary interrelationships, hence opening the possible support of further primary and secondary endogenous channels, which is likely to benefit the victims by their joining existing social capital. Public money and other resources used for this may appropriately fit the permanency required by positive systemic networks, and therefore for medium- and long-term recovery. Given the need to survey and prop up the hospitality conditions of affected people, it might be necessary to set up hopefully short-term refugee camps, including the use of schools, stadiums or the like, in the interim. The direct coordination with local authorities and leaders, and their active participation, will be of paramount significance to speed the clearing of provisional refugee quarters. So activities of coordination, information and persuasion plus appropriate cash transfers and channelling of remittances are bound to come a long way towards systemic and personal recovery. Statistics and training, from the likes of local authorities, police, army, trade unions, religious institutions, social clubs and schools, on the above requirements can come cheaply and can be extremely useful as an *ex-ante* public activity. In addition, 'owner-driven reconstruction', which directly tallies with endogenous channels and initiatives, has received more attention lately. This can of course be supported with cash transfers and other financial instruments, as part of an *ex-ante* public policy (Özerdem and Jacoby 2006).

Migration

Public policy, hopefully *ex ante*, should also be able to produce and count with normal statistics of migration patterns, so as to evaluate what migration is induced by disaster effects (and the response to them) and what responds to standard behaviour. Migration-sensitive assessments should build on people's own adjustment strategies (i.e. basic endogenous adjustment), so that the design of public and international response takes into consideration and taps positive (economic and/or social) migration behaviour as distinct from distress migration or displacement (Stark 1993; WFP-ODI 2005). The aim would be, as a rule, to support positive migration and discourage disaster-induced or distress migration, although the latter might be necessary too, so again financial support to ease migration costs might be required (see also Box 6.2 for illustration).

Insurance and loans

Formal insurance, like other market activities, is typically a systemic item that belongs in secondary horizontal interrelationships and is therefore related to impersonal endogenous responses or bridging capital. A good deal has been written about it, and a plethora of new financial instruments have been created, such as weather derivatives and weather bonds, to compensate and partly prevent disaster effects, whether in urban or agricultural areas (Giarini 1984; Kunreuther 1996; Keipi and Tyson 2002; Kunreuther and Pauly 2004; Arias and Covarrubias 2006). What we know about insurance is that it is not taken up voluntarily, even when available in hazardous locations, except by a small minority. This responds to a mix of psychological and economic considerations. On the one hand, it is well known that people do not even react to a damaging event that has a low probability of occurrence, even if its effect is deemed massive (for themselves and/or their communities). Recent experience with actual disasters may change that perception, but it has also been shown that such feelings are not long lasting. Market insurance might generally be an unaffordable luxury for most people, especially when the economic choices are narrow and people are poor. The latter may be too poor to avoid deriving a livelihood in vulnerable settings, which might be the only possible option open to them (e.g. floodplains, ravines and the like). This may exclude them from the insurance market, as both the insurer risk may be too high and the potential insured too poor to afford it. In addition, middle income people, by having more influence in public policy, especially as electoral constituents, may always expect some public bailout after disasters on top of the standard charity response, i.e. the 'charity hazard' (Browne and Hoyt 2000).

Insurance and other risk-sharing systemic solutions via the market, for those who could afford it, should be preferred to exogenous bailouts. It must therefore be encouraged as it would be an endogenous mechanism that reinforces and gives resilience to both the economy as a whole and its participants. But this normally crashes with the coverage failure of voluntary insurance, mainly for the reasons indicated above, so a role for public intervention and mandatory insurance must be considered in a balanced manner. Complementary to public efforts to creating voluntary markets for insurance, via guarantees, subsidies or reinsurance, it seems necessary for public policy to force key systemic players into compulsory insurance (and its required vulnerability reduction adjustments to qualify for it), as it is done in some countries (Schwarze and Wagner 2007). In most OECD countries, there is some form of compulsory inclusion of disaster cover in mandatory insurance requirements for property and cars. For example, in the USA and the UK mortgage borrowing requires the purchase of insurance that includes some disaster types and levels. In the former, there is a high complementary subsidization while in the latter this is mostly private with some public guarantees. In many developing countries, there is some premium-subsidized crop insurance. For example, the premium subsidy is well over 50 per cent in Chile (average) and India (for small producers), while it is around 8 per cent in Argentina and 10 per cent in Mexico, although the actual surface coverage is not proportional, as it is not compulsory. Developed countries, by means of a variety of public-private schemes, show some significant crop insurance coverage, such as Spain 40 per cent or the USA 36 per cent, both operating under high subsidization (Saldaña-Zorrilla 2006). Whether it is with subsidization or otherwise, mandatory insurance should aim principally at all middle and large businesses and also most housing of middle and upper-middle households. The importance of this cannot be overstated enough, as even if most workers and poorer households are not insured, the preservation of their employment and hence livelihoods via the insurance of their employers would be systemically paramount for their fast recovery. Of course, this leaves out poor businesses that cannot afford insurance, for which some kind of *ex-post* palliative response has to be designed, such as grants or soft loans, if insurance subsidization is deemed too costly. At any rate, this is likely to reduce significantly the cost of *ex-post* public response, whether with foreign support or not.

Whether with the benefit of insurance or not, it is important to acknowledge that a good deal of rehabilitation and repairs is endogenously done by the affected people themselves without reference to exogenous responses. So the propping-up and support of these activities should be considered an essential part of positive public policy. However, certain traits of public and international response may act at variance with these activities. For example, the promise of large bouts of aid may frustrate endogenous responses, as participants may delay activities to prevent being excluded from the aid benefits. Or worse, the scattered nature of international commitments (i.e. in the hands of multiple NGOs and other institutions) is likely to create serious coordination problems, duplications, omissions, wrong competition and so on, delaying further the required rehabilitation and reconstruction, e.g. 2004 Asian tsunami recovery (TEC 2007). Here is where cash transfers or preferential loans and not least the use of microfinance institutions (for micro loans and *ex-ante* micro insurance) can play a useful complementary role (Pantoja 2002; Miamidian *et al.* 2005). These mechanisms should support and be balanced against people's endogenous reactions so as to prevent discouraging self-repairs and rehabilitation. For example, the use of cash transfers to top up endogenous expenditure or also the use of trained experts' advice to orientate endogenous efforts can go a long way in this direction, especially if the aim is to rehabilitate, while reducing potential disaster vulnerability (materials, design, procedures and the like). One permanent lesson, which is not always observed, is that rehabilitation and reconstruction should be channelled through, and receive strong input from, domestic and local institutions, i.e. endogenous channels and sources (Cosgrave 2007). The possibility for corruption and fungibility should be balanced against the systemic local efficacy of the public and international response. Some corruption or response fund deviation is unavoidable, and there is little point in zero-tolerance policy, as by trying to kill the mosquito you may end up by knocking down the Ming Dynasty porcelain jar. Once this is recognized, the issue would be to attempt to control it within some sensible boundaries, via some transparency, monitoring and penalization, but not by trying to eliminate it at the expense of more effective systemic recovery. Pre-disaster arrangements in this direction, as general policy, should be an essential part of *ex-ante* public policy (see also Box 6.4 for illustration).

Systemic public policy and institutional networks

As we anticipated earlier, after disasters have destroyed and/or damaged the capital stock and income directly, there will be suppliers that cannot supply, as they have lost their customers; demanders that cannot demand, as they have lost their suppliers; and producers than cannot produce, as they have lost their input providers. Here is an important role for *ex-ante* and *ex-post* public response, via (i) facilitating the contact between frustrated economic participants and new sources/destination of demand and supply, including foreign ones, and (ii) speeding up recovery of affected participants so that they do not lose their regular connections with demanders/suppliers. Frustrated participants will necessarily take the required initiative themselves to look for alternative markets and early solutions to come out from their predicament, but this can be facilitated and orientated by public policy. That is, public response can support endogenous reactions not only via appropriate information, but also via incentives and disincentives associated with subsidies, taxation, supply storage, demand for stock piles, and not least creating and/or reinforcing marketing infrastructures and the like. Public activity should aim at a twofold systemic balance. On the one hand, it should seek to prevent the macroeconomy from undergoing unnecessary negative indirect effects that may translate into losses of future GDP; and on the other, it should prevent that directly affected localities are bypassed by macro considerations, rendering them less effective in re-establishing their positions after recovery by default. This of course represents also the requirement of *ex-ante* public activity in arrangements leading to collating and disseminating information as well as financial backing to facilitate the joining of disaster affected participants to new economic networks.

Trade unions and employers' organizations

In countries where there are regular trade unions, these are useful endogenous institutions that may be used as point of contact to transmit information and/or channel response resources, whether cash or in-kind ones. National ones will normally have branches across sectors and over the whole country. Trade unions have practice and communication routines instituted and not least are normally trusted by their members. They can also be more easily monitored than ad hoc emerging groupings. Non-members can also be reached by trade unions in affected areas, under the aegis of national ones, as they will operate at the level of both the firm and the industry, but this will require some checks to prevent lopsidedness, for example via employers' organizations. Employers' organizations normally have national presence and a regulatory body and experience. They can become extremely useful in the aftermath, as it is likely that they will seek to create goodwill and again can be more easily monitored than autonomous emergent groupings. It is likely that in the early aftermath both trade and employers' unions check on each other in a cooperative fashion, so non-union members will have a better chance of being reached than it would otherwise have been. At the same time, employers' organizations will have better information about damage and failures of their business members than rapid surveys by outsiders, even if overestimations are to be expected. These may contribute to discipline recovery in a less wasteful way.

The use of trade unions and employers' organizations do require a coordinating public body, so that their actions can be properly channelled towards emergency and rehabilitation. Here is another useful *ex-ante* public policy, i.e. the creation of a coordinating body, associated with an economy ministry, which should have appropriate routines and up-to-date information about these organizations as well as some kind of mandate in cases of emergency. In addition, the International Trade Union Confederation (ITUCC) has participated in disaster fundraising and linking activities to local trade unions, e.g. Indonesia, Sri Lanka, India, Burma, Nepal and many others, and not least has had an important presence in climate change conferences and issues. And local trade unions have normally played an important role in relief and rehabilitation and beyond (see websites for ITUCC; ITFGlobal; www.labournet.de/internationales/pk/turcp1105.pdf; etc.). ILO has worked with both employers' organization and trade unions in the case of disasters. This means that there is some experience that should be further explored for *ex-ante* public policy along the lines above (see www.ilo.org).

Mobile phone access

Mobile phones have become ubiquitous and extremely useful in countries where fixed lines are not or cannot be available. Mobile phones and mobile-based internet access have become simple and expedite mechanisms to put together buyers and sellers at short notice, e.g. fishing boats can phone alternative ports, picking the one with the best prices for their catch. The distribution of mobile phones, where signals are available, can also put together senders of remittances and their dispersed recipients after a disaster, and not least can be used to produce personalized and efficient information about disaster issues, such as gathering points for food/cash distribution, refugee camps, extended family communications and the like. But it can also serve as crowdsourcing for information about the state of things around the disaster area and region so as to both help emergency and rehabilitation and network shifting. Here is yet another *ex-ante* public policy, i.e. distribute mobile phones and help create signals in disaster prone areas of difficult access. These can both be useful in the aftermath of disasters and run through to normal times, regularly incorporating people into systemic networks, i.e. facilitating their endogenous behaviours (Crowe 2012).

The armed forces and religious institutions[5]

It is well known that the use of the armed forces, especially the military, is necessary, especially during the emergency and partly during early rehabilitation. In addition, they are normally trained to deal with natural disasters and other emergencies. In countries where they are not openly partisan and/or corrupt, they can and normally do play an important role and are trusted. For countries that are not at war or civil war, whether actual or potential, the use of the military is a valuable organized and effective force, which is not particularly costly, as they receive the same income support from the government, whether they are used for war or not. This is, of course, a reason not to use them beyond emergency needs, as they are likely to substitute regular workers, who may have been rendered unemployed by the effects of the disaster impact. So the response can contribute more to systemic recovery by employing regular workers than by using the military, which mostly operate outside the economic system, as *deus ex machina*. Public response policy should of course consider the best mix of these two sources of recovery resources, as it probably does, but should privilege those that directly feed the economic system for the reasons exposed in this book.

In turn, religious institutions, like the Synagogue, Church, Mosque or others, are typically inbuilt in culture and social structure and normally play a useful role in especially the early emergency, which goes beyond purely spiritual comforting and general proselytizing, even if they run on such agendas. In countries where they have significant presence and therefore coverage, and are not tainted by political leanings, let alone corruption, they are normally trusted and can be useful for information and response organization and not least as a conduit for in-kind aid, cash transfers, remittances and the like. So an *ex-ante* public policy of linking religious institutions, which are often funded by taxpayers, with public actions via training and procedures for disaster situations, can go a long way to make the disaster emergency response more expedite and effective. The particular details, of course, should be discussed in each case well before disasters, so as not to hurt sensibilities. But actual disasters themselves might create conditions to ease the establishment of such disaster preparedness (see www.cwserp.org/training/and other religious websites). It is however true that a religious institution may tend to cater less for people from other religions than for those of their own persuasion, which should be checked by means of a balanced approach.

Conclusion

Endogenous reactions from businesses and communities are of paramount importance. The failure of exogenous responses, whether domestic or foreign, to tap them is bound to lead not only to short-term wastage and a catalogue of unnecessary insufficiencies, as shown in the case of the 2004 Asian tsunami, but also to long-term wasted opportunities for securing a recovery in terms of systemic consistency and functionality. Network bypassing seems to be a normal state of affairs after disasters by both firms and people. The role of public policy, whether *ex ante* or *ex post*, would be to prevent an excessive lopsided recovery that unnecessarily affects indirectly the locality that was directly impacted by the disaster, by insulating the national economy at its expense, i.e. by excessively supporting, purposefully or otherwise, the national economy networks, especially those associated with the market, at the expense of significantly severing the local economy from them.

This chapter showed some reactions and behaviour, especially from endogenous sources, which can be usefully supported by public policy so as to secure a systemic consistent recovery of both the disaster affected area and the country. We express the need that exogenous responses should be in tune with the inbuilt reactions of people and markets, with a view of securing systemic sustainability, i.e. functionality. In such context we analytically presented the cases of cash transfers and in-kind aid, remittances and their infrastructure, shelter provision and migration, insurance and loans, and general systemic public policy. The aim was to show the importance of learning about people's reactions in disaster situations for public policy and in passing to show that networks are ubiquitous at all levels of societal action. An appropriate policy support and enhancement of community networked reactions can reduce the local-national tension, and the effectiveness of recovery both in itself and in terms of general development. In this context, in the next three chapters we deal with economic networks at macro, sectoral and business levels and therefore the importance of endogenous reactions that are consistent with supporting societal functionality.

4 The networked macroeconomy and disasters

Introduction

In this chapter we focus on the macroeconomy as a whole, via both an aggregate and a disaggregate outlook, to show the likely networking substitutions induced by direct disaster effects within it. Short and longer functioning macroeconomic effects can only happen via indirect (flow) effects, i.e. derived from the direct disaster effects on capital stocks and populations, while cumulative effects result from a mix of direct and indirect effects, as shown below.

Indirect consequences of direct disaster effects on societal entities (human capital, labour, children, etc.) can only cause a long-term effect if they are simultaneously (i) univocal, i.e. they represent a unique cause and effect pattern, and (ii) unsubstitutable, i.e. they cannot be substituted as part of permanent endogenous processes, like market and social reactions, or as part of public policy-induced counteractions. For example, it has been shown as regards the effects of Hurricane Mitch on Nicaragua in 1989 that children in the disaster areas may have suffered from nutritional deficiency (Baez and Santos 2007; Santos 2008). Assuming that the standardized WHO weight-for-height ratio is an appropriate measure of undernourishment and/or disease, the effect of this on human capital, i.e. education, energy and intelligence, is hardly straightforward. Will these affected children be at a socio-economic disadvantage for the rest of their lives? Or will they just be at a disadvantage if they exert themselves beyond normal energy usage and intelligence? Can they compensate for early malnutrition in adulthood life? If the answer to the last two questions is yes, then in terms of potential productivity this effect would go unnoticed at both micro and macro levels. If the answer is yes to the first question, then this will affect a group of individuals in their economic (and probably social) role, as their human capital would be less productive than it would have been otherwise. But then, even if that was true, it would be unlikely to have an effect on the macroeconomy, as this labour, as any general labour, is likely to be both not univocal and substitutable for similar or better quality labour and/or capital. In addition, the same studies above showed that school enrolment and work increased significantly for children in the affected areas, partly as a cash-for-requested-behaviour policy, meaning that their human capital may have developed better than it would have been otherwise, probably compensating for the potential negative effect, at least at a personal level, from the very outset. These observations, like any other below, are set as normal rules, as there may always be some counterexamples, as in any socio-economic analysis.

Cumulative disaster effects can be defined as any effect on the resilience of stocks or flows, which is unimportant or undetectable at first, but tends to gain strength over time, coming out in full swing after capital stock undergoes several debilitating impacts from natural disasters, e.g. a building collapsing only after experiencing a third natural impact due to subsidence movement on structural foundations or a dam experiencing faster waterlogging after low intensity weather events upstream and the like. These consequences are more likely from the secondary forces of primary natural events, e.g. an earthquake leading to subsidence or stormy weather leading to landslides (Albala-Bertrand 1993). Slowly developing disasters, such as drought-induced famines or breeding grounds for vectors of disease that lead to epidemics, are more likely candidates for cumulative effects, which if not checked may suddenly break out into a major disaster. This is highly unlikely in the case of sudden disasters. But at macroeconomic level, if a disaster has no discernible longer-term (functionality) effects, then it is unlikely that it will have cumulative effects. But even if there were some cumulative effects on some structures, society is a living organism, so gradual and more definite checks on it would likely come endogenously, making them irrelevant at macro level over time, unless the economy depended fully on a staple export like copper, and all the mines collapsed, which is highly unlikely. The problem would be to distinguish when a change is societally induced by cumulative disaster effects and when it is a standard discontinuous trait of development, which is even more difficult to assess quantitatively than standard longer-term economic effects of disasters, as shown in Chapter 1.[1]

We start below by differentiating a disaster from a catastrophe, as this encapsulates the main traits associated with the societal capacity of response to systemic failure so that basic functionality is not impaired. We then enter an analysis at an aggregate level, via an economic argumentation and model, and end up with a disaggregate analysis of the networked economy via input–output sectoral interconnectedness.

Disaster escalation and catastrophe

Let us emphasize that as long-term effects can only happen via indirect (or flow) effects, then the issue of counter-flows at macro and local levels becomes paramount. As proposed by Albala-Bertrand (1993), the implicit or open purpose of macro response would not be the reconstruction or restitution of destroyed and damaged stock items, but the counterbalancing (counteraction and compensation) of their potential flow effects, so as to re-establish the macro functionality of the economy as a whole. This can happen without full reconstruction, but it does normally require effective rehabilitation. This can be clarified by showing how a disaster can escalate.

A way to introduce this is by means of a distinction between a disaster and a catastrophe. A catastrophe is an extreme and sudden disaster whose intensity affects a social system in such a way that (i) the endogenous (inbuilt) capacity and the exogenous (policy) options of the system are greatly surpassed, i.e. most economic resources become unavailable (destroyed, damaged, inaccessible or immobilized) and most normal institutions become fragmented and ineffective (failure of normal rules and incapability of governance), so further systemic disintegration and deterioration is unstoppable; (ii) assuming that the initial impact was economically local, the localized failure is so intense that it pervades the whole system in the same way as in the previous point, i.e. the system has no viability within the same institutional arrangements and resources; (iii) external aid, domestic or foreign, even if available, cannot re-ignite the system, but only support its now helpless victims. That is to say, the system stops operating as such, requiring a fundamental change, which is a long-term and costly endeavour. This can be the case of a harshly defeated country in a war, like Germany after the First World War, or the destruction of the institutional cohesiveness of a multi-national/ethnic country, like Yugoslavia after the Soviet Union demise (Albala-Bertrand 2000a, 2000b) or Iraq after the 2003 US-led invasion. But except and arguably for Montserrat after its volcanic eruption that started in 1995, this scenario is unlikely in the case of natural disasters for countries as a whole.

For a disaster to escalate towards an economic catastrophe, following our definition above, three conditions are required: (i) direct (stock) effects have to be economically widespread, massive or pivotal; (ii) indirect (flow) effects have to be uncontainable; and (iii) institutional effects have to be so perverse that functional recovery, via economic rehabilitation and reconstruction, becomes unachievable. So the economic system is rendered unviable and victim relief must be the most that external aid can achieve, as in some complex emergencies (Lateef 1982; Nafziger *et al.* 2000; Nafziger and Auvinen 2002; Di John 2008). A natural disaster becoming a catastrophe is then unlikely and, arguably for Montserrat (see Box 4.1), no example can be provided in modern times. In other words, a catastrophe, as defined above, might only happen if a disaster renders economy and society into either inert objects or fully disorganized social entities, which are unlikely propositions, especially in the context of localized disasters.

Societal reactivity via domestic and foreign linkages in a diversified economic environment is paramount in explaining why naturally induced disasters might not have the dramatic negative economic effects that are so commonly portrayed in the mass media and other sources, let alone become a catastrophe. That is, the networked economy via market behaviour and information, economic diversification and integration, public institutions and expenditure, communities' reaction and self-help, and general domestic and foreign interactions are likely to endogenously and exogenously help counteract, if not outweigh, actual and potential disaster effects. At the macro level, these processes might be enhanced by globalization, which would make the possibility of disaster escalation towards

Box 4.1 A proper catastrophe: the 1995 Montserrat volcano

Montserrat is a small Caribbean island which, before the volcanic eruptions that started in 1995, had a population of some 12,000 inhabitants and enjoyed a middle GDP *per capita* of some US$4,000 (in ppp). This was an open economy with a very low share of GDP and employment coming from agriculture. Most of the GDP came from services and then industry, where tourism featured prominently. The island had a well-integrated population, with well-developed communications and services infrastructures. The volcanic eruptions had widespread economic consequences, as if it did not destroy or damage most infrastructures and residential capital, affecting any options for markets and business activity, it became a health hazard to be around, which meant the exodus of most of the island population. That is, this is the case in which disaster effects are not economically localized but economically widespread, so the expectation would be for strong and uncontainable indirect effects, as it happened. Some two-thirds of the population left the island, while insurance and other foreign companies withdrew and ports and airports closed (Clay *et al.* 1999; Benson and Clay 2004), making the island unviable as an economic proposition. Half of the island is still expected to be uninhabitable for many more years. Ever since 1995, the current economy has mostly existed on the back of financial support from the UK, but not as an autonomous economy with self-capacity to progress. Today it has a population of around 5,000 people, meaning that some people have returned.

This is the case of a disaster with widespread indirect economic consequences, which could be classified as an economic catastrophe, as whatever the island's level of domestic networking and *per-capita* income it would have become unviable as a proper economic entity. Its external historical linkages with the UK have however served it well to keep a minimum of the economy afloat until it becomes habitable and viable again.

catastrophe highly unlikely. Notice however that even in the absence of exogenous responses, especially associated with foreign aid, a good deal of this counteraction would happen anyway, as society and the economy are not inert but living organisms. But accepting that a catastrophe is highly unlikely does not mean that a disaster cannot be devastating, especially for the directly affected locality, households and businesses, but it does mean that societal response mechanisms, even if defective or slow, are likely to be always available. That is to say, as long as societal functionality is not badly impaired, the system is bound to counteract negative effects and recover, as is always the case after disasters, even if this is especially trying for the directly affected locality. In other words, natural disasters are unlikely to affect the capability of a societal system to be viable, i.e. to survive shocks by being resilient, to secure general continuity by being responsive to local failures and to develop by expanding and deepening its functional features (see Chapter 2).

An aggregate macroeconomic argument

In the general context of networking, let us start with an aggregate macroeconomic analytical argument about the likely indirect effects of localized disasters on the economy. We start by sustaining that even if the capital stock lost to a disaster was not completely replaced, it would be unlikely that the economy would be significantly affected in the short term, let alone in the medium and long terms. This can be shown by means of a macroeconomic argument based on well-supported facts about both localized disasters and the way economies, especially developing ones, actually work.

In the case of localized disasters, as defined in Chapter 2, we know that capital losses to disaster are heterogeneous and normally lopsided towards the less productive type of capital. We also know that most losses are to the capital stock rather than to income and that reconstruction investment is likely to be of better quality than that of the capital lost. In turn, for any economic system it is well known that the growth of output does not depend only on the contribution of the capital stock, but also on labour power, technology, organization and other societal requirements such as peaceful order, lawfully coded competition, institutional cooperation and legally backed trust. It is also accepted that if new investment opportunities are available, these are more likely to be taken up by the private sector when they are less risky, especially when private investment is publicly supported and protected. It is also accepted that public investment in infrastructure normally complements or 'crowds in' private investment (Taylor 1983, 2004; Aschauer 1988; Albala and Mamatzakis 2004). Furthermore, economies, specially developing ones, exhibit large levels of unused or underused productive factors, in terms of idle capacity and underemployed labour and other resources, which may be one of the contributing reasons why inflation is, as a rule, either not significant or very short-lived after localized disasters. In the case of developing countries, idle capacity is mostly due to lack of domestic demand and markets, primary exports and lack of export diversification, lack of domestic credits and savings, lack of foreign exchange and expertise, and not least lack of access to and information about investment opportunities and know-how (Thirlwall 2011). In developed countries, capital idleness might be a private policy option to smooth jumps in demand, while labour unemployment may be due to lack of employment opportunities for a growing population. Of course, their levels depend much on the stage of the business cycle and the state of the economic environment, e.g. after the 2008 Great Recession. Some of these constraints are normally weakened, if not lifted, by the disaster response, both public and foreign, which might induce a positive systemic contribution.

In the context of a disaster situation, i.e. taking the impact and the response as an interactive process (see Albala-Bertrand 1993), economic and other societal networks would normally generate *endogenous* reactions from within and from outside the disaster area. For example, reactions by frustrated suppliers and demanders via network shifts that seek alternative market sources, or market reactions that fill profitable gaps left by the disaster losses or private investment that complements new (disaster) public investment or that follows new information about investment opportunities opened up by the disaster. These would all represent systemic behaviours that help business and recovery, and general economic development. There will also be economic counteractions via the use of buffer stocks, like savings and inventories plus fast imported inputs, to partly make up for the initial losses to both final and intermediate goods. Buffer stocks and remittances, which may be complemented with cash transfers and easy loans (see Chapter 3), in a disaster aftermath, are bound to contribute to contain negative spreading effects from the disaster zone to the rest of the country and therefore contain negative multiplying effects on the national economic machinery (Albala-Bertrand 2004/1993). The more diversified and openly integrated the economy was, the more important would these networked reactions be. In other words, the disaster itself endogenously creates domestic and foreign economic incentives and reactions, which are reinforced by public and foreign exogenous responses. New concessional foreign exchange could even relax a foreign-exchange constraint if this was present before the disaster, as can be shown via a two-gap model (Taylor 1994, 2004), increasing investment and hence growth. The stimuli from disaster-induced incentives may also unlock and create economic opportunities, inducing a reconstruction investment multiplier larger than the disaster loss multiplier, making the recovery less costly to undertake and more rapid to succeed than it would have been otherwise. But the main argument about networking and localization would actually hold even if there were no multiplying effects from the disaster response, when the multiplier was equal to unity (Albala-Bertrand 2004/1993). Both endogenous and exogenous reactions require physical and institutional conduits and networks to be usefully deployed. That is, the more sophisticated and all-embracing these networks, the more effective the likely counteractions from disaster-induced incentives and reactions, and the faster the rehabilitation of infrastructures. The converse case is also true; weaker domestic networks make for both weak endogenous reactions and systemically weak absorption of foreign aid and response (see Box 4.2).

An aggregate macroeconomic model[2]

Within the above dynamic societal framework, an economic model to assess the output effects of a localized disaster can be articulated by following the Albala-Bertrand (2004/1993) model. The basic relationship is that a unit of capital loss (via capital productivity) will always have a lower impact on future output than one unit of capital replaced with new investment (via the multiplier). On this count, the potential negative effect of the disaster impact is always smaller than the positive effect of the disaster response. This is because the value of the productivity of capital is always smaller than the value of the investment multiplier, even if the latter were equal to unity, i.e. no multiplying effect. Let us show this by analytically distinguishing between impact effect, response effect and total effect, in a networked context of endogenous and exogenous societal networks and counteractions.

Box 4.2 Malawi and network weakness

This is a small landlocked country in Southern Africa and one of the most densely populated and poorest countries in the world, currently with a GDP *per capita* of around US$700 (in ppp) and over half its population under the poverty line. Of its 14 million people, some 80 per cent of them represent the rural population, which mostly derive their livelihood from agriculture. The share of agriculture in GDP is around 45 per cent. Its export ratio is around 15 per cent, agricultural exports representing around half of it (tobacco in turn accounting for around half of it). This is an economy that strongly depends on international aid and it is included in the IMF-World Bank Heavily Indebted Poor Countries (HIPC) programme. The country is among the most sensitive to climate in the semi-arid region of Southern Africa, so food security is an extremely important endeavour. Potential and actual variations of rainfall patterns, from especially the El Nino Southern Oscillation phenomenon (ENSO), on cereal output, especially maize, can therefore be very costly. Climate forecasting is an essential informational policy tool for both the government and especially small commercial farming decision making, which has been improving over time with the backing of international organizations. Small farmers however do not normally have the means (credit, savings, etc.) to adapt to forecasting.

This country has a recognized centre of allegiance in a multiparty type of democracy, which only started in the mid-1990s, but public administration has been subjected to inefficiencies and corruption and its country coverage is uneven. Communications have been expanding, especially mobile communication, but this mostly covers urban areas, so cellular subscribers are still less than 10 per cent of the population. The country has been developing credit and marketing structures, but they are still precarious. Therefore, this is a country that would qualify as network underdeveloped, both in coverage and strength. But it seems to be well connected internationally, belonging to most of the institutions set up by the OECD for the poorest countries. This means that, on the one hand, geographically localized disasters might not spread over the rest of the country given absence of linkages. But on the other hand, where linkages are present, a geographically localized disaster might spread more intensely with less effective counteraction, given the weakness of linkages. International aid network linkages, however, are bound to compensate for the weakness of endogenous domestic (market) reactions.

Benson and Clay (2004) show that as regards the droughts of 1992 and 1994, which were mostly geographically widespread disasters, the economy seemed to have bounced back and outweighed the losses within a year or so, on both occasions. Not all agricultural output undergoes similar output falls, as they are not equally sensitive to rainfall variation, like many types of tobacco crops. A good deal of this can be attributed to the fact that these droughts were short term in nature and that there was a generous exogenous foreign and public response in the aftermath (ibid.). The facts of fast agricultural recovery from foreign supported resilience to droughts and the vagaries of rainfall patterns seem to be common to most of Africa (Benson and Clay 1998). Therefore, despite the expectation that a climatic disaster in a poor country like this may be macro-economically trying, the particularities of agricultural production, the short-term duration of the impact and public/foreign support tend to make them short-lived. The same study also shows that variations in rainfall patterns tend to be less significant on both agricultural output and GDP towards the end of the studied period, i.e. the early 2000s, with less severe fluctuations of (now positive) growth rates, as compared to the early 1990s. So again, macro effects from short-term climatic disasters do not seem to have been important in the medium run, let alone the long term for macroeconomic functionality. But this is the case of a country with weaker endogenous resilience on the back of poor integrative linkages and less economically localized types of disaster, which is still unlikely to recover quickly without significant international support. For as long as domestic networking is not both widespread and efficiently compensatory, the economy would be unlikely to be able to wean itself off foreign dependency on this score.

Impact effect

The output that can be produced with a given stock of capital normally represents only a fraction of the value of the capital stock, normally around 40 per cent of it (i.e. the ratio of total output to total capital, or average productivity of capital, is around 0.4). That is, 2.5 units of average capital would normally produce around 1 unit of average output. But given that disasters affect more the less productive capital types, like residential and infrastructure capital, the average productivity foregone to the disaster will be lower than the average, say half of it. That is, other things being equal, 5 units of capital loss would represent 1 unit of foregone output. By the same token, given that the less productive capital is the more affected within any capital type (i.e. old housing and infrastructures, obsolete capital and the like), say half of it again, then 10 units of average capital loss would represent around 1 unit of average foregone output (i.e. the output-to-capital ratio would actually be only equal to 0.1). Hence, other things being equal, 10 units of capital lost to a disaster would only represent about 1 unit of future output loss. Or conversely 1 unit of capital loss would represent a one-tenth loss of future output. If we also allow for non-capital contributions, then the impact of capital losses on future output will be even smaller, but to make our point we can stick to the moderate capital-output ratio above. To compensate for this omission and to simplify, we also ignore direct inventory and income losses, e.g. goods in storage or in production process or some savings, which are normally significantly less important than capital stock losses. After all the corrections above, this can be represented by the *potential loss in the growth rate of GDP from capital loss* as:

$$g_{Y1} = d/c \tag{4.1}$$

Where g_{Y1}: growth rate of GDP, $d=D/Y$: capital loss-to-GDP ratio, and $c=\Delta K/\Delta Y$: incremental capital-output ratio, which is the inverse of the incremental productivity of capital. So if $c=10$ (i.e. the productivity of capital would be 0.1) and $d=5\%$, then $g_{Y1}=0.5\%$, which represents the growth rate that would potentially be foregone due exclusively to flow effects from the direct disaster loss to the capital stock after one year, all other things being equal.

Response effect

Investment has a dual role in the economy: on the supply side, it represents additions to the capital stock and, on the demand side, direct income. So reconstruction investment, while replacing the losses to the capital stock, also increases the aggregate demand and therefore income directly. One unit of reconstruction investment will represent one unit of income, and significantly more via the multiplier. That is, one unit of expenditure on autonomous investment would normally represent more than one unit of new income at the end of the year, as this expenditure will undergo several market rounds over the year, which is what we call the multiplier. This of course requires the existence of underemployed resources, which is a normal feature of most countries, especially developing ones. It also requires the lifting of some domestic and foreign constraints via increased information and coordination as well as public support and foreign exchange availability, which are normal disaster response features. So if we conservatively assume a multiplier equal to two, then the replacement of one unit of capital loss would represent about two units of new income. If we also allow for the fact that the capital replacement is normally of better quality than that of the loss, the positive effect would be greater, but for the purpose of our general argument we can ignore this fact. After all the corrections above, this can be represented by the *potential gain in the growth rate of GDP from reconstruction investment* as:

$$g_{Y2} = m\Delta v \tag{4.2}$$

Where g_{Y2}: growth rate of GDP, m: income multiplier, and $\Delta v = I_R / Y$: variation in total investment-to-GDP ratio due solely to reconstruction investment (I_R). So if $m=2$ and $\Delta v = 5\%$, then $g_{Y2} = 10\%$, which represents the growth of GDP that would potentially be gained due exclusively to reconstruction investment after one year, all other things being equal.

Total effect

Taking the impact and response together, then a unit of reconstruction investment would have 20 times more impact on income and output than one unit of capital loss. That is, one unit of capital loss would represent a one-tenth loss of output, while one unit of capital replacement would represent two units of new output. In other words, to recover the possible negative effect of disaster loss on future output, reconstruction investment can be only one-twentieth of total capital loss, in the first aftermath year. That is, if capital loss represented 10 per cent of GDP, then the required investment-to-GDP ratio would have to be only 0.5 percentage points more than it would have been otherwise. As this investment ratio is normally around 15 per cent of GDP, the post-disaster ratio would be required to be around 15.5 per cent of GDP, which is not an onerous additional effort. Most countries do fulfil such a requirement within a year or so. It can also be shown that, after the first post-disaster year, the required investment ratio can be even more moderate than in the first year to keep GDP unaffected, as if there were no disaster. So equalizing the loss and the gain in the growth of GDP (i.e. $g_{Y1}=g_{Y2} \Rightarrow d/c=m\Delta v$) and solving for Δv, we will have the reconstruction investment ratio required to keep the growth of GDP unchanged, as if there were no disaster, all other things being equal. That is, the *compensatory required investment* would be

$$\Delta v = d/mc \tag{4.3}$$

So if $d=10\%$, $m=2$ and $c=10$, then $\Delta v=0.5\%$. This means that if the ratio of capital loss-to-GDP were 10%, which would represent a large disaster, it would be enough with an addition of 0.5% (or 0.5 percentage points more) to the standard investment ratio to keep the economy as if there were no disaster, all other things being equal.

An application of this model to seven large disasters in Latin America appears to confirm the patterns above. For example, the large Guatemalan earthquake of 1976, which reported a loss-to-GDP ratio of 17 per cent, required a total expenditure ratio (including both investment expenditure and other expenditures – the latter was omitted above) of 1.2 percentage points more than it would otherwise have been in the first post-disaster year, and significantly less afterwards. In all the cases in this study, the required investment ratio was generally fulfilled, making potential growth losses more than compensated either in the year of the disaster or within the first two post-disaster years. That is, even in the worse cases, the negative disaster effects on the economy were relatively short-lived and more than compensated for afterwards. For a full description, presentation and application of the model, see Albala-Bertrand (2004/1993).

In this light, only rarely has a localized disaster a negative impact on GDP in the medium term, and even in the first accounting year, which means that functionality is rarely affected by localized disasters. If anything, because of the new disaster-associated opportunities, not necessarily related directly to reconstruction, and the unlocking of potentials due to public expenditure, domestic finance and foreign exchange, as well as endogenous stimulus and information related to the response, there may be a significant acceleration of growth. This will normally be confined to the first two or three post-disaster years, especially but not only in the case of earthquake disasters (Albala-Bertrand 1993; Charvériat 2000; Murlidharan and Shah 2003; Benson and Clay 2004; Noy and Nualsri 2007; Raddatz 2009; Cavallo and Noy 2010).

A disaggregated macroeconomic argument

The above model does not let us appreciate how network interactions between and within economic sectors, whether in the disaster area or outside it, can help explain the outcome above. So it is necessary to analyse the workings of the economy towards this end in a more disaggregated manner.

Box 4.3 Bangladesh and increasing localization

Bangladesh is a large and poor country with a population of some 150 million inhabitants, and a GDP *per capita* of around US$1,100 (in ppp), which undergoes recurrent cyclones, floods and droughts. A severe cyclone in 1970, when the country was still East Pakistan, killed some 300,000 people, and seemed to have catalysed the ensuing civil war and independence from Pakistan (Albala-Bertrand 1993). From late 1970s onwards, the Bangladeshi economy improved significantly with important domestic structural changes and domestic and trade liberalization, including a more professional monetary management. Also some important export diversification ensued, moving towards light industrial goods, like clothing (which represents over 45 per cent of exports, with agriculture representing some 3 per cent), from which most public tax revenue is derived. This has significantly shifted output from agriculture and primary sectors to industry and services, the share of agriculture in GDP being now around 18 per cent. More than half the population still live and derive their livelihood in rural areas, which makes people more vulnerable than the macroeconomy to climatic disasters. These reforms have induced both private-sector development and foreign direct investment (Benson and Clay 2004). The human development index (HDI) has also evolved positively, from 0.37 in 1980 to 0.55 in 2005, while exports to GDP moved from around 5 per cent in 1980 to 17 per cent in 2005. These are all indicators of an evolving economy that diversifies, opens up internationally and better integrates its population into societal networks. These development processes are always accompanied by a movement towards increased networking and livelihood options, which may increase the country's macroeconomy disaster resilience over time.

Disasters in such a large country are always geographically localized, and mostly economically localized, especially from the 1980s onwards, even when they are recurrent. This does not mean that localities cannot be badly affected and that disaster-induced injuries and mortality are unimportant. The macroeconomy however seems to be less vulnerable to disasters, correcting itself, helped by some variable doses of international aid, in the short to medium terms. This means that current disasters can significantly affect the rest of the macroeconomy only if they affect the less volatile non-agricultural sectors, and both networking options are not easily available and public response is not forthcoming. As shown by Benson and Clay (2002, 2004), over time the macroeconomy has become less and less vulnerable, with any disaster-induced negative fluctuation in GDP and agricultural output being compensated for if not outweighed within two years. It shows also how the non-agricultural sectors remain stable, helping the compensating process. For example, after important floods in 1998, there were large-scale imports carried by the private sector to fill the temporary food gap over the period. This was a substituting endogenous response backed by public policy, 'limiting pressures on prices and public finance' (ibid. 2004: 12). It also shows that remittances and the development of micro finance for the rural poor played important roles in mitigating and increasing resilience to natural disasters.

The above has happened both as part of the development process itself, but also as part of *ex-ante* and *ex-post* foreign-helped public policy aimed at anticipating and mitigating potential disaster events, reducing macroeconomic risks and hence enhancing the macroeconomic resilience and response to local failures. These development programmes, whether general or disaster-focused, have been mostly financed by external aid, which after disasters may have reallocated resources, bringing forward commitments rather than increasing them systematically (ibid. 2004). This should not however be considered as a serious problem in itself, as long as the project is systemic, i.e. integrated into the structure and dynamics of the country's development. That is, response in terms of disaster projects should be part and parcel of the development path of disaster-prone countries. Budgetary resources may also undergo significant reallocations, but again it is the development quality rather than the fact of reallocation that should count. In other words, what should be assessed is their role in the overall long-term functionality of the macroeconomy. Of course, a good deal of early emergency expenditure might have little development implication other than to palliate victimization, which is a cost that should also be taken into account for a complete picture.

What about longer-term macroeconomic effects? There is little evidence that GDP, investment, employment, exports and the like were affected whether positively or otherwise beyond two to three years after the event. Public finances and balance of payments though can carry increased deficits for much longer, but there is little or no evidence that the persistence of long-term deficits is disaster induced. Much depends on budgetary policy, but it seems that public deficits did not change significantly after disasters, especially towards 2000 (ibid. 2004). But again, it is the use of the deficit in terms of macro functionality that should be assessed and not the fact of it. For as long as the deficits are the results of necessary (systemic) development projects and can be sustained by either growth and/or external aid commitments (and/or capital flows), then these longer-term effects might be trivial, meriting little or no concern. This of course requires a study of deficit funded projects and resources and indeed public finances, which are difficult to track from official statistics, as expenditure and revenue flows may fall in items that are not disaggregated enough, including some creative accounting, but some attempts have been done about it (Benson and Clay 2002). Only a purposeful country study might help disentangle such expenditures and revenues, which is certainly beyond the scope of this work.

So, as a conclusion, Bangladesh will keep being exposed to climatic disasters, but it seems that its more robust diversification and continuing less dependent output from agriculture are bound to make the expected geographically localized disasters even more economically localized than currently. At the same time, such developments can only mean a more effective and all-embracing set of networking, offering more counteracting options to the potentially (indirectly) affected activities and people. So we can anticipate that the macroeconomy is unlikely to undergo negative effects on basic functionality, and thus on the economy, in the medium term, let alone the long term. It is again the potentially directly affected localities that should be the focus of *ex-ante* disaster policy at national and local levels.

Maximum potential interconnectedness

Just to have an idea of how impossible it would be to analyse the working of a fully disaggregated economy, we show the following appreciation. It should be easily understood that in an economy the maximum number of links among the maximum number of participants or nodes would be a very large number. The following three definitional equations contain the main possible linkages that can analytically be identified in an economy, disaggregated into three different but interrelated networks, N_1, N_2 and N_3.

$$N_1 = \{P[(P-1)+E_N]+P[(P-1)+E_I+E_C]+H[P+E_H]+G_M(P+H+E)\} \text{ (Real Side)} \tag{4.4}$$

$$N_2 = \{(F_D+F_E)(P+H+G)+F[(F-1)]+F_E]+BF_{DB}\} \text{ (Financial Side)} \tag{4.5}$$

$$N_3 = \{G_T(P+H)+E_T(H+P+G)\} \text{ (Transfers side)} \tag{4.6}$$

Where P: number of domestic producers, E_N: number of available external markets for inputs, E_I: number of available external markets for investment goods, E_C: number of available external markets for consumption goods, H: number of domestic households, $G_M(P+H+E)$: number of government interactions with domestic producers for final goods, households and available foreign markets, F_D: number of domestic financial firms, F_E: number of available foreign financial firms, G: government (a unit), B: central bank (a unit), F_{DB}: number of domestically operating banks, $G_T(P+H)$: number of government interactions via transfers (taxation and subsidies), $E_T(H+P+G)$: number of external interactions via transfers (remittances, grants and other net unrequited flows or transfers).

These three sets interact within and between them, making up the formal economic system. Set N_1 represents the real side of the economy, which underpins and drags the other two sets. Set N_2 is the financial side of the economy, which is meant to facilitate the real side of the economy, providing strong positive and negative interactions on it, and often taking unwarranted and unsustainable autonomy from the former, resulting in the well-known and mostly unproductive bubbles and their damaging bursting. Set N_3 represents all those net unrequited flows in the formal economy such as remittances and government transfers. Again, these have strong influences on the real economy and its financial side, especially the ones associated with government policy. Behind these interactions are wage earners and profit seekers, who are the motive forces of the economy. Finally, the above sets represent only the formal economy, which in many developing countries greatly underestimates actual output and economic activities. Informal activities are a dynamic, if unstable, source of livelihood and can be huge. In cases of disaster, they are an important resource for personal recovery. The informal sector does have important connections with the formal one, but they are less important the more developed and sophisticated the economy becomes (Thomas 1992). In settings where the informal sector is supposed to be large, the formal economy may have an important drag on it, so concentrating on the formal economy and generally allowing for systemic interconnections with the informal economy might provide a better measurement than ignoring the latter altogether.

Assuming that both the actual number of linkages and their strength were known for a whole country, and also assuming that these are stable, then with the use of computers it would not be too difficult to create average networking indicators. Once we focus on a particular sector, region or group of activities, then we can create indicators via the proportion of these actual linkages with respect to the total and even produce some measures of linkages associated with the money-transaction levels between them. However, we don't know the actual number of interactions, either their strength or whether they are individually stable. It can be seen that even giving very moderate numbers to the nodes above, the total number of interactions, whether mono- or bi-directional, will be huge and fairly unworkable, let alone if we deal with the actual numbers of economic participants.

A network mapping would be out of the question, as it would become little else than a meaningless and useless blot. This is the reason why network mappings are confined to very few nodes and links, making for a very incomplete societal picture (see Chapter 2). In reality, not all nodes are connected with each other directly, but that would still make for an enormous network map of linkages, even if the degrees of node separation (i.e. how many links to reach a particular node) were also very small. So at best this can be done for very simple connections and very small groups of participants, as in standard network studies, which would necessarily be partial and unrepresentative of a dynamic system and, therefore, of little use for a proper political economy and macroeconomic approach. So there is then a need to assess them either nationally grouped via input–output tables or summarized via national accounting.

For an explicit network analysis, an input–output framework of already grouped units (industries, sectors and/or regions) is the only possible route at macro level, keeping always in mind that within each grouped analytical unit there are large networks of seemingly alike participants or nodes. The input–output framework is then a network of networks, which explicitly via matrix presentation and algebra takes care of (i) what unit is linked with which other unit, (ii) how strong is such direct connection and (iii) how strong is the pull/push of a particular unit on all the other units directly and indirectly via backward and forward linkages. This is a great advantage over standard network analysis. The latter takes usually explicit care of the links of a very small group of participants, normally extricated from society as a whole. But even here it has serious difficulties in assessing the strength or importance of links, which normally depend on some proxy measure of qualitative variables (Jackson 2008).

A measure of localization in the context of input–output relationships should answer how many, what type and what proportion of participants were affected by direct disaster effects. From here, we should try to establish how many, what type and what proportion of interconnections are affected by direct disaster effects, in terms of both existence and strength. This should take care of the importance of both the affected units in the national economy, disaggregated according to economic sector, and the networking options or substitution potential (SP), as defined in Chapter 2, of both the directly affected participants and the indirectly affected ones.

Hopefully this should be regionally and sectorally disaggregated, according to the disaster pattern, which can only be done with appropriate inter-regional input–output (IRIO) tables, which are rarely available, so a combination of standard input–output (IO) tables, which are more often available, and national accounts will be the normal available approach. If the disaster is geographically localized, as most disasters are, then information about the locality and region that contains it would be important. But whether the direct effects are geographically localized or widespread, sectoral information will be paramount in assessing the *economic* localization of the disaster and the alternatives open to the productive units that are directly affected and those that are indirectly affected. As regards direct disaster (stock) effects, we normally count with summary data coming from the first assessment, usually differentiated between infrastructures, agriculture and business capital stocks in connection to the affected zone vis-à-vis the country at macro level (e.g. ECLAC reports on disasters). Despite its shortcomings (see Chapter 1), this will give us an idea of loss distribution even if the actual levels are less reliable. What we rarely have is a good and reliable disaggregation of stock destroyed and damaged. Most of the information comes as a ratio of GDP rather than the capital stock. So what we will normally lack is the proportion of capital stock losses according to sector and region, which is a real insufficiency, as this is the specific information that can give us a more accurate idea of potential indirect (flow) effects, so we are forced to work with flow measures, as shown in Chapter 5.

The analysis of networking and localization

Taking into account the aggregate macroeconomic argument and the network approach above, an analytical framework for the relevant networks can be based on the framework proposed by Albala-Bertrand (1993), which is mostly embedded in the input–output framework and the circular flow of income at macroeconomic level. To be sure, this should not be confused with the input–output model, which we criticized for this task in Chapter 1. The point here is to use it in a loose way to account for general interconnectedness and its strength so as to focus on the areas where endogenous reactions and exogenous responses, and therefore resilience, have to be forthcoming to counterbalance for potential indirect effects, i.e. to counteract the potential spreading of flow effects. To this purpose, we call *supra-networks* the encompassing interconnectedness of the government institutional apparatus with intra- and inter-networks, which mostly depend on comprehensive policy derived from both short-term expectations and longer-term development policy aims. We call *intra-network* the interconnectedness between producers and *inter-network* the interconnectedness between producers and households.

Supra-networks

Supra-networks refer to vertical open-loop economic policy decisions of government and international institutions vis-à-vis economic agents (firms and households). These networks operate a good deal via the financial system. This open loop is due to the fact that income withdrawals from the economic circuit (i.e. savings, taxes, imports, debt servicing and the like) and income injections or reintroductions (i.e. investment, subsidies, loans, exports and the like) are both separated in logic and time. Some of these, like public discretionary spending (e.g. some subsidies and public works), some debt built up, and others are not mediated by the relatively stable behavioural patterns associated with input–output relations and propensities to consume. The public budget accounts for the expected income to be received and expenditures to be executed by the government over a year. Its structure reflects social and economic policies, representing preferences and priorities of the government and their political persuasion. Many types of subsidies and taxes are clearly discretionary, meaning that a government of different persuasion can and normally does alter them towards its own preferences and priorities.

In the case of disasters there may also be discrepancies about how to spend the contingency item in the budget. Should this or that sector and people be bailed out? If so, with which financial levels and with which distribution? For large disasters, the contingency reserve in the public budget is normally not nearly enough. Then should these be financed out of taxes or new money creation? Should debt financing come from domestic or foreign quarters? Should some current projects be substituted or extended to cover for disaster response requirements? It is not unusual that new taxes are temporarily created to finance expenditures on relief, rehabilitation and reconstruction. In addition, the government may increase its debt either domestically with the Central Bank (e.g. quantitative easing) or internationally with bilateral and multilateral institutions. So there is a good deal of discretion both in the way new income is created and new expenditures are allocated that goes beyond the standard politically induced discretion on such scores. This means that especially the public expenditure side, whether current or capital, may not be mediated by relatively stable behavioural patterns. Public expenditure depends on policy and expectations, which are never far from political ideology and especially short-term political aims. Hence, factual evidence, changing political aims and a mix of agents' perceptions, can sway the expenditures and taxation income in a range of ways. That is why we represent these as open loops, which will be closed in different ways, in different times, by different governments.

Figure 4.1 shows some of the supra-links. The straight arrows represent flows of income from firms and households to the government via taxation, loan (from public bonds or directly) and flows (profit or losses) of public firms and utilities. In turn, the curved arrows represent open loops, which are made of transfers (social security, subsidies and the like), debt repayment (e.g. public bonds on maturity), payments for public investment and public works carried by the private sector, public insurance and re-insurance, etc. Finally, the straight interrupted arrows from international institutions to the government represent also an open loop of income to the country via the government or to the private sector with public guarantee. Subsidies go to particular groups of firms and people,

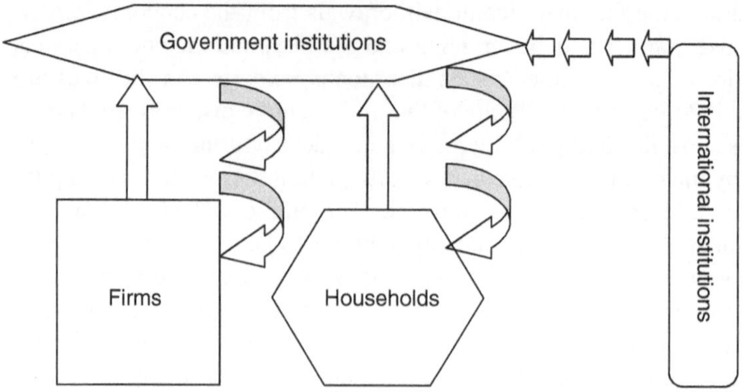

Figure 4.1 Some supra-network links.

especially those under the effects of disaster. So these links are hierarchical and supra-national, which represent vertical relationships or the so-called linking capital, as described in Chapter 2. These can be described as open loops in the economic circuit, which can be closed sporadically in accordance with background expectations and policy. This closing is less stable and less predictable in abnormal times, like economic recessions (notably the 2008 Great Recession and sequel), political instability, wars and large natural disasters. These operate above and go beyond intra- and inter-networks, influencing the behaviour, multipliers and stability of the economy, whether purposely or not.

Transmission effects

Private expectations and public policy associated with incentives or otherwise are paramount in characterizing possible response consequences. First, if the disaster shock is considered as permanent, the agents' behaviour would reinforce the downturn (e.g. no compensatory behaviour, capital flights, outmigration, bankruptcy and the like). Second, if the shock is considered as transitory, agents will keep prevailing policies, compensating recessive factors and make the downturn shorter-lived. Third, if agents expect public and foreign aid, then agents' behaviour may either reinforce the positive upturn or delay recovery as external aid, to the disaster zone, is awaited. In addition, if public and foreign responses act at odds with endogenous response mechanisms, by bypassing them or unnecessarily superimposing on them, then local recovery will likely be systemically negative and wasteful. In slowly developing disasters, in turn, expectations and behavioural patterns would not change overnight but along a progressive revision.

Summary

Government action and international assistance may be highly significant in pre-empting the appearance of negative expectations which reinforce recessive and/or depressive tendencies. A simple indirect measure of possible supra-linkages can be the level and coverage of taxation, the level of social expenditure and the human development index (HDI). The first one may provide an indication of both government capacity and linkage, the second one the inclination of the government towards social development and welfare. And the latter one may provide a summary indication of a socially sensitive and influential government. But none of them is enough is itself, as contradictions can arise in all of them, e.g. an HDI can be compatible with very poor standards of income distribution and social mobility.

Intra-networks

Intra-networks refer to the economic linkages within and between economic sectors or industries. The actual linkages however are between constituent firms or producers, whether within or between sectors or industries. This refers to the connection of each firm with some other firms, as generally shown in Figure 2.3 (Chapter 2). As is well known, a sector or industry normally cuts across regions, e.g. tourist firms and resorts can be scattered all over a country, agriculture production can come from many areas of a country, textile firms can be located in many regions, and so on. This is an extremely important consideration in the case of disasters, as many firms can be badly affected by a disaster, but the industry or sector can remain unscathed via substitutions, shifts, new entrants and the like, especially within the substitution potential of affected countries, making the indirect disaster effect less important or irrelevant at macro national level.

Figure 4.2 shows in a simple way some relationships that a firm can have with other firms, when disaster strikes. The rectangular shape represents economic sectors A and B. The rectangle on top represents foreign markets and the elliptical shape represents the economic disaster area. The latter involves one firm in Sector A (FA4) and two in Sector B (FB4 and FB5). Lines without arrows represent bi-directional links, while those with arrows indicate direction of trade. FA1 is related to FA5 of the same sector and to FB4 of sector B. The latter happens to be directly affected by the disaster. So initially FA1 is indirectly affected by the disaster, just as FB1 would also be. FA5 supplies FA1 and exports part of its output abroad. FB2 in turn represents a full enclave as it imports all its inputs from, and exports all its output to, foreign markets. So FB2 is less likely to be indirectly affected by the domestic disaster. And if it was directly affected it would not create intra-links negative flows, but it may affect foreign currency levels. The other firms are of course related directly and indirectly to most if not all other firms, but to avoid a confusing spaghetti junction, we keep it simple as it is. Likewise, most if not all firms produce also for final

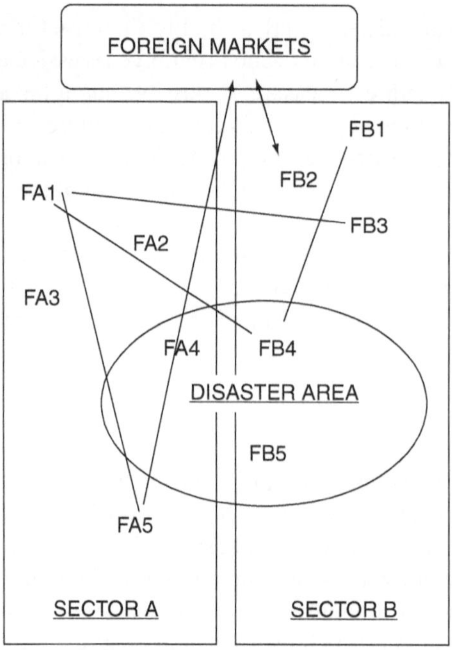

Figure 4.2 Some links between firms or intra-networks.

demand (i.e. consumption and investment), but that is part of the inter-networks, which we deal with in the next section.

Let us assume that the linkages above are the ones just before the disaster. In principle, FB1 can substitute FB4 with either other firms in Sector B or via foreign markets or both. For this, it can create new links with FB3 or FB2 or with other firms of that sector (not shown in the diagram). It can also create links to foreign markets for the first time. The point is that if this network shift is possible, then indirect effects will be short-lived and therefore unimportant for the macroeconomy. We will show in Chapter 6 that network shift is normally possible and should be encouraged, keeping in mind the necessary balance between the local and the national, as the firms directly affected (FA4, FB4 and FB5 in the diagram) may be significantly bypassed, making their recovery more difficult.

Intra-network linkages are typically input relationships via market exchange. It is more likely that firms will relate to other firms via wholesalers than directly. But direct firm-to-firm trade is also important, especially in less developed areas. Wholesalers are normally more than one in any region and have the advantage of (i) buying and storing a range of different goods from several firms, (ii) buying and storing similar goods from more than one firm and (iii) selling goods to more than one firm. From a wholesaler viewpoint, a network shift is a change in the purchase and sale structure of a given wholesaler. And from the viewpoint of a firm, if customary wholesalers fail, a network shift is a change of wholesale outlet and/or provider. The analysis that follows is in many ways the response of wholesalers to incentives and initiatives of input demand from frustrated firms. So, in the context of wholesalers, each firm produces intermediates for other firms and demands intermediates from other firms to satisfy its final output. This input demand can be variable according to the production pattern and the general economic environment. That is, some firms will accumulate a level of inputs high enough to keep production for, say, a month without replenishment, while others will follow a 'just-in-time' pattern that requires continuous replenishment. The former is more costly (given amounts and storage space), but safer in the case of both up-fluctuations of demand or disruptions of linkages like disasters. The latter, on the other hand, is less costly but demands a pretty good market coordination and expedite physical access, which makes it vulnerable to serious disruptions. The normal case is inclined to the former in especially developing countries, but much depends on the type of production. For example, perishables (like most food components) will be closer to just-in-time types of replenishment, while non-perishables and less bulky items (like cloth components) may prefer the alternative one. The latter, especially, depends strongly on the quality and trustworthiness of market participants.

To clarify the issue of direct interconnectedness, it should be kept in mind that:

- a given domestic firm can be domestically connected to several domestic firms and various external firms (whether via importers or directly);
- not all firms are directly connected to a given firm domestically or externally;
- not all firms are connected with equal strength and frequency;
- input trade can be done directly firm-to-firm or intermediated via wholesalers;
- firms are not of equal size, productivity and resilience; and
- they don't have the same political economic access and influence.

Indirectly, however, each domestic firm can be connected to all other domestic (and participant foreign) firms, e.g. a clothing firm purchases material inputs from a textile firm, in turn the latter purchases inputs from a cotton firm, and then the latter does the same from firms producing seeds and fertilizer, and so on and so forth. The clothing firm may also require new machinery and labour for an output increase, exerting again a sequence of investment and material input demands down the line, affecting any firm related to these requirements. This can be measured via customary backward and forward linkages via input–output tables (Albala-Bertrand 1999; Raa 2005) or other more elaborate measures associated with system complexity (Ferreira *et al.* 2007). In practice firms are neither so vertically integrated nor so stable, especially in the presence of shocks like disaster. Network decentralized diversification of supplies and demands is more likely in more sophisticated economic environments, which means that given inputs could come from many sources at the same time. So shocks can open opportunities for the more resilient ones and/or for new domestic and foreign entrants. That is, any firm can delink and purchase the required input from anywhere available domestically or from abroad. This might be a good economic decision associated with lower prices, better quality, more expedite availability and the like. But this may also affect the domestic firms that were supplying these goods originally, affecting employment and livelihoods, which is also likely to happen with fast trade globalization (Albala-Bertrand 1999, 2006; Alvarez and Lopez 2008). This delinking and relinking may be even more intense in the wake of disasters, as short cuts might be preferred for faster macro recovery. This may be systemically positive and consistent with longer-run macro development, but it may also be locally harmful in the short to medium terms. As said, a systemic policy balance should be struck between the national and the local in disaster aftermaths.

At this level, there are also supporting networks associated with the financial system and public sector flows, which channel credit, savings, subsidies, taxation and the like. We assume that these flows are mostly dragged by decisions in the real side of the economy, but there are strong interactions both ways. If we want to look for indicators of productive networking, indicators related to the real side of the economy will primarily be more compelling. But this can be complemented with financial variables for a more complete picture, when required.

Transmission effects and their economic context

The effects and counter-effects via main transmission routes at this level can be observed and analysed via both sectoral and regional input–output multipliers. In a mechanical input–output system, any loss of one unit of final or intermediate output demand for a particular sector will have indirect consequences elsewhere, as we critically showed in Chapter 1. But the fact is that market and non-market reactions of real economies can and normally do compensate for such an indirect loss, if not in the short term, at least in the medium term, let alone in longer terms. Compensations can happen within the same structure, via buffer reactions, if the disaster setback is considered short-lived and the economic environment unchanged. This may create some compositional change, as the economic participants are unlikely to have all the same buffer response capacity. Compensations may also happen via structural change, associated with network shifting at the sector, regional and/or national levels, i.e. relinking with new firms within the same sector, as shown above, whether they belong to the same region or not. If available, this can also be complemented with technical change, output type change and other forms of diversification, especially when the economic environment has undergone significant changes, whether the initial setback was short-lived or not. After large sudden disasters a combination of both types of change, compositional and structural, is likely to happen, while in slowly developing disasters, like droughts, let alone complex emergencies, structural change is a more likely candidate. We concentrate on sudden disasters, as slowly developing ones and complex emergencies elicit additional societal impositions and changes (Albala-Bertrand 2000a; Nazfiger *et al.* 2000; Nazfiger and Auvinen 2002).

There is an analytical and empirical need to distinguish between income loss and capital stock loss, as loss transmission will be pretty different in one case as compared to the other. First, if income is lost, we saw in Chapter 1 that to assess its economic consequence in an inert input–output model was highly unrealistic given the living nature of an economy. The counteractions to this income loss should however be seen mostly as part of inter-networks, which we deal with in the next section. Second, if capital stock is lost, which is mostly the case, to transform capital stock losses into potential income losses, as if these actually happened, is a non sequitur. In Chapter 1, we showed the economic and technical inconsistencies associated with such a procedure. However, to assess which sectors or regions can potentially have higher national spreading effects via pre-disaster backward and forward linkages as well as their potential for substitutions would be a more useful and qualified starting point.

The general context for transmission effects via intra-networks looks as follows:

- Most sudden disasters are regional in nature and rarely significantly affect materials inputs directly or for too long.
- In the less industrialized countries, most interregional trade is trade in final goods (mainly consumer goods) rather than intermediate commodities. This may affect the circular flow of income rather than input–sectoral relations.
- The capital stocks of firms are normally not badly affected by natural disasters, so capacity might not be the main productive problem, but distribution, as infrastructures can be badly affected in the short run.
- Disasters normally affect the main industrial service infrastructures (e.g. water, electricity, gas, roads). These can create bottlenecks and affect sectoral productions. These disarticulations are normally both very localized (i.e. they affect only a few firms of a sector) and normally short-lived, initially via rehabilitation and circumvention and then via reconstruction.
- Reactions, such as circumvention of affected infrastructures, bypassing the affected units and/or locality, will help compensate for direct local failure at national level, especially.
- As partly shown in Box 4.4, productive substitutions like resorting to buffer stocks (inventories and savings), idle capacity of unaffected areas, existing unemployment and underemployment (within and outside the disaster area), new productive entrants, imports, price adjustments, credit adjustments, new technology, fast new investments, solidarity and general domestic and foreign responses, may prevent the spreading of most of the potential indirect losses and more often than not compensate the macroeconomy for existing direct losses.

Box 4.4 Example of possible counteractions

Let's clarify this with an example. Assume that in a pivotal sector, i.e. one with high backward linkages, a single machinery that produced, say, bricks for construction, is lost, then at the firm's level, the shortfall can be counteracted via either more capacity usage of existing machineries within that firm or by using brick inventories or both for the short period until the lost machinery is replaced. If this is not available, then at the industrial level, the shortfall can be compensated for by unscathed firms increasing capacity usage or selling their own inventories, therefore benefitting other firms of the same industry at the expense of the directly affected firm. If this was not available, then the shortfall can be filled up via imported bricks, benefitting importers. In the short run, if none of these substitutions was available, then that would partially affect construction projects that were using this source, unless they themselves had some inventories to keep going in the interim, or unless they can change the order of construction to delay the use of these bricks, which is also a substitution. They can also bid for existing brick supplies, pushing the price up, but that does not make the shortfall disappear in the short run. Finally, if none of this is available, then construction projects may have to be delayed until the machinery is replaced. All this may affect costs, but construction output is likely to resume within weeks. As it can be seen, there are a lot of 'ifs' before output (construction works) actually falls. On the other hand, in the longer run, if none of the substitutions above are available and the shortfall is deemed to be long-lasting, then it is likely that the construction industry will shift gradually to alternative technologies, e.g. by using more iron, cement, glass and so on at the expense of bricks, as has actually happened in virtue of more efficient technologies as part of the process of development. But of course the latter is unlikely to happen from sudden disasters, which are typically short-term initial shortfalls at macro level, even if at micro level the initial affected firm does not recover at all.

- Rapid rehabilitation of infrastructures may in addition help re-establish economic flows locally. In such a context, the economic performance as a whole, at national level, will be hardly affected, even if there were significant local losses or initial changes in cost structures.
- Transport, fuel, food and water are economic areas of primary importance for recovery, as they are basic requirements for the operation of the economy, i.e. transport for distribution, fuel for productive means and food and water for people and industries. Both *ex-ante* and *ex-post* preventive and reactive activities, whether endogenous or exogenous, normally act with determination on these areas after disasters (e.g. see ALNAP papers).

Heterogeneity of producers

Producers are not homogeneous, so firms or units of different size and productivities are bound to coexist with each other. Larger units would have many more possibilities than the smaller ones to withstand both direct and indirect disaster effects, as they may have a better quality of fixed assets and location as well as more subsidiaries and diversification, i.e. less vulnerability to direct effects and less exposure to them. Larger units are also likely to have higher profits and solvency, higher liquidity and inventories, higher client power and market access, better business connections and higher political influence, i.e. both less vulnerability to indirect effects and more resilience to counter them. As a corollary, the smaller the unit, the higher its economic vulnerability, even in the absence of disasters. In other words, pre-disaster economic and political vulnerability and resilience greatly explain disaster vulnerability and resilience in the aftermath, as shown in Chapter 6. For example, if a flood imposes a shortage of supplies, then given the greater influence and client power of larger units, these are likely to be supplied first from alternative supply sources. Only then may smaller units also be supplied, which may put them out of business by lack of required input or lack of markets.

In addition, there may be an economic, and partly a social, rationale in satisfying first the larger units. On the one hand, they are likely to be the bigger employers, securing livelihood of employees and so helping faster recovery. And on the other, larger units may require less input per unit of output, as they are likely to be more efficient. So the disaster recovery of output levels, especially at national level, is likely to be faster and less wasteful if recovery reliance is primarily placed upon larger units. That is to say, precisely the units which are less affected might be the ones which benefit relatively more or deteriorate relatively less after disasters. This is *mutatis mutandis* a bit like the 'too big to fail' dictum of public response policy in the case of the Great Recession. But in our case this refers more to the endogenous resilience conditions of larger firms, including their political influence, than to systemic public policy orientated by such political influence. This may bring a post-disaster change in both the technological structure of sectors and the market shares of firms in the affected areas, as less efficient units are put out of business and market shares of larger units increase. This may make it even more unlikely that the negative indirect effects on gross output be long-lasting. Of course, this also implies the destruction of local livelihood associated with smaller and less resilient firms. We deal with firms under disasters in Chapter 6.

Summary

Inbuilt economic mechanisms at national level, especially market responses, associated with exogenous responses could well prevent most indirect disaster input effects within and between economic sectors, securing a fast recovery of macro functionality. Endogenous mechanisms via inventories, prices, idle capacity, new entrants, foreign trade, credit, associated with the overall linkages of the disaster area as well as the internal differentiation of productive units, in terms of size and productivity, may render unwarranted the claim that indirect effects are important for the economy in the short to medium terms, let alone the longer term. This should be even more so in the presence of exogenous public and foreign responses under the not always fulfilled assumption that they are to complement economic activities and stimulate endogenous responses, hopefully avoiding inefficient bypassing and dependency suffocation. We should look at the backward and forward linkages on which the economy operated just before the disaster as well as the sectoral, regional and national substitution potential, so that we can then assess what is the existing resilience of the most affected nodes or firms and their connections. This must however be seen in conjunction with income effects, i.e. inter-networks and effects.

Inter-networks

Inter-networks refer to economic linkages between households (as income earners and consumers) and producers (as suppliers of final goods and services) through the circular flow of income via market exchange. This refers to the connection of each household with some firms (producers or distributers) as generally shown in Figure 2.3 (Chapter 2). As is known, most firms, apart from producing for intermediate input demand, will also produce for the final demand. These are income relationships, which are normally expressed in terms of aggregate demand, i.e. consumption, investment, government expenditure, exports and imports. Imports imply that households can buy directly or indirectly from foreign producers, so other things being equal, imports will compete with domestic production of final goods. The issue after disasters would be to secure compensatory levels of demand. These can come from savings, remittances, formal loans, informal loans, government transfers and works, and general foreign and domestic aid. Figure 4.3 helps visualize some of these demand flows.

In this figure, F: domestic firms, FF: foreign firms and H: households. The households H2, H3 and H6 (enclosed in a square and shaded) are assumed to have been directly affected by the disaster. We assume also that no firm was directly affected by the disaster, but the normal case is that there will be both firms and households that are directly affected by disasters. So mutual interactions will likely follow similar patterns as the ones described in intra-networks and below. The shapes in the diagram below are self-explanatory. The direction of the arrows indicates direction of money (payment, transfer or loans). We have included the government for completeness, but that belongs to supra-networks. It is to be understood that rarely do households relate to firms directly, but via retailers. So the arrows simply indicate some of the firms that the household mainly connects via retailers. In the above diagram there are no arrows from the financial sector to firms or to the government and vice versa, but they should be assumed implicit. They have been omitted to both concentrate on households and avoid too many arrows. So to this effect let us focus on household H3.

Let us assume that the diagram above presents the linkage situation after some disaster reaction and response took shape. Household H3 was directly affected by the disaster, but is in a rather privileged position as it now receives

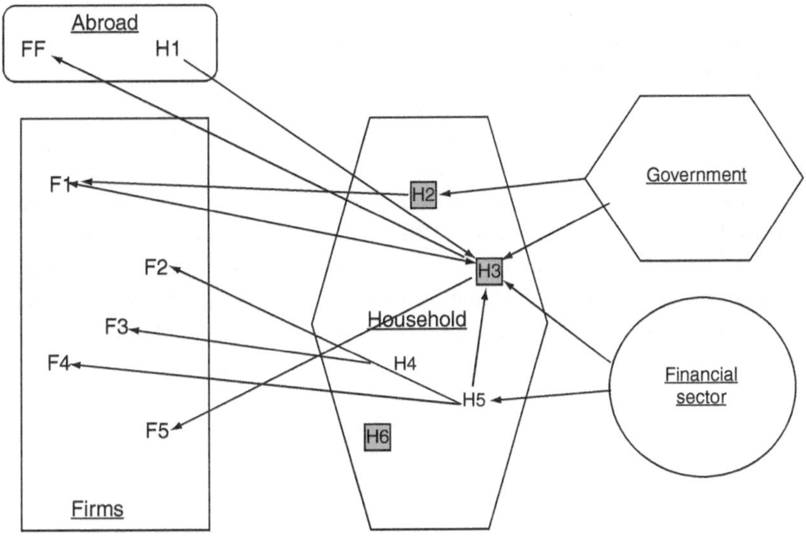

Figure 4.3 Some links between firms and households or inter-networks.

transfers from the government, loans from the financial system, informal loans from H5 (which was not directly affected by the disaster) and not least remittances from H1. It can also be seen that H3 buys now (assuming that he did not do it before) from foreign markets (directly or via importers). It also buys now from F1 and F5 showing some useful diversification. We assume that before the disaster F3 purchased from other firms that were directly affected by it, so it has now been forced to look for alternative unaffected firms and retailers, whether in the disaster zone or outside, to satisfy its needs. This would be a case of network shift via demand shift in search of alternative suppliers. In turn, H2 receives transfers from the government and can keep buying from F1, assuming that that was what it did before. H6 however was directly affected and completely severed from domestic and foreign markets and assumedly without savings and domestic support from the government and community. This is a household rendered totally disenfranchised by the disaster. It will probably be a candidate for relocation in a refugee camp. Now, notice that the demands from H6 to any firm that it used to buy from have been severed, so these firms themselves might be indirectly affected and be looking for alternative consumers in alternative markets, which would be a case of network shift via redirection of their supplies to keep production and sales at a level. Of course, this is just analytical, as one household is unlikely to make much of a difference, so the description above assumes a large number of households and firms affected in such ways.

As said, most of this exchange will be intermediated by tertiary sector service providers (i.e. distributers via corner shops, supermarkets, specialized vendors, importers and other traders). The role of these firms is to make available the output from producers to households and investors. Disasters may upset the tertiary sector badly, although this is not normally so, but its recovery is also normally faster and less onerous than that for infrastructures, especially now that firms can be located in cyberspace via the Internet. Lastly, flows associated with the financial and public sector networks do have an important bearing on consumption and investment behaviour and levels. The credit-based economy leading to the 2008 Great Recession is a clear witness to this. Inter-networks can be measured by means of both backward and forward linkages of final good demand by sector of origin, derived from extended input–output tables. These are however rarely available, let alone on an interregional basis. So the usual way is to resort to national accounts and their regional disaggregation, complementing them with some knowledge of the sectors and firms directly affected by the disaster, as shown in Chapter 5. With this knowledge we can then assess what is the existing resilience of the most affected sectors and firms, especially in connection to their macro substitution potential.

Transmission effects

Let us assume that price adjustments are sticky, which is normally the case, and slower than quantity adjustments to clear markets. On this scenario let us first assume that agents hold elastic expectations, i.e. an exogenous demand fluctuation is considered as permanent by market participants, which is rarely the case in disasters, then a standard income multiplier would work as follows. Any autonomous variation of expenditure will be instantaneously met by an equivalent variation in production to absorb it. In general, if the variation is positive, this will be met out of idle capacity and new employment, from the pool of the unemployed or underemployed, and if it is negative by cutting down capacity usage and employment. So the multiplier will amplify the initial demand loss, via several market exchange rounds, by some factor over time, e.g. one unit of demand lost to the disaster could become two units of potential loss over time. This is a derived, or indirect, flow effect. Alternatively, under the assumption of inelastic expectations, i.e. an exogenous demand variation is considered as transitory by agents, which is the normal case in sudden disasters, then the multiplier will look quite different. The multiplying effects are potential, as these represent flows that could be counteracted by the wider economy, including the initial losers, which is more likely in the case of sudden disasters. Economic agents will attempt to counteract the shock via households' dissavings and firms' disinvestment (faster inventory reduction), if these are available. In addition, exogenous responses via transfers, credits and new response demand are bound to reinforce the loss counteraction. This will happen in an environment of endogenous network shifting and bypassing of the affected links. So even if the directly affected agents cannot recover fast or at all, the macroeconomy is bound to insulate them and compensate the economy for the potential flow loss.

As long as these fluctuations are absorbed by these adjustments, disequilibrating variations in output and employment will be avoided and the multiplying effect will be stopped in its tracks, so the final accumulated reduction in gross output will be equal to the initial direct loss of income. It can be shown that if each income unit of disaster loss is fully compensated through dis-savings and disinvestment (which represent past value added), both negative sectoral interaction (intra-network effects) and negative income multipliers (inter-network effects) will be prevented and the final income loss (current value added) will be equal to the initial direct disaster loss. In this case, the economy will be at the pre-disaster level of equilibrium between supply and demand and functionality would not be affected. But if, on the other hand, only the percentage of consumption propensity is compensated for out of savings (i.e. the average proportion of income that is devoted to consumption; say, 70 per cent of it), then the multiplier will be stopped in its tracks and the final equilibrium after the disaster will be at a lower level of income, i.e. equal to the pre-disaster period minus the initial loss of value added, but this is likely to be ephemeral and recovered in the next period, as functionality would not then be affected (Albala-Bertrand 1993). In both cases, macro functionality would be effective to recover the levels of output in the short term.

Inflation pressures

Disaster-induced inflationary pressures can happen at inter-levels and intra-levels. There however appears to be no clear case, especially in the medium to long run, whether empirically or theoretically, for relative prices to vary significantly, let alone for inflation to become systematic. A disaster is normally geographically rather than sectorally located, so there will normally be unscathed productive units of the same sector in other locations (and even in the disaster area). This implies that it would normally be possible for unaffected units to make up for the loss by using idle capacity (if capital were affected), buffer stocks (if production and income were affected), from new supply entrants (if production or capital were affected), and foreign trade (if production were affected), which will normally be complemented by public and foreign responses. Under these conditions, if we assume that communications between regions are acceptable (i.e. disruptions are short-lived), transport costs do not vary significantly, and information about both new business opportunities and macro coordination is fairly adequate, then the excess demand for goods in short supply does not need to bring changes in relative prices, except only transitorily. Of course, price increases that are not speculative may stimulate socially useful supply increases where they are needed for recovery. In addition to substitution effects of price variations, rationing and cooperative behaviour after disasters as well as expectation of aid will also act as price moderators. Public policy, whether *ex ante* or *ex post*, should tap on these linkages and traits so as to secure a shorter-lived inflationary pressure. For example, it seems that there were important inflationary pressures in Banda Aceh after the 2004 tsunami disaster, but they were not so for Indonesia as a whole (Blanco *et al.* 2008). This may be an indication of inappropriate national policy, which despite the overgenerous foreign aid, may have over-insulated the national macroeconomy at the expense of Aceh. We discuss this disaster in Chapter 5.

Summary

A disaster loss on inter-sectoral income flows, according to various assumptions, will be translated into a contractionary economic situation (when multipliers fully operate), into a fall once and for all (when buffer stocks prevent the multiplying transmission), or into an unchanged equilibrium of supply and demand (when there is full compensation). Macro functionality is unlikely to be affected even in the short term. In turn, although in real disasters the level of prices does not vary significantly, the real multiplying effect of an exogenous decrease in supply can also be prevented through price adjustments. Lastly, in least developed countries, the normally weak economic linkages of affected areas with the rest of the economy are likely to make the spread of the indirect effects of little relevance for the country-wide economy. In addition, it is also likely that the positive multipliers from disaster response are more significant than those from disaster loss, which may make the recovery even faster (Albala-Bertrand 2004/1993). Here is then the importance of both emergency and early rehabilitation of pivotal infrastructures as well as information on alternative linkages, which is mostly a role for the government, but also increasingly from private citizens via crowdsourcing and other forms of emergency management and information (Crowe 2012).[3]

As an overall conclusion, indirect effects of economic disarticulations on the economy as a whole would appear less significant than normally portrayed, except in some unlikely circumstances, as shown by Albala-Bertrand (1993).[4] There then seems to be little theoretical support (as shown above) or empirical evidence (see Chapters 1 and 5) for the usual claims about the importance of indirect macroeconomic effects of disasters. In addition, if we also consider the standard exogenous public and foreign disaster responses, then indirect effects are even more likely to be mostly potential, if not short-lived phenomena, which with some systemic and prompt assistance can be further averted and/or compensated for.

Conclusion

In this chapter, in the context of networks and macro functionality, we analysed what behaviours and derived flow effects from capital stock destruction can be expected in a living societal system. At an aggregate (macroeconomic and sectoral) level, we attempted to show why disasters are unlikely to have the medium- and long-term effects that are so commonly portrayed in the media, but also from more specialized quarters, and why the spectacularly photographed destruction of the early hours is likely to be counteracted if not outweighed, at flow levels, in the short term. First, we showed in the context of general networks and the concept of functionality why a disaster is unlikely to become a catastrophe, which we defined explicitly. In addition, in Chapter 2, we differentiated between isolation (a state of things) and insulation (a societal response) to stress the way networks may secure systemic functionality in a situation of disaster. Second, we showed via a macroeconomic argument and a simple model what was required to counteract the potential effects on GDP from capital stock losses from a disaster, concluding that the effort in terms of additional investment over normal investment-to-GDP was quite modest to secure it. We recalled some examples of major disasters that appear to confirm such a result. Many other examples are available in the literature, some of which were presented here as boxes. Third, we moved from the single national aggregation towards sectoral disaggregation to show how the input–output economic interconnectedness or networking can help explain such an outcome. We differentiated these interrelationships into supra-networks, intra-networks and inter-networks, indicating that all of them interact with each other in an institutional or political economy context. We showed here how endogenous responses via buffer stocks, prices and network shifting can prevent negative disaster flow effects to spread over the economy, which, associated with standard exogenous responses, may render unwarranted the claim that indirect effects are important for the economy in the medium and the longer term, but also often in the short term.

5 Regional disaggregation and two examples

Introduction

Supra-, intra- and inter-networks are spread over a national territory with variable international connections. The latter connections are what we normally identify with globalization, but this is more all-embracing than normally portrayed.[1] Standard input–output tables are only produced sparingly in any country, normally every ten years or so, which may make them unreliable for analysing aggregate sectoral linkages or networks when a large disaster happens too distant from the production year, especially in the case of fast changing developing countries. What is required are tables as close to the disaster year as possible.

Sectoral networks are normally spread over the territory of a country, and given that most disasters, apart from being economically localized, are geographically localized (see Chapters 2 and 4), then regionally disaggregated tables, called interregional input–output tables (or IRIO tables) could be of great use. These are however less available than standard input–output tables (or IO tables), and carry the same timing problem. In addition, the regional disaggregation that encompasses a disaster zone may be too large to be of use without further qualification and information, as was the case of Sumatra encompassing its most affected Aceh province in the 2004 Indonesia tsunami, as shown below. So IO and IRIO tables (or simply IOs and IRIOs), may be too aggregate to analyse a localized disaster without complementary statistics, but can still be a good starting point. In the absence of timely IOs and timely and regionally appropriate IRIOs, the only alternative is to complement such tables with yearly national accounts. The latter are often, but not always, disaggregated into regions, but they may also have the problem of being disaggregated into too large regions. So information about the main sectoral firms actually affected would be normally necessary, but this information is usually highly scattered, unsystematic and incomplete, which is one of the main reasons for our proposed surveys in the Appendix.

Interregional connections and switching

Figure 5.1 helps to visualize how the indirect disaster effect on businesses can prompt their linking with unaffected firms and consumers whether within the

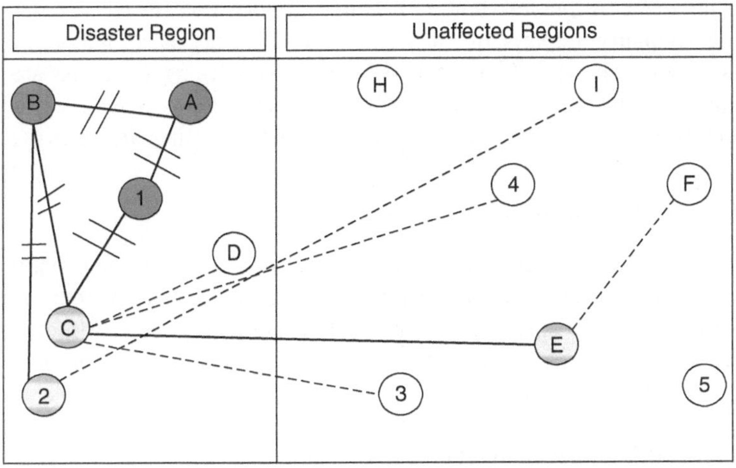

Figure 5.1 Interregional network switching.

same disaster region or outside it, i.e. what we have been calling network shifting.

As we indicated earlier, firms and consumers will normally link up via wholesalers and retailers, but to avoid a spider web of crossed lines, we implicitly assumed that fact and simply connect them directly. In the diagram above, we use capital letters for firms and numbers for consumers enclosed in circles. Fully shaded circles mean that the firms or consumers have been directly affected. Partially shaded ones mean that firms or consumers have been indirectly affected. Circles without shades mean that they are unaffected by the disaster. Heavy lines with two crossed bars mean then the link has been totally severed by the disaster. Dotted lines mean the available options open for indirectly affected firms or consumers. Finally, unlinked circles simply mean that they are unaffected, but not useful options for indirectly affected firms or consumers. The diagram shows that firms A and B and consumer 1 are all out of functions. Because of this, firms C and E and consumer 2 are indirectly affected, as their standard links with the former have been cut off by the disaster. Their available options are as follows: firm C can replace firm B by linking with firm D of the same region and with consumers 3 and 4 of the unaffected region. In turn consumer 2 can now replace firm B with firm I of the unaffected region. Finally, firm E is second-degree (indirectly) affected by the potential failure of firm C, which is first-degree (indirectly) affected. It can then link up with firm F, if need be.

The above shows that if (i) alternatives links are available, (ii) the information about them is prompt and (iii) the link is possible without excessive additional cost, then most of the initial potential indirect effects can be substituted, compensating the macroeconomy for the functionality failure of the directly affected economic units and, therefore, stopping indirect flow effects in their tracks. This of course assumes that these alternatives exist and that there will be coexistence of affected and unaffected economic units, of similar sectors, both in the disaster region and in the country. Imports, of course, can also be an alternative link-up, if need be, which are not shown in Figure 5.1. All these alternative network links are normally available in the case of localized disasters, as defined in Chapter 2, especially in countries with some economic diversification and marketing structures.

The use of IRIO, IO and national accounts

In the absence of appropriate standard IO tables, let alone IRIOs, only regionally disaggregated national accounts can be resorted to to analyse indirectly both the potential for flow effects to spread to the national economy and the substitution potential to counteract it. So some indicators for the task can be devised for three cases, i.e. (i) when IRIO tables are available, (ii) when only IO tables are available and (iii) when only National Accounts are available. Indicators derived from these cases should provide information to set up a few quantitative measures as follows:

- A measure of the importance of the affected region in the country's economy via simple aggregate ratios.
- A measure of the importance of the most affected regional economic sectors as a share of the national economic sectors and as a share of the region's economy again via simple ratios.
- A measure, from disaster assessments, of the sectoral proportion that was affected in the most affected regional economic sectors. From here ratios of substitution potential (SP) at sectoral, regional and national level can be created. Ideally these proportions should refer to the capital stock, but normally are a ratio of flow variables, i.e. in GDP or gross output terms, which may make them only indirectly useful.
- And, hopefully, a measure of interregional and inter-sectoral trade linkages via backward (Bw) and forward (Fw) linkages.

We aim to produce measures of Bw and Fw linkages as well as of SP, in the political economy context where these happen. We show below examples of cases (i) and (ii), as case (iii) comes implicitly in the analysis of the former two.[2]

Two cases: Indonesia 2004 and Chile 2010

Indonesia has IRIO and IO tables around the time of the earthquake-induced tsunami that affected the Indian Ocean, while Chile has only IO tables around just before its very strong earthquake.

Indonesia

On 26 December 2004, a massive earthquake (Richter degree 9.0) struck off the West coast of Northern Sumatra. The earthquake induced a large tsunami that affected many Indian Ocean countries. The five most affected countries were India, Indonesia, Maldives, Sri Lanka and Thailand, where over 225,000 people were reported to have been killed by the tsunami, displacing some 1.7 million people, with total damage and losses of the order of US$10 billion, Indonesia bearing about half of the total (TEC 2006). Setting aside the usual problems with the misreporting of general effects and the overestimation of direct (stock) effects, let alone indirect (flow) effects (see Chapter 1), this was a very strong disaster.

Indonesia is a large archipelagic country, made of large islands like Sumatra and Java as well as scattered small ones over its territory. It has a population of some 220 million inhabitants and enjoys a lower-middle GDP *per capita* of around US$3,500 (in ppp). Agriculture share in GDP is around 20 per cent, with a rural population of around 50 per cent. Its exports-to-GDP ratio is around 45 per cent, while agricultural share in exports represents around 10 per cent, and both fuels and manufacturing take some half of it, in about equal shares. It also counts with a medium-level Human Development Index (HDI) of around 0.61, falling to around 0.50 when adjusted for inequalities (UNDP 2011). In addition, it exhibits a Gini coefficient of inequality of around 0.38, which is on the low level and has some 18 per cent of people under the international poverty line (i.e. less than US$1.25 a day (in ppp)), which is on the medium level (World Bank 2011).

The Aceh province, the region most devastated by the 2004 tsunami, with a population of around seven million, has at least twice as much poverty and significantly more inequalities than the country as a whole. Despite being an oil- and gas-rich region, this industry is however a low employer. In addition, and up to the disaster, Aceh endured a three-decade-long civil war, which can partly explain such a poor social indicator. Its main industries are mostly extractive and light, representing also its main exports (e.g. petroleum and gas, textiles, electrical appliances, chemical fertilizers, food, rubber and tourism). Indonesia has been receiving ODA aid of US$2.5 billion, mostly on the back of Aceh tsunami pledges. It has a high foreign debt that has steadily been falling over later years. Despite some reforms, addressing financial and public sectors, financial markets are still underdeveloped and infrastructures inadequate, with also important inequalities between regions (Blanco *et al.* 2008).

The 2004 earthquake-induced tsunami in the Indian Ocean affected mostly the Northern-West coast of Sumatra, the Aceh province, especially the northern tip of Sumatra, Banda Aceh, Aceh Barat and Aceh Besar, causing a large number of casualties, some 2.3 per cent of the province's population (around 160,000 dead or missing), and many times more displaced people, the poor and women being disproportionately represented (Cosgrave 2006; TEC 2007). Most of the physical losses were for housing and infrastructures, while productive sectors suffered only secondary damage, except for agriculture and fishery, which are mostly associated with the poorest sections of the affected region. Oil and gas production and exports were already in decline, but were not badly affected. Given that these are the main economic activities of the region, with little linkages towards the whole country, there was never a serious economic analysis that claimed that the tsunami was going to affect Indonesia's macroeconomy in any significant way, to the point that most international organizations, like the IMF, kept the growth rate for 2005 slightly lower (IMF 2005), which actually improved. If anything, the overgenerous aid committed for emergency and reconstruction of the affected areas, especially Aceh, may have rapidly compensated for any possible spread effect and in passing contributed positively, even if secondarily, to GDP. However, discounting the dramatic short-term effect on people, the longer-term disaster response effect on the Aceh province may have proved to be highly positive: the end of a 30-year civil war, more autonomy and public resources (increasing some five times since 2004), addressing infrastructure, economic and political dragging problems, and not least the high unemployment, excess inequality and excess poverty levels of the region (World Bank 2007, 2009; Blanco *et al.* 2008; Akita *et al.* 2011). It is too early to judge whether this will sustain and enhance in the future, but it is a good start from a dire tragedy.

National macroeconomic effects were therefore meant to be unimportant from the outset, even without reference to international aid. The disaster was very geographically localized, affecting only a very confined area of economic activity in very heterogeneous ways. The low impact on main economic sectors made the disaster economically localized too. In addition, the main sectors (oil and gas production, oil refinery and oil manufacturing) are mostly semi-enclave exporting sectors with little indirect impact on the rest of the economy, so were not bound to transmit negative effects in a significant way, eliciting less demands on endogenous and exogenous macro counteractions to keep the national macroeconomy at a similar level to that which would have prevailed without the disaster. In addition, Sumatra's main industrial centre, Medan, was not directly affected at all. This city has a good deal of trade interaction with Aceh province, so some indirect effects were to be expected. There were some important inflationary pressures in Banda Aceh after the 2004 tsunami disaster, but not equally so for Indonesia as a whole. This was short term and back to trend level within a year. Construction material, as expected, and some food and textiles were the most affected by excess demand and inflation in the region (Blanco *et al.* 2008). This may be an indication of inappropriate short-term national response policy, which despite the overgenerous foreign aid, may have over-insulated the national macroeconomy at the expense of Aceh, i.e. partly bypassing the disaster area.

Statistics and indicators

Let us see this story via interregional input–output statistics (IRIO) and National Accounts statistics.[3] The 2005 Indonesian IRIO is disaggregated into five regions and 35 sectors or industries (see Resosudarmo and Nurdianto 2007). The regions are however too aggregate to properly deal with the disaster. Sumatra appears as one single region, but as shown above, only the northern-west province of Aceh and in particular its most northern tip were actually strongly affected by the

Table 5.1 Regional output structure

Regions	*GO/TGO*	*F/TX*	*X/TX*
Sumatra	0.21	0.21	0.21
Java and Bali	0.64	0.64	0.63
Kalimantan	0.09	0.07	0.12
Sulawesi	0.04	0.04	0.02
East Indns	0.03	0.03	0.02
Sum	1.00	1.00	1.00

Notes
T: Total; GO: gross output; X: exports; F: final output.

disaster. So some outside refinement via national accounts and associated information would be required to deal with the potential for spreading effects. So let us go from the most regionally aggregate to a more focused disaster area. Table 5.1 and Table 5.2 show Indonesia's regional output structure and its regional linkages, respectively.

At an interregional level without sectoral disaggregation, the IRIO in question shows that Java & Bali and Sumatra are the main output producers and exporters, the former some three times as much as the latter, whether in gross output (GO), which includes intermediate plus final output, in final output (F), which includes exports, or exports (X). The other three regions, Kalimantan, Sulawesi and East Indonesia, are significantly less important in all scores. Sumatra imports

Table 5.2 Regional linkages

Regions	*Sumatra*	*Java and Bali*	*Kalimantan*	*Sula*	*East Indns*	*TBw*
	Backward linkages					
Sumatra	1.56	0.17	0.02	0.00	0.00	1.75
Java and Bali	0.05	1.66	0.06	0.01	0.01	1.79
Kalimantan	0.02	0.09	1.56	0.00	0.00	1.67
Sulawesi	0.01	0.18	0.04	1.52	0.00	1.75
East Indns	0.00	0.09	0.02	0.03	1.38	1.52
Average						1.70
	Forward linkages					*TFw*
Sumatra	1.56	0.14	0.01	0.00	0.00	1.71
Java and Bali	0.05	1.66	0.01	0.01	0.00	1.73
Kalimantan	0.04	0.41	1.56	0.02	0.01	2.04
Sulawesi	0.01	0.10	0.01	1.52	0.02	1.66
East Indns	0.02	0.27	0.00	0.01	1.38	1.68
Average						1.76

Notes
TBw: Total backward linkages.
TFw: Total forward linkages.

only some 3 per cent of its total gross input requirements (not in the table), but it exports some 21 per cent of its final output, which represents also about 21 per cent of total exports. In terms of final output, Sumatra produces some 21 per cent of Indonesia's output, while Java & Bali produce some 64 per cent of it, while the other two regions, Sulawesi and East Indonesia, are very secondary on this score.

The linkages in Table 5.2, whether backward or forward, should be read from left to right, which simplifies its visualization. As can be seen, most of the direct and indirect input demands and supplies are for sectors operating within the same region. For example, the direct and indirect input demand per unit of final output in Sumatra is 1.75 (backward linkage), i.e. one unit of final output production requires 1.75 units of intermediate inputs. But only 0.19 of it is for inputs from other regions, mostly from Java and Bali (0.17), which is geographically proximate. That is, only 11 per cent of all input requirements come from other regions, which represents Sumatra's interregional (domestic) imports. In turn, Sumatra supplies intermediate inputs, directly and indirectly, mostly between sectors of the region itself (1.71). Only 9 per cent of it goes to other regions, mostly Java and Bali, which represents its domestic regional exports. This shows a lack of strong links between regions, which has been studied and analysed elsewhere (e.g. Resosudarmo and Nurdianto 2007; Fideus and Widyasanti 2010). At this level of aggregation it can also be seen that despite the lack of strong links between regions, Sumatra has over-average backward linkages (TBw), which means that a strong failure of some of its most important sectors may have strong effects in Sumatra itself and then in Java and Bali and from here on the rest of Indonesia. And it would also appear as heavily affecting foreign trade and therefore the inflows of hard currency.

If we now look at both the actual sectors that were affected by the disaster and the particular area where this happened, then we could derive a more accurate and useful picture. Setting aside the important direct stock losses to social sectors (especially housing) and infrastructures (especially transport) (Blanco *et al.* 2008), the economic sectors most affected were identified as agriculture and fishery, which are also among the main employers of labour together with construction and trade. In an unspecified and very general way industry and trade was also reported with some important stock losses (Bank Dunia/World Bank 2005). We know that trade can recover fast after infrastructures are rehabilitated, especially in the presence of outside aid. As regards productive sectors, some 60,000 hectares of agricultural land were reported as damaged due to carrying debris and salinization, affecting soil, irrigation systems, harvesting storage and other land facilities. In turn, over 4,500 fishing boats and some 20,000 hectares of fish ponds were reported as lost. Industry associated with fishing and agriculture was the most affected (ibid.). When analysing longer-term effects, if we concentrate on agriculture and fishing we take a good deal of the rest with it.

We recall once more we are looking for effects that can affect the functionality of an economy and therefore its medium- and longer-term performance. And we also recall that if its short-term (one-year) activity is not badly affected, then the longer-term one is unlikely to be. Sumatra as a whole is an important contributor to output in both agriculture and fishing, these sectors together representing 32 per cent of the national sector in gross output terms, respectively. In terms of final output, the two together represent 36 per cent. But national agriculture represents about 5 per cent of national final output, while fishery represents about 1 per cent of it. For exports, these two sectors together represent about 2.5 per cent of them. In other words, in national terms the most affected sectors are secondary to the economy, but an integral part of it, so they cannot just be dispensed with. Table 5.3 below presents the linkages of these two sectors with some agriculture disaggregation.

Again, Table 5.3 should be read from left to right. In terms of direct and indirect input demands and supplies, backward linkages and interregional imports (IndsRest) are smaller than average, except for livestock; and forward linkages and interregional exports are larger than average, except for crops, livestock and fishery. It can also be seen that Sumatra demands little from the rest of Indonesia, except for livestock production, and supplies little to the rest of the economy, except for forestry output. In turn, the rest of the economy (IndsRest), outside its own sectors, on average demands only 0.04 intermediate units (or around 5 per cent) from Sumatra for each unit of final demand and supplies 0.05 input units (or around 6.5 per cent) for each unit of gross output the rest of the economy produces. So in terms of intermediate input linkages alone, we would expect that a blanket destruction of the capital and labour on which this production mostly depends is bound to have some potential widespread effects over Sumatra, but not significantly over the rest of the economy, which is an indication of low network levels between main regions (main islands). But again this is still too aggregate to deal with the actual economic localization of the disaster over the Aceh province.

The Aceh province represented some 11 per cent of Sumatra's gross regional output and only 2.3 per cent of Indonesia's final output in 2004 (Akita *et al.*

Table 5.3 Linkages of affected sectors

Sectors	*Sumatra*	*IndsRest*	*TBw*	*Sumatra*	*IndsRest*	*TFw*
Paddy	1.09	1.07	1.16	2.11	1.11	2.22
Crops	1.17	1.07	1.24	1.77	1.18	1.95
Livestock	1.53	1.24	1.77	1.54	1.17	1.71
Forestry	1.22	1.08	1.30	2.37	1.30	2.67
Fishery	1.22	1.13	1.35	1.59	1.11	1.70
SmRest	1.59	1.20	1.79	1.49	1.15	1.64
IndsRest	1.04	1.72	1.76	1.05	1.72	1.77
Average			1.48			1.95

Notes
SmRest: Rest of Sumatra.
IndsRest: Rest of Indonesia.
TBw: Total backward linkages.
TFw: Total forward linkages.

2011). We know that most of this value, including foreign exports, was due to the chronically declining oil and gas, coal mining and refineries industries, which were reported to be not badly damaged after the disaster. Table 5.4 shows Aceh's GDP structure.

It can be seen that Aceh's agriculture and fishery together represented some 20 per cent of Aceh's GDP in 2004. So assuming that the disaster provoked a blanket destruction of Aceh's agriculture and fishery, then that would represent some 2.2 per cent of Sumatra's output and less than 0.5 per cent of national output. We also know that the destruction was not blanket, as not all Aceh's land and agriculture, and coastline and fishery were equally affected, e.g. Aceh's east coast was not badly affected, except in its northern-most tip. So the disaster must have compromised directly a smaller fraction of these two sectors than above.[4] Keeping in mind this fact, for the sake of argument, let us assume that the destruction was blanket for these two sectors.

Given that we are taking a longer-term view about how capital and labour destruction can have an indirect spreading flow effect, we have been assuming that main transport infrastructures and indeed main housing are not indirectly affecting production importantly in the affected areas after emergency and early rehabilitation is over, which is short-term activity, normally over in the first few weeks. Reconstruction however can take significantly longer, from a few months to a few years. Most main infrastructures were rehabilitated fast, and almost fully reconstructed about a year after the tsunami, by means of a massive reconstruction process on the back of an overgenerous international aid. But meanwhile it was clear that the disaster could not have important effects on Indonesia's output, as setting aside the emergency itself, the rest of Indonesian regions had enough leeway to compensate for Aceh's potential output losses. Following our concept of economic localization, we can then look at some useful ratios derived from the IRIO table and the table above:

Table 5.5 gives us general indicators of the disaster localization and potential counterbalance, which we call 'substitution potential' or SP. The SPs are simply

Table 5.4 Sectoral share of Aceh GDP

Sector (% share of Aceh GDP)	*2003*	*2004*	*2005*	*2006*
Agriculture and fishery	17	20	21	21
Oil, gas and mining	36	30	26	25
Manufacturing (incl. oil and gas manufact.)	20	18	16	14
Electricity and water supply	–	–	–	–
Building/construction	3	4	4	5
Trade, hotels and restaurants	11	12	14	15
Transport and communication	3	4	5	5
Banking and other financial	1	1	1	1
Services	8	10	13	13
Total	100	100	100	100

Source: BPS (Indonesia Official Office of Statistics).

Table 5.5 Localization ratios (LR) and substitution potential (SP)

Ratios (%)				
	Aceh/Inds	*Aceh/Smt*	*Smt/Inds*	*Aceh/Aceh*
Sct/Fn	0.5	2.2	2.3	20
Sct/Sct	7.3	20	36	
Fn/Fn	2.3	11	21	
SP (times)				
	Inds/Aceh	*Smt/Aceh*	*Inds/Smt*	*Aceh/Aceh*
FnSct	200	45	43	5
Sct/Sct	14	5	3	
Fn/Fn	43	9	5	

Notes
Fn: Final output.
Sct: Agriculture and fishery together.
SP: Substitution potential.
Smt: Sumatra.
Inds: Indonesia.

the inverse of the ratios above, which gives an idea of the number of times the unaffected areas are to the directly affected area, in terms of the variable in question. In terms of the actual sector affected (agriculture and fishery) to final output (first row in table) for Indonesia-to-Aceh the SP is over 200 times (i.e. 100/0.5) and for Sumatra-to-Aceh this is over 45 times (i.e. 100/2.2) and for Aceh itself it is 5 times (100/20). In terms of the actual affected sector to the same sector (second row), the values are 14 and 5 respectively. So given that the capital stock loss in Aceh was not blanket, then the above SP values are likely to be significantly larger. Notice also that the figures above are all yearly ones, but a good deal of the actually affected sectors and firms were back in business from a few weeks to a few months after the disaster, which compounds the positive SP with actual recovery, making the flow effects even less significant.

Recall that there are two types of potential substitution via sectoral and via general network shift or network bypassing. That is, network shifts when unscathed firms of a given sector take over the production of affected firms of the same sector and when potential losses of GDP from the affected area are counteracted with increases of GDP in other areas, whether including the affected sectors or not. A typical case of the latter is the productive activity of rehabilitation and reconstruction of affected infrastructures and housing.

The SPs above show that in principle unscathed functional resources are large and that the fraction directly affected of agriculture and fishery can be bypassed by the rest of the country many times over. This assumes that both demand for this sector has not been greatly compromised, which given the levels of aid was highly likely, and that there is enough idle capacity in the unaffected fraction of sectors, which given their low capital requirements (e.g. fishing boats) and standard levels of underemployment may be an acceptable assumption. Still, we would like to learn how firms in general would actually react in the presence of disasters, which is what we deal with in Chapter 6.

Given the above it is hardly surprising that international organizations, like the IMF and the World Bank, did not significantly revise down the growth prospects for Indonesia, even for the first year after the disaster. Indonesia's actual growth rates after the event were actually higher than expected before the tsunami, even if at the expense of Aceh's. In the latter, excluding the declining oil and gas, the positive real GDP growth rate fell from 3.7 per cent in 2003 to 1.8 in 2004 and 1.2 in 2005, jumping up to 7.7 in 2006 (Bank Dunia/World Bank 2007). This is an indication of network shift and bypassing, as Indonesia real GDP growth rates increased from 4.8 per cent in 2003 to 5.0 in 2004 and 5.7 in 2005, and were then 5.3 and 6.3 in the next two years. The strong increase from the end of 2005 in Aceh was primarily due to the reconstruction effort and derived activities. The construction sector, although small, has strong backward linkages, especially in employment, and grew by 48 per cent and 14 per cent in 2006 and 2008 respectively. The transport sector also underwent significant, but lower, growth than the construction sector. The inflow of funding and reconstruction input demand, including labour, did create significantly larger inflation in Aceh than the rest of Indonesia for about two years to then converge to about the levels of the country. Poverty and unemployment declined on the back of this massive aid and reconstruction effort (Blanco *et al.* 2008).

Lessons

The above analysis shows a few usable points. First, an IRIO is an important, even if insufficient, statistical instrument to analyse sectoral potential linkage effects. Second, IRIOs are normally too aggregate to properly analyse the effects from a localized economic and geographic area affected by a disaster on the rest of the economy. This is again an indication of what we criticized in Chapter 1, i.e. an IRIO, let alone an input–output model (which is aggregate for a country as a whole), can deal badly with the issue of localization and is even less able to do so if endogenous counter-reactions, both insulating and recovering the disaster area, are ignored. Third, the indexes of sectoral and national substitution potential (SP) are useful general indicators as a complement of other information, coming especially from IRIO, IO or national accounts. Fourth, the fact that in this disaster case there was such an amount of overgenerous aid, if contentiously used by the government and NGOs (Telford and Cosgrave 2006; TEC 2007), hides the fact that important endogenous reactions, associated with networks, national characteristics and general policy, must have happened independently of it. And fifth, the analysis above shows, at the macro level, significant network shifts from the affected areas to the rest of the country, as Aceh's economy showed declines or modest growth, especially in non-construction productive sectors, while the country showed strong growth as a whole. This is an indication of localized network bypassing, i.e. frustrated normal demands from the disaster area, and supplies to this area, that bypassed Aceh, which may have been even more pronounced in the absence of the high levels of aid funding.

Chile

Chile is a high-middle income country with a population of some 17 million.[5] It is a long and narrow country located in the southernmost west coast of South America. On 27 February 2010, just before the new presidential mandate transmission, a very strong earthquake (Richter degree 8.8) affected Chile, especially in its south-central territory. This happened in a context of economic slowdown (2008) and recession (2009), coming from the Great Recession, which was still to be overcome. To top that, a salmon virus seriously affected its aquaculture, salmon being the second most important export. And in addition, in early 2010, a new government came into office, replacing a coalition that had been there for 20 years, which was bound to produce early administrative disruptions and maladjustments. The earthquake epicentre was under the seabed not far from the coast, which originated a tsunami that struck some of the Chilean coastline. The first waves from the tsunami hit about 34 minutes after the earthquake, but others came several hours later, damaging some properties and businesses and killing some 200 people. Most of these people died due to a botched and incompetent managing of early warning, especially for the waves that came later (Galleguillos-Jara 2010). In all, around 500 people died, some 40 per cent of them from the tsunami. Chile did not ask for international aid.

A few weeks after the disaster, the official and much challenged figures (see Chapter 1) of economic damage and losses were set at US$30 billion, with some 200,000 houses destroyed and a similar quantity with damages only. The official report also claimed that some 11 per cent of total capital was lost to the disaster. Most of this was in infrastructure (transport, utilities, etc.) and the capital of social sectors, i.e. housing, hospitals and schools, which in its estimations accounted for around 70 per cent of the total, while productive sectors were 30 per cent. Most of the latter were private. The report also estimated that of the US$30 billion, 25.6 per cent corresponded to expected losses of GDP due to interruption of activities and production (Gobierno de Chile 2010). This latter figure, as argued in Chapter 1, is nonsensical as it does not take into account substitutions, bypassing and network shifting plus the new stimulus created by the very emergency, rehabilitation and reconstruction. Setting aside the emergency, especially for a country with a long experience with earthquakes, most of the effort and speed in both rehabilitation and early reconstruction was on these areas, especially on infrastructures, educational premises, hospitals and housing. In turn, the main affected economic sectors were especially non-industrial fishing and small and medium firms, where the government put most of the effort, particularly by giving subsidies and soft, but small, credit to micro, small and medium firms. A year later, it was reported that some 50,000 firms (micro, small and medium) benefitted with these types of loans, which seems to have included some standard small credits for these sectors, earthquake notwithstanding. In addition, some 1,000 non-industrial affected fishermen benefitted mostly via grants, allowing them to replace and repair their boats and equipment (CORFO 2011). Agriculture and fishing, which were still under recession, and light industrial sectors, which were just recovering, were generally not badly damaged, except in very localized areas and sectors, such as oil refineries, cellulose and paper production, which also represent important foreign exports from the zone. In the latter case, most of this industry is concentrated in the directly affected area, where a couple of the most important factories in the country could not resume activities for a number of months, but more than fully recovered a year after the disaster (ECLAC 2010a, 2010b; SOFOFA 2012).

At the end of 2010, ten months after the disaster, the country was growing stronger and creating more employment than expected before the disaster. However, a number of sectors in the disaster zone either grew by a lower rate or had not quite recovered their immediate pre-disaster levels. The region of Valparaiso (Region V), the second most important in Chile, which was just outside the disaster zone, grew at unprecedented GDP growth rate levels, 7.5 per cent as compared to 5.2 per cent for the country as a whole (INE 2011).[6] Valparaiso's Regional Economy Secretariat for the Economy Ministry stated that:

> The earthquake stimulated a process of expansion of the Valparaiso region, given that it had to substitute the supply of the regions that [directly] suffered important losses of their productive capacity ... [The Valparaiso region] has managed to lead the country's economic growth of 2010 ... After overcoming the first effects of the earthquake, the process of expansion and dynamism continued: this shows that the region was capable of waking up from a lethargy of many years. It is important to stress that the Valparaiso region had never before occupied the first ranking of these indexes...
>
> (Silva Malig 2011)

This shows massive demand and supply shifts from the directly affected regions to this important (only peripherally affected) region, which stimulated other sectors and industries, especially manufacturing, mining, transport and communications, and commerce, restaurants and hotels. This is what we have called network bypassing or network shifting from a disaster that frustrates otherwise stable network patterns of economic activity. Most of it is normally an endogenous reaction of firms and consumers seeking to satisfy demands and supplies that are constrained and frustrated by the disaster, but this also responds to the additional aggregate demand created by the needs of emergency, rehabilitation and early reconstruction. It is to be seen for how long this development can keep its momentum. On the other hand, the directly affected regions and especially some firms in them may find it difficult to regain the economic position that was lost to Valparaiso.

Statistics and indicators

As said above, Chile does not count with IRIO tables, so let us see the above via national accounts and input–output statistics. The most affected areas were three regions (O'Higgins, Maule and Bío-Bío), with population of over 3.5 million, representing some 20 per cent of the country total. Other regions were only peripherally affected with generally minor effects. Table 5.6 shows the importance of these three regions in the total economy and their sectoral composition in terms of pull and push effects, i.e. backward and forward linkages, while Table 5.7 shows the normal substitution potential (SP) of the region via the national economy.

In 2009, the year before the disaster, the three most affected regions represented some 16 per cent of the county's GDP, 22 per cent of total employment, 41 per cent of total non-mining primary sector employment and 14.3 per cent of mining employment. The GDP share of the regions' main sectors were manufacturing (3.4 per cent), personal services (1.9 per cent), agriculture and fishing (1.6 per cent), construction (1.3 per cent) and transport and communications (1.1 per cent). It can also be seen that the share of regional sectors in the respective sectors varies from 50 per cent in agriculture, cattle and silviculture (sector 1) to 9 per cent in mining (sector 3) and a range of important shares in between, especially manufacturing and utilities. It can also be seen that both backward and forward linkages for non-mining primary sectors and also for utilities were above average, and around average for manufacturing and transport/communications, meaning that the former had some over-average push and pull strength on the rest of the economy, although they represented only a small fraction of the national GDP. In addition, not shown in the table above, the affected region contributed 19 per cent of total exports, especially from the first two sectors together and the sub-manufacturing sector producing wood, furniture and paper, which represented around 1.5 per cent and 5.5 per cent of total national exports, respectively (ECLAC 2010a, 2010b; Banco Central 2012).

Table 5.7 shows that the substitution potential for many regional sectors with production of the same sector (SRGDP/SGDP) is low, especially the non-mining primary sectors (1 and 2), but also manufacturing, which indicates the importance of this region for such sectors. Still, the general substitution potential, whether within the region (SRGDP/RGDP) or within the country (SRGDP/GDP) is significantly larger, which indicates a generally strong response capacity to make up for initial production impairment from the losses to the capital stock.

On this account, it would appear that the disaster was bound to have strong indirect flow effects on the economy, especially over the first year. For example, a report by the confederation of industry (SOFOFA), in May 2010, expected that the growth of the manufacturing activity over the same year was going to fall to a range of 1–2 per cent, from previous levels of around 4 per cent (SOFOFA 2010).[7] But this account is both too aggregate and does not take into consideration the fact of network shifts and public response, which would make it highly misleading if presented without qualifications, as many newspapers and vested

Table 5.6 Characteristics of affected region

Sector	*SRGDP/ SGDP*	*SRGDP/ RGDP*	*SRGDP/ GDP*	*SGDP/ GDP*	*SRE/SE*	*SRE/E*	*SX/X*	*X/GDP*	*BW*	*FW*
1 Agric. cattle and silviculture	50	9.3	1.5	3.0	40.7	21.8	5.5	2.2	1.9	2.1
2 Fishing	29	0.7	0.1	0.4	Inc. in 1	Inc. in 1	0.1	0.0	2.2	3.1
3 Mining	9	8.2	1.3	15.3	14.3	1.0	48.1	19.3	1.6	1.2
4 Manufacturing	28	20.6	3.4	11.8	18.8	11.6	34.5	13.8	1.9	1.8
5 Utilities	54	11.1	1.8	3.3	22.4	0.5	0.0	0.0	2.0	2.6
6 Construction	17	8.2	1.3	7.7	21.7	8.7	0.0	0.0	1.7	1.2
7 Trade, hotels, restaurants	11	6.6	1.1	10.1	18.8	18.1	0.8	0.3	1.8	1.6
8 Transport and communications	16	6.7	1.1	7.0	18.3	7.3	9.0	3.6	1.7	1.8
9 Financial services	6	7.2	1.2	19.4	12.9	5.9	1.9	0.8	1.4	2.3
10 Housing services	14	4.7	0.8	5.6	18.6	24.8	0.0	0.0	1.3	1.0
11 Personal services	16	11.4	1.9	11.5	Inc. in 10	Inc. in 10	0.0	0.0	1.4	1.1
12 Public administration	18	5.3	0.9	4.8	Inc. in 10	Inc. in 10	0.0	0.0	1.4	1.1
Sum/total/average		100.0	16.3	100	20.8	100.0	100	40	1.7	1.7

Source: Calculated from Banco Central de Chile.

Notes
SRGDP: Sectoral-regional GDP.
SRE: Sectoral-regional employment.
SX: Sectoral exports.
BW: Backward linkage.
FW: Forward linkage.

Table 5.7 Normal substitution potential of the region

Sector	*SGDP/ SRGDP*	*RGDP/ SRGDP*	*GDP/ SRGDP*	*GDP/ SGDP*
1 Agric. cattle and silviculture	2.0	11	66	33
2 Fishing	3.5	140	858	245
3 Mining	11.5	12	75	7
4 Manufacturing	3.5	5	30	8
5 Utilities	1.8	9	55	30
6 Construction	5.7	12	75	13
7 Trade, hotels, restaurants	9.5	15	93	10
8 Transport and communications	6.4	15	92	14
9 Financial services	16.5	14	85	5
10 Housing services	7.3	21	130	18
11 Personal services	6.2	9	54	9
12 Public administration	5.5	19	116	21

Source: Calculated from Banco Central de Chile.

Notes
SRGDP: Sectoral-regional GDP.
SGDP: Sectoral GDP.
RGDP: Regional GDP.

parties normally do as a matter of fact every time there is a disaster anywhere. First, the effects on these regions and sectors were hardly blanket, especially on manufacturing and construction. Second, on other sectors, the potential for indirect effects were relatively short-lived, like those on transport and communications, which are normally rehabilitated well before re-construction starts by both temporary re-establishment of same affected networks, the use of alternative ones or the provisional creation of others. In turn, agriculture and especially fishing suffered mostly at the non-industrial level and were still recovering from both the 2009 recession and the salmon virus, which affected badly the production and exports of salmon. Third, among the industrial sectors most affected were fishing and fish manufacturing (preparation and conservation),[8] cellulose and paper production, oil refinery, basic plastics and synthetic rubber, glass production, and basic iron and steel production. All these sectors started to show a strong recovery from both the previous year's recession and the disaster from the second and third quarter of 2010, although by the end of the year fishing manufacturing, cellulose production and paper production were still under their levels a year earlier.

Table 5.8[9] shows the substitution potential (SP) of these sectors in the national economy in 2009, in terms of total growth output GO (i.e. including both intermediate and final output) and final output F (i.e. including government and private consumption and investment plus variation of inventories and exports). It also shows the SPs of the manufacturing sectors in manufacturing total for gross output and final demand.[10] We can see that among the backward and forward linkages of the actually affected subsectors, it is only fishing (1–4) and wood and cellulose/paper manufacturing (5–7), mostly for backward linkages, that may have some important indirect effects on intermediate demands and supplies. The share of sectoral exports in total exports is important for sector 4 (fish and shellfish) and 7 (cellulose). The latter, as said above, had some important firms in the disaster region, which were directly affected. As can be seen, for both manufacturing and the national economy, sectors 4 (fish and shellfish), 7 (cellulose) and 8 (fuel) have above average importance. Given both the highly localized (i.e. disaster region only) and partial destruction of these activities (i.e. only some firms in the disaster region), and therefore their high general substitution potential,[11] it was unlikely that that was going to affect economic functionality in any significant way. Most of this localized production was bound to be affected only in the short term, from a few days to a few months, as it actually happened (Banco Central 2012).

According to official information, by the last quarter of 2010, the regional GDPs of the three most affected regions were just above their levels of the last quarter of 2009, while all the other regions, except for a couple not related to the disaster, were already showing strong growth rates (INACER 2011; INE 2011). But these most affected regions were already showing a strong growth acceleration towards the end of that year, which continued over 2011, especially in the most affected region of all (Bío-Bío). By the first quarter of 2011, all disaster affected sectors, including fishing, were strongly growing, especially in Bío-Bío. This of course does not mean that all firms in affected activities had recovered, but that as a whole the regions, let alone the country, had recovered more strongly than expected. This was due to a combination of strong domestic consumption and investment demand after the recession, partly as a result of the public response to the disaster, although construction only picked up towards the end of 2010 and over 2011, as part of massive disaster reconstruction programmes. Construction normally has an above average pull factor in terms of intermediate demands, but a stronger one in terms of both (direct and indirect) employment creation and consumption expenditure by its workers. The GDP growth in 2011 was 6 per cent, again a very strong growth for a second consecutive year after the disaster (Banco Central 2012).

Therefore, only a fraction of the data in the table above was actually affected. And most of what was affected was relatively short-lived. From the viewpoint of substitution potential (SP), as shown in Table 5.8, which contains the most specific subsectors directly affected, it seems that the damage was unlikely to produce flow losses of significance, which were likely to be compensated over the year, as most of it had the potential for substitution from unaffected areas and regions, apart from imports, as it actually happened. The lack of interregional input–output tables for Chile prevented us from knowing how the affected regions interact with the rest of the country via both intermediate inputs and final demands, which would have been useful complementary information for functionality assessment.

Table 5.8 Characteristics of most affected subsectors (%)

Sectors	*National SP (times)*			*Manufacturing SP (times)*		*Sectoral linkages*	
	GO/SGO	*F/SF*	*X/SX*	*MGO/SMGO*	*MF/SMF*	*BW*	*FW*
1 Aquaculture	203	n.a.	n.a.	n.a.	n.a.	1.7	1.8
2 Extractive fishing	331	1,345	1,212	n.a.	n.a.	0.5	1.3
3 Fishmeal and oil	360	380	94	72	68	1.5	1.1
4 Fish and shellfish products	92	62	20	18	11	1.7	0.1
5 Wood production	200	223	70	40	40	1.3	0.7
6 Wood goods	265	263	93	53	47	1.3	0.6
7 Cellulose production	95	79	26	19	14	0.9	0.5
8 Fuel production	57	95	79	11	17	0.2	1.2
9 Basic chemicals	106	115	36	21	21	0.8	0.7
10 Rubber goods	837	1,125	381	167	202	0.5	1.0
11 Plastic goods	159	270	226	32	48	0.6	1.0
12 Glass and glass goods	700	1947	1,136	139	349	0.6	1.1
13 Basic iron and steel	148	541	108	30	97	0.8	1.4
National averages	111	111	111	45	45	0.8	0.9

Notes
SGO: sectoral gross output.
GO: gross output.
F: final demand output.
SF: sectoral F.
X: exports.
SX: sectoral X.
M: manufacturing.
MGO: GO for M.
SMGO: Sectoral MGO.
MF: F for M.
SMF: Sectoral MF.
BW: backward linkage.
FW: forward linkage.

Lessons

The lack of an IRIO prevented us from learning how regions are interrelated with each other, so we have to complement the national IO tables with regional national accounts, but the latter do not deal with such networking directly. The Chilean case shows again that too aggregate regional statistics can be highly misleading, as they implicitly assume that the disaster affected regions and/or sectors homogeneously, which is extremely unlikely. We know however that only a specific area of Chile was badly affected. When using regional accounts without qualifications it would appear that the disaster had significantly more negative effects on functionality than it actually did. We learned here that not all sectors were affected, and those affected were not equally so. We also learned that there was enough potential capacity for substitution from less affected quarters, whether in the same regions or outside them and whether within the same sectors or around them. And we also emphasized that affected economic and social infrastructure is rapidly substituted via rehabilitation and/or circumvention. All this also shows that economic functionality was never in peril.

Conclusion

We first showed a diagram to help visualize the way network switching could happen when affected economic participants coexist with unaffected ones, whether within or outside the disaster area. We suggested that if there was prompt information about potential alternative links and the switch was not too onerous, then the switch will be sped up, substituting the potential indirect effects that potentially can come from the directly affected participants. This would then compensate the macroeconomy for the functionality failure of the directly affected economic units. Then, we showed that an input–output approach can benefit if it is partitioned into regional input–output tables so that domestic interrelation between regions can be assessed, especially if the disaster area coincides with one of the regions or at least can be pinpointed within the generally affected region. To this effect, we showed two examples, one where regional input–output (IRIO) tables were available (Indonesia) and one where only input–output (IO) tables were available (Chile). We concluded that although IRIO tables were generally useful, their regional partitions were too aggregate to deal directly with the disaster area, so national accounts and other information were required. In the case of only IO availability, there was no way to learn directly about the interconnectedness of regions, but only to assume it via usual regional disaggregations of national accounts in terms of final output. From here we produced the values of backward and forward linkages and the ratio of substitution potential (SP), which we introduced in Chapter 2. This ratio indicates how many times the potential or actual reduction in output, coming from a directly affected sector in the disaster zone, can be compensated with output from the same sector whether within or outside the disaster zone, or alternatively with output from other sectors. It showed that SP ratios were generally large for the actually affected sectors. Not surprisingly, both Indonesia and Chile more than substituted their potential flow effects over the first few months, ending up with higher than expected GDP growth rates a year later. Not surprisingly too neither cases suffered important functionality losses and were growing strongly only a few months after the disaster. This good result was also due to exogenous domestic and foreign responses, but the role of endogenous market and non-market responses cannot and should not be underestimated.

6 Systemic consistency, business and network shifting

Introduction

In the two previous chapters we dealt with the macroeconomy as a networked viable system. We approached the network structure by means of aggregated nodes (sectors, industries or regions) and equally aggregated links (flows of goods, money and information) in the context of the input–output framework. We indicated that a disaster impact is rarely congruent with an economic sector, i.e. a sector is a collection of firms that are normally spread all over a country and rarely confined to a single geographically localized spot, where a disaster could happen. We showed this in aggregate via interregional input–output and input–output statistics as well as regional national accounts, with illustrations for Indonesia and Chile. We also anticipated that even in the disaster zone, not all firms and consumers are equally affected and that firms and consumers may also be linked to foreign firms directly or otherwise. So after a disaster has struck, there would be, in the disaster area, directly unaffected units or nodes coexisting with directly affected ones (firms, households, public organizations and other societal institutions). And outside the disaster area, there would also be indirectly affected ones with unaffected units (including foreign ones). This means that there would normally be ground for network shifts within a sector and between sectors, i.e. indirectly affected units that relink with new units or nodes within the same sector (whether within or outside the disaster area) or between sectors, bypassing the fully affected ones so as to keep their functionality and, as a side effect, contributing to keep that of the whole system. This also represents new opportunities for unaffected units to take over the production and roles of the affected ones, especially outside the disaster zone. And this is the origin of the tension between the local and the national, which is often stimulated by the ways in which the exogenous response actually comes about, which we further illustrate here via boxes associated with the policies presented in Chapter 3.

In this chapter, we first further the concepts of systemic consistency and its policy criteria. We then deal with businesses and their networks under disaster endurance, attempting to illustrate some of the important issues and learn some lessons. What is the possible range of direct and indirect effects on firms? What types of firms are more vulnerable? Which are more resilient? How do they fail?

How important is network bypassing? We then retake our model of Chapter 4 to show why network shifting behaviour should be tapped by public response policy to make functional recovery faster and less costly at both macro and local levels. We then show what a desirable network context should be to secure effective systemic recovery after disasters. We end up the chapter and the book with an appendix that contains a suggestion for domestic surveys after disasters, backed by international organizations, with the aim of directly building up the knowledge about business networked reactions under disasters for a gamut of countries and disaster types, which can help the design of policy response for a faster and more effective systemic recovery after disasters.

Systemic consistency

Disasters primarily affect vulnerable local communities, as disaster impacts and direct effects are for the most part either geographically or economically localized. And from here, they may affect the wider whole via flow or indirect effects. Disasters do not however affect vulnerable communities equally, as heterogeneity of effects is normally observed. Even widespread disasters (e.g. Sahelian droughts) do not normally affect all communities equally. This simply means that there may be some resources and capabilities to resort to in the aftermath. So focusing on this, we can establish a pair of analytical criteria: value criterion and boundary criterion.

We define our *value criterion* as follows: any public and/or foreign (especially) exogenous action that helps facilitate, enhance, support or create useful endogenous reactions is to be promoted. As a corollary, any exogenous action that bypasses, frustrates, suffocates or destroys useful endogenous mechanisms, if it is not to be resisted, should be modified so that it can be systemically absorbed, minimizing negative side effects. In turn we define our *boundary criterion* as follows: an endogenous reaction is economically useful if it feeds and is part of local and national societal networks, especially associated with markets and public development activities. Not all endogenous reactions are systemically useful, as some are just a necessary palliative without further systemic consequence or permanency, especially during the early emergency, e.g. search and rescue, but should and normally are publicly supported. Some other endogenous reactions are simply a-systemic and counterproductive, e.g. panic, looting, speculation, fragmentation, free-riding on public aid, and so on. Of course, some palliative reactions do have a bearing on the speed of recovery and can also be enhanced by public response and policy, especially in terms of pre-disaster measures, e.g. warning systems and trained reactions, first-aid information and training, emergency locations and network information, etc.

The above recognizes that stable community livelihoods depend directly or indirectly on societal networks, especially economic ones associated with both permanent public activities and the market. This means that the re-establishment, enhancement, development and integration of local authority, people and businesses, within national economic networks, should be considered the very aim of a systemic disaster response. Formal local authority is the first point of contact to coordinate external responses (public, NGOs, foreign), but also the first point of exogenous response expectation by the affected people, so failure at this stage is bound to transmit elsewhere, eliciting fragmentation and potential conflict. Hence the effective re-establishment of local authority and enforcement should be paramount to prevent such potential negative traits and therefore support cooperative behaviour and orderly recovery. In turn, family businesses, whether formal or informal, represent a good deal of direct local livelihood, while larger businesses normally represent the most important source of stable livelihood (Tierney 2006). Therefore, response measures that tend to facilitate the long-term stability and creation of competitive business will indirectly secure the stability and development of long-term livelihoods. For example, even if very few households take formal insurance against disasters, the insurance of formal business, including the protective requirements to qualify for it, can go a good way towards speeding up recovery of the whole community, therefore increasing disaster resilience.

Empirical approaches often examine how usual risk-adjustment mechanisms, such as remittances, insurance, borrowing, asset sales, saving usage, informal labour, disaster-induced opportunities or migration, are used to help counteract disaster effects. Many of them often focus on affected people's ability to smooth consumption (Townsend 1994; Ligon *et al.* 2002). These studies are useful, but concentrate more on how the coping mechanisms palliate the plight of victims than how they are used for systemic recovery. We take here the opposite view and look to enquire about how disaster affected people's (endogenous) compensatory reactions, which are aimed at confronting disaster effects, can contribute or frustrate systemic recovery. This is then coupled with the positive or negative impact of public response on such adjustment mechanisms, within the described systemic context.

This should be analysed within the permanent systemic tension we have advanced earlier. Systemically, public information and subsidies to divert supplies to the disaster area and to create systemically *sustainable* demands for these goods and services in the area (i.e. controlling for oversupply and inflation) should be considered as positive actions for the economy. Contrariwise, if public actions, whether by design or default, partially insulate the national economy from the disaster area at the expense of the area, then this should in principle be considered as negative. In an extreme case, all supplies and demands can be compensated outside the affected locality so that the national economy does not undergo significant output/income loss, but then the local economy is fully bypassed, which may impair its economic re-insertion into domestic and foreign arenas and therefore its development possibilities. By the same token, a policy balance between positive and negative aspects of foreign trade and capital flows should actively consider the formalization of well-funded and well-managed public and private mechanisms of response to potential disasters (Benson and Clay 2004), representing *ex-ante* policy actions.

The tension between the national economy and the affected (economic or geographic) locality is permanent and a good deal of it falls outside direct public

Box 6.1 Cash transfers illustration

An assessment by Save the Children (2005), following the 2005 earthquake in Pakistan, reported that many businesses had been destroyed or affected, with their supply being down to some 75 per cent from their pre-disaster levels, mostly due to lack of demand, rather than to productive capacity failure. The size of the directly affected market, relative to Pakistan's, was small and most output used in the affected area was actually produced outside the area, especially from Rawalpindi and Islamabad. There was then no expectation for prices of food supplies to increase significantly as a result of the earthquake. The lack of demand for food was mostly due to the provision of massive in-kind relief and also migration of Muzaffarabad city's wealthier households to other unaffected cities.

Prices for transport on the other hand rocketed by well over 50 per cent in some areas, mainly on the back of reduced supply of local transport, from direct disaster effects on stocks (and drivers) and on repair shops, but also from a strongly bid-up price by relief agencies for local transport, as a consequence of which food prices increased by some 15 per cent in the villages. The recommendation was clear: markets had to be quickly assisted, including support for reconstruction and shopkeepers, by means of a phased increase in the provision of cash transfers, rather than in-kind aid (Save the Children 2005; Save the Children USA 2006). A market assessment in the most food-unsecured areas was also carried out, concluding that food relief in urban areas would likely hinder market recovery. So food aid distribution was retargeted mostly to rural areas (Donovan *et al.* 2005; Hoskins 2006; WFP 2006).

The Pakistan government played a leading role in the response, which included a large cash component, reaching some Rs45 billion (US$747 million) by mid-2006. These cash interventions included grants to repair damaged houses by means of instalments of Rs25,000 and Rs50,000, to the point that by July 2006 grants had been provided to three million of the estimated four million houses damaged by the earthquake. In addition, there were also compensations for the injured and the relatives of the dead, with additional World Bank support to some 250,000 families with no breadwinner, amounting to Rs3,000 per month for six months (Khan 2006; Earthquake Emergency Recovery Project 2006; Government of Pakistan 2006).

In recent cash projects in Pakistan, but also in places like Kenya and Kashmir, Save the Children has encouraged the formation of 'community livelihoods committees', which are meant to act as peer discussion groups about what to do with cash grants, but without imposing conditions on how the money should be spent. The aim is to facilitate discussions among recipients about how they might make the most productive use of the cash, opening possibilities to use cash transfers also for investment. Recipients have generally spent part of the cash on livelihood-investment activities, feeling some peer pressure to make good use of the grants. This has also encouraged community recovery, with some recipients pooling part of their money to rehabilitate a road to a key market or to negotiate better prices when purchasing community animals (Harvey 2007).

The report also indicates that international assistance was again overwhelmingly in-kind, but there were some examples of cash-based responses. Catholic Relief Services (CRS) provided cash grants of US$35 to help people transport shelter materials and hire additional labour (Causton and Saunders 2006). Save the Children provided grants of Rs12,000 to 4,250 poor households and Rs75,000 to village shopkeepers to support livelihood recovery (Save the Children USA 2006).

Another aspect of cash transfers is that they can use, and have used, remittance distribution systems, as it has been shown that these are agile and often re-established very quickly after disasters. For instance, in Gonaives, Haiti, following Cyclone Jeanne in 2004, staff working in remittance transfer agencies had reopened their partially flooded offices within three days, restoring internet links, enabling people to contact relatives overseas and arranging for both cash payments and in-kind deliveries to be made (Fagen 2006; Savage and Suleri 2006).

As an additional example, cash transfers in the aftermath of the 2004 tsunami were important, although they were not a regular feature in all places. In Thailand, the government provided cash grants for the relatives of the dead and the injured. It also provided temporary income tax exemptions. In India, people received US$2,264 for each death in the family, US$22 per person per month for four months to cover basic needs and US$22 per household for basic household goods. The government also provided cash to repair and replace fishing equipment, pay school fees, provide grants to women in fishing communities and increase pension benefits, but also for agricultural reclamation and support to orphans. In Sri Lanka, the government provided US$1,515 in compensation for deaths, US$25 for household items, US$50 in emergency resettlement allowances, US$8.50 a month for approximately 12 months and four unconditional transfers of US$198 per household. It also provided cash transfers for people with damaged and destroyed houses (Deshingkar and Aheeyar 2006; Schubert 2006).

Whatever it is, cash transfer response has the double benefit of supporting affected people directly, by empowering them to choose purchases, and not least supporting systemic networks, especially local and national markets. And it has duly started becoming a more mainstream type of response.

control, as it is mostly the result of independent actions from market and social participants. Therefore, a balance has to be found so that neither the local economy is sustained by public resources for its own sake (as this can be at odds with development, be economically inefficient and financially unsustainable in the longer term) nor the local economic failure is counteracted by the rest of the economy bypassing the affected locality, insulating the national economy. So there are two balances to account in the wake of disasters: that between the local and the national and that between exogenous and endogenous responses. Standard public and foreign response policy, as shown in World Bank (2010), can be further directed towards such balances, via direct and indirect stimulus and *ex-ante* and *ex-post* actions, so as to help secure them in the disaster aftermath.

Consistency criteria

As regards the locality, the issue is about the consistency between public (and international) response (mostly exogenous) and local response (mostly endogenous) in terms of systemic viability. Public response, just as the international one, can act against or as a facilitator of inbuilt (systemic) relationships and responses, whether at primary or secondary levels. We may classify public response as (i) *directly inconsistent*, if it leads to unnecessary local dependency, by suffocating local markets via excess or inappropriate in-kind aid, e.g. Malawi 1992 (Clay *et al.* 2003) or imposing an exogenous administration that takes over local management and decisions, e.g. Aceh (Telford and Cosgrave 2006); and (ii) *indirectly inconsistent*, if it leads to the national economy taking over the affected locality, leading to the rundown of local viability. As a rule, any time the national GDP does not fall, but local GDP does, might be an indication of the national bypassing the affected locality.

On the other hand, public response policy can act in favour of, and therefore be consistent with, local inbuilt institutions and reactions, by means of cash transfers that stimulate local markets, policies that stimulate remittances and policies that stimulate interconnectedness via mobile phone distribution, and/or by means of helping centralized coordination, information and the use of cash transfers and remittances. Public response policy can also reinforce the local administration and recovery by channelling information, goods, cash and required coordinating directives via alternative permanent local institutions, especially those with national presence and some level of trust, such as trade unions, employers' organizations, religious institutions and the like, i.e. resorting to both primary and secondary institutional relationships (see Chapters 2 and 3). Behind these reactions and activities is the conception that just like the social body as a whole, most individuals, households and businesses do not respond to disasters just to palliate adversity, but to preserve both their livelihood and social status, also preserving their community and domestic linkages, general relationships and institutional mobility. This is not just an abstract depiction of requirements, as the experience with the 2004 Asian tsunami showed how little regard was paid to these important areas of systemic consistent recovery.

The yearly reports by the Tsunami Evaluation Coalition (TEC), which are the result of one of the best funded, most all-embracing and deepest studies of any natural disaster, show a catalogue of insufficiencies and/or outright mistakes associated with the actual practice of international and public disaster responses. Although most governments, NGOs and other international agencies do seem to subscribe to the Hyogo Framework for Action (from the UN International Strategy for Disaster Reduction in January 2005), the general lessons went rapidly astray, locking into some standard bureaucratic routines, which proved to be at odds with a systemically appropriate response. The Hyogo Framework sought to make disaster response more effective by establishing some main operational priorities, which (in our terms) amount to give disaster reduction (and by implication disaster response) priority to local and national institutions via endogenizing assessment, monitoring and early warning, while creating a culture of safety and resilience, as well as securing preparedness for an effective response (World Conference on Disaster Reduction 2005). Instead, the tsunami response showed (i) significant and wasteful lack of coordination between the myriad of disaster agencies themselves and between them and domestic institutions, (ii) a bypassing and disregard for local and national capabilities, (iii) an often inappropriate type of in-kind aid in both consumer and capital goods (e.g. sweaters, boats and the like), (iv) a lack of accountability and transparency in response funding and use, (v) an inadequate risk analysis about affected people's own reactions and behaviours, (vi) an insufficient if not misleading information about reconstruction plans and general activities, which failed to incorporate local input and understanding to such purpose, and so on.

It is not surprising that the report's first recommendation is the need for 'a fundamental reorientation from supplying aid to supporting and facilitating communities' own relief and recovery priorities' (Telford and Cosgrave 2006: 110). From here, it recommends that international agencies need to coordinate effectively with domestic institutions and that 'all actors need to make the current funding system impartial and more efficient, flexible, transparent and better aligned with principles of good donorship' (ibid.: 122). It then asks for a fundamental reorientation of especially international agencies to achieve these and other recommendations, envisaging difficulties and resistance to change, associated with bureaucratic inertia (Cosgrave 2007; TEC 2007). These reports and their analysis, criticisms and recommendations are more oriented towards the international community than the domestic public action, but can be partly extended to the latter, as all the problems, insufficiencies and failures would not have been so prominent had domestic governments themselves not invested international agencies with such an autonomy and deposited so much faith in them, whether by design or default.

Box 6.2 Shelter issue illustration

After the 2004 tsunami, the provision of shelter was the most urgent task facing Aceh. In the longer term, there was also an additional need to relocate and rehouse a large number of displaced people, who lost their land to submersion as well as excess risk. This also includes non-owners, i.e. many poorer members of coastal communities in Aceh did not own their land, but rented it from wealthier Acehnese or 'squatted' on state land. Although the estimates vary widely, in some versions, in Aceh alone, over 600,000 people were made homeless and some 25,000 families needed relocating to new land. There were some 15,000 households of renters and squatters who did not have anywhere to live, who had to be resettled on new land before they could be given houses (Oxfam 2006).

In addition, over 150,000 hectares (1,500 sq km) of agricultural land were made unfit for growing crops after being inundated with salt water and mud. According to FAO, up to 15 per cent of western Aceh's agricultural land may be permanently lost. Initially, some important markets were lost, or access to them was no longer available. For example, a report by ALNAP (2008), after the tsunami, stated that fishermen in Aceh could not sell fish, as people did not want to buy them from fear that they had eaten the dead, and recommended that agencies be able to provide assistance to help re-establish markets from the very outset.

As an example of a typical endogenous reaction, host families provided the majority of the accommodation for internally displaced persons (IDPs) in Indonesia in the first six months. According to various official estimates, between 400,000 and 500,000 people were accommodated with host families. These host families play an important role in nearly all emergencies, 'but while there is a great deal of literature on camps for the displaced, there is very little on host families. This reflects the undervaluing of local capacities by the international aid community' (Telford and Cosgrave 2006: 50). But as a good example of international practice, the Swiss Development Cooperation project supported with cash grants families hosting IDPs in Banda Aceh.

As in most cases of displacement, there were problems with documentation and the type of land tenancy/ownership that affected people held. Only around 25 per cent of land in the tsunami-affected areas of Aceh was statutory titled land, i.e. registered under government laws with paperwork held by landowners and in National Land Agency offices. The other 75 per cent of land was not registered, but instead governed by *adat* processes, i.e. undocumented traditional forms of tenancy and ownership.

Renters, squatters and the landless represented the bulk of the 70,000 people that had to be housed in some 150 government barracks, scattered across Aceh. Only in June 2006 (one and a half years after the tsunami) did the government issue regulations on the resettlement of renters and squatters. Under these regulations pre-tsunami home owners are entitled to free land for a basic 36 square meter house, while pre-tsunami renters receive around US$2,800 and squatters US$1,150. Oxfam gave instrumental support for the barracks-dwellers, with engineers and health workers providing support to those most in need, and monitoring sanitation and public health in the barracks in Aceh Besar and Banda Aceh.

The problem was how to resettle the refugees from the barracks. That is, a state-run resettlement process risked dumping the poorest Acehnese into economically inappropriate areas, besides creating slums. Alternatively, one initiated by the homeless vis-à-vis unaffected communities, with state support, seemed to be a better solution. Unaffected communities can then donate, rent or sell the required land, which in passing may turn previous renters or squatters into owners. Shelter is linked to livelihoods, as the location of the home is strongly associated with livelihood strategies. This is a common problem with resettlement projects, as they may shift people far away from the sites of their livelihood.

As an example of an endogenous process well backed by public (and NGO) response, in the Jaya sub-district of north-western Aceh 1,130 people in 14 villages lost their land to the tsunami. They needed 44 hectares for resettlement. Villagers and sub-district officials found appropriate new sites for each village and negotiated with landowners before taking the case to the district authorities, who then took the case to the BRR (the Indonesian Agency for Reconstruction and Rehabilitation) and provincial government. The new land was then effectively acquired by the government and came under the joint titling programme to ensure equal ownership rights for men and women. This also guaranteed that vulnerable groups of people would be rehoused close to their pre-tsunami livelihood areas. This is a good example of an endogenous community-led process, receiving financial and legal support from the provincial authorities, which was also well supported by Oxfam by means of both advocacy and shelter teams, which worked with the villagers and local authorities through the entire process.

As an example of poor public response, acting against endogenous reactions, the governments of India, Indonesia and Sri Lanka decreed early on that a key part of reconstruction would involve the creation of 'buffer zones', i.e. 'safety' areas of between 100 m and 500 m from the sea line to provide protection from future sea waves. This proved to be of doubtful safety use and highly likely politically motivated, which was strongly resisted by original dwellers, mostly poor fishermen. In Sri Lanka, for example, repair or reconstruction of homes within this zone was prohibited, but hotels that had suffered less than 40 per cent structural damage were allowed to remain within this area. It looked more like securing prime costal land for the international tourist industry than to protect against a highly unlikely future tsunami. In Aceh, there was initially no government support to reconstruct within the buffer zones, but cash transfers proved useful for own reconstruction and repairs by dwellers who were not prepared to accept being extricated from their traditional livelihood and location. The rule was abandoned or relaxed a few months later, but that unnecessarily delayed the whole process of reconstruction (Oxfam 2005).

This brought additional problems, as reported by Ingram *et al.* (2006). The resettlement process that came on the back of the buffer zones also resulted in unfavourable social conditions for the displaced ones. For example, in a resettlement camp in the Matara district of southern Sri Lanka, over a thousand people of different societal backgrounds were brought to live together. As they put it:

> This is a drastic change from the small traditional villages of a few hundred residents where people lived before the tsunami. A sense of community is difficult to attain in large resettlement camps with non-traditional groupings of socio-economic and cultural classes. Thus, community networks, which are crucial for fostering adaptation and learning from disaster, may have been severely disrupted. A failure to address long-term needs, such as social and cultural issues when selecting resettlement camp locations for coastal communities has potentially made it difficult for people to cope with the trauma of the disaster and may increase vulnerability to social conflicts.
>
> (Ibid.: 609)

Here is then another example of the importance of community networks. The above example shows how a wrong resettlement policy, emanating from hierarchical relations or linking capital can unnecessarily destroy important levels of social capital (especially bonding and bridging capital), which had been built up over a long period and are essential for survival, stability and development (see Chapter 2).

Business and networks

Productive units, as private businesses or otherwise, are the very foundation of community networks and livelihoods, as they provide gainful employment and in-house training, consumer goods and necessary services, introduction of technology and know-how, and not least a number of related societal institutions and networks like trade unions, social clubs, sports clubs and the like. But they normally receive scant attention from disaster studies, as these mostly focus on household emergency concerns, especially shelter, food, health and education, and also on the reconstruction of physical capital, especially infrastructures and housing. This omission might have to do with the fact that businesses are supposed to have greater response autonomy than households or public infrastructures as well as the fact that the most pressing and distressing direct disaster effects, associated with physical destruction and damage, affect the general population from the outset. However, most disaster assessments count indirect effects from business interruptions as part of the total cost of a disaster. We have already shown that this is unwarranted at macro-national level. It is only true for particular businesses, which are directly affected and cannot easily recover or at all, rather than for the economy as a whole. To extend these (potential) losses to the national level is a clear case of fallacy of composition, which assumes that what is true for the part is also true for the whole. As indicated in Chapter 1, this is a source of unwarranted, fallacious and un-checkable overestimation of disaster losses.

We assume that networks involve horizontal and vertical inter-relationships of (individual or institutional) actors within and between the market, state institutions and formal and informal non-state institutions and associations (see Chapter 2). These interrelations are carried out by complex processes and are the basis of any community at any levels (Kilduff and Tsai 2003). At the economic level, despite their complexity, they can be analytically aggregated and divided into industries, sectors or regions, especially by means of the economics of input–output relationships. We however need to look at the basic unit that composes such aggregates, which is the productive unit or more particularly the business. That is, a unit that legally seeks to obtain a regular and increasing income in the form of profit via the production of goods and/or services by following and exploiting market rules. So we look first as to how these units can be affected by disasters and then as to how they normally react to such situations.

On the basis of a few studies that were carried out for especially developed countries, more particularly for the USA, we attempt to show the state of knowledge about business effects and responses after disasters, and then to anticipate indirectly what that would be in developing countries.

The range of business effects

After disasters have destroyed and/or damaged the capital stock and income directly, there will be suppliers that cannot supply, as they lost their customers (whether directly or the access to them); demanders that cannot demand, as they lost their suppliers (whether directly or the access to them); and producers than cannot produce, as they lost their input providers (whether directly or the access to them). That is, there will be (i) disaster unscathed market participants that cannot satisfy their needs, as they lost their regular supply, demand and/or credit flow channels, and (ii) there will be directly affected participants that can no longer participate in the market, as they lost their means of participation, i.e. capital, labour and/or income. Frustrated participants will necessarily take the required initiative themselves to look for alternative markets and early solutions to come out from their predicament, but as shown in the previous chapter this can be facilitated and orientated by public policy.

Disasters may impose direct and indirect business losses. Capital losses and damage to business functionality may end up in closure or losses of production and productivity, which may in turn result in job losses, negatively affecting community incomes, putting household and community recovery in greater difficulties. In turn, losses of lives and household impairment may also affect the production process of businesses within the directly affected zone and community via employment difficulties such as problems of labour availability and labour productivity. These are likely to affect supply and demand links, even if physical distribution channels are not primarily affected. And losses to distribution channels and access as well as impairments of fuel distribution and utility services (especially water, electricity, gas and sewage) may also affect them, even if business premises are unscathed. In other words, direct and indirect effects are likely to feed back on affected and unscathed firms through their standard networks.

In the context of Figure 2.3 (Chapter 2), but focusing on a single firm, we can account for its main productive networks. A firm or productive unit will normally have intra-links (between firms) and inter-links (with final consumers) and will operate in an environment of economic conditions, government policy and business/government expectations (supra-links). A disaster can affect a productive unit directly via stock losses on business capital, labour and physical linkages, such as transport and service infrastructures. But it can also affect this unit via flow effects derived from intermediate inputs availability, utility services disruption and of course the demand for its output. The latter if unchecked may feed back to its own demand for intermediate input, its output level, its income from sales, its credit position, its customer base, its share of the market, and so on. But this is not the same for unaffected firms competing in the same markets, as they could now take over the unsatisfied demand, gaining business position and extending their share of the market. In turn, unaffected but frustrated

Table 6.1 Range of business disaster effects

Direct effect on	*Indirect effect*
Capital Labour Management	Output/sales quantity Output/sales quality Network switching
Infrastructures: Transport Utilities	Network disconnection Service flows Network switching
Population Housing	Customer base Network switching
General environment and societal disruption	Community environment Business environment Network switching

consumers can switch their demands to these unaffected firms within and outside the disaster zone, complementing the bypassing of directly affected firms. This may make it significantly more difficult for directly affected firms to regain their pre-disaster positions, as now their customer base may have, at least partially, shifted away from their pre-disaster consumer patterns. So from the viewpoint of a single firm the disaster can affect it in five analytical dimensions, as shown in Table 6.1 and described below:

1 Directly via losses of capital, labour and management. This is bound to have a fast indirect effect on the quantity and quality of output/supplies/sales of the firm. If capital is fully destroyed, then new production will stop. If labour is not easily available, then both the quantity and the quality of output are likely to suffer. If management fails under stress, then again both quantity and quality may fail. This will affect revenues and so on.
2 Indirectly via losses of transport infrastructures, affecting flows derived from the failure of physical access, affecting the connection between a firm and input suppliers, wholesalers and retailers, i.e. affecting the access to customary markets. If the latter ones have also endured losses to their capital then the problem will compound. Losses of transport infrastructures are normally the most pressing for firms in the disaster zones (Gordon *et al.* 1997; Tierney 2006).
3 Indirectly via losses of utility infrastructures, affecting service flows such as water, electricity, gas and sewage. Although this is normally a short-lived problem, it is nonetheless a pressing one immediately after a disaster strikes. This normally translates into various degrees of interruption of economic activities.
4 Indirectly via losses of its customer base. This may arise from a disaster affecting consumers themselves, both via unemployment from firms that were directly affected or via direct disaster victimization on the population (death, injury, residential damage and displacement). But it may also arise because markets become inaccessible and shifty. This is likely to impinge on falls in the level, patterns and composition of demand. The latter may increase the proportion of basic need goods, so firms supplying non-essential ones might suffer most. This then feeds back in terms of losses of revenues and so on.
5 Finally, indirectly via general changes of community and economic environment. This is important, as when the business environment has changed and is unlikely to return to pre-disaster patterns soon or at all, firms may struggle for survival if they proceed on the assumption that everything will soon be about the same as it was before the disaster. The failure to acknowledge major environmental changes leads many firms to struggle against the odds for a long time before failing. Pre-disaster business patterns are likely to be exacerbated after a disaster, which means that firms that were in precarious conditions before the disaster are likely to fail faster after it. Although it may well be the case that for some of them, government aid acts as a lifeline to keep them alive for longer than it would have been otherwise.

All the above normally happen with different weights, affecting firms in varying degrees. These are all related to community and economic networks within and outside the disaster area. As such, these effects are not linear, and reverberate and feed back in negative loops to given firms via losses of sales, revenue, profit, savings and credit, and on the strength and commitment to recover. But if firms can somehow be flexible enough to adapt to the new situation and the outside response from the government and community can help on this, then the trend might be reversed. Notice that the counterpart to business failure in the disaster zone is demand shifts to alternative networks towards unaffected firms. If the switch is large, let alone permanent, then the affected firms cannot possibly survive without major changes, whether in output composition, location or the like.

All the points affecting demand and personal incomes are related to firms via loss of labour, productivity and ambience changes. The demand can then be under a number of effects, which are not necessarily independent:

- income effect via loss of employment;
- substitution effect on demand towards essential goods and services;
- saving-debt effect from loss of housing and migration; and
- switching effect from losses of standard markets and suppliers.

Changes in consumption composition, away from non-essential expenditure, and loss or disconnection with standard markets and suppliers are the incentives for demand shift and network bypassing. Therefore, fully unscathed firms, whether within or outside the disaster zone, would be the route for network shift and disaster zone bypassing.

It is also to be noticed that business decisions also affect vulnerability and resilience to disasters. For example, convenient locations for required resources, from easy access to intermediate inputs to transportation routes that lead to important markets and ports, bypassing the availability and quality of human resources, may cluster businesses in risky locations. As local communities develop around such businesses, the community itself would be under serious potential losses, were there to be a strong disaster event.

General network bypassing

When local businesses are impaired or impeded to produce and supply largely non-affected demands, then given competitive market practices, non-affected businesses are likely to do so, taking advantage of the situation. And consumers and firms that need such goods are also likely to look for alternative sources, stimulating and complementing a network demand-supply shift, which mutually reinforces each other. In this case, the directly affected firms are then likely to be bypassed at least in the short term. A much referred case is that of the Japan earthquake in 1995, which especially affected the city of Kobe:

Box 6.3 Remittances illustration

Pakistan's earthquake of 8 October 2005 killed over 70,000 people, affecting over three million people in the North-West Frontier Province and Kashmir. This affected a mountainous and remote area of some 30,000 square kilometres. Estimations are always tricky, but it was reported that some 600,000 homes, 6,000 schools and 500 health facilities were destroyed, severely affecting livelihoods.

International remittances played a significant role in the aftermath of the earthquake. A large number of people from the earthquake-affected areas who worked abroad (mostly in Saudi Arabia and UAE) send regular remittances, which recovered relatively quickly from the earthquake initial infrastructure and documentation disruption. While remittances were initially severely disrupted, they significantly increased in the following year. Given the severity with which the local economy was affected, external sources of income such as remittances were essential for recovery.

An empirical survey, carried out under the aegis of ODI (Overseas Development Institute), selected a representative village in each of four affected districts: Riyali (Muzaffarabad), Chamiati (Bagh), Chitta Batta (Mansehra) and Kot Gala (Battgram). Interviews were then conducted in these four villages, followed by six focus group discussions: two with women, three with farm workers and one with humanitarian agencies. Remittances represented between 15 per cent and 100 per cent of recipient household income (Savage and Harvey 2007).

Informal endogenous methods to carry out remittances were preferred to formal ones, i.e. both the Hundi (or Hawala) system and the personally carried transfer (mostly by remitters themselves) were preferred. The former was the most widely used method of sending remittances, as it is preferred because it is quick, efficient and accessible, requiring less documentation and is cheaper than formal alternatives. In turn, personal transfers carried out by hand are regarded as speedy and safe, representing the second most popular remittance method. Formal (banking) transfer mechanisms were regarded as confidential and secure, but slow and expensive, so they tended to be used only for larger transactions.

As an example of public policy tapping existing endogenous behaviours, we can refer to the incorporation of people into the formal financial systemic network. Before the earthquake, 68 per cent of recipients and 44 per cent of non-recipients did not have bank accounts, considering them time-consuming and requiring too much documentation, but also because of lack of accessibility and education about them. However, after the earthquake, some 90 per cent of recipients and 74 per cent of non-recipients ended up with bank accounts. This was a direct result of the government's cash-transfer programme to affected households, which could only be received through a bank account. Apart from reinforcing the systemic nature of remittances, this measure also incorporated otherwise isolated individuals into financial networks, which should be considered systemically consistent with development.

This is again an indication of the need for public policy to have a combined approach after disasters: facilitate regular remittances, encourage new avenues for them and support poorer dwellers directly (e.g. via cash transfers), who normally do not receive remittances. More than half of respondents stated that they received external help from national and international NGOs, and 40 per cent stated that they were assisted in some way by the government. None of the remittance recipients reported having to sell assets to meet needs after the earthquake, despite the immediate reduction in remittance flows that followed the disaster. Several non-recipient ones, however, reported selling jewellery and livestock to pay for shelter and health care. External assistance seems to have filled the gap left by the initial drop in remittances for those who regularly receive them. But non-recipients, by having to sell livestock, may have been putting in peril their own longer-term livelihood. This is then an important role for direct public action.

In terms of remittance use, the study is also telling: over 40 per cent of respondents indicated that they were used for daily expenditure, such as food, clothing, health care and school fees. A third of them reported that, in addition, they used them to pay off debts, refurbish the home, pay wedding expenses and arrange dowries for their children. And some 20 per cent stated that they also used the remittances for housing construction and investment in real estate. So the role of remittances is all-embracing and fundamental for their survival and livelihoods, and not least social status.

Lastly, as regards the permanent need to support local economic networks, key informants, such as traders and farmers, reported that local markets would have taken much longer to recover without remittance resources. Many markets reopened in temporary accommodation to meet remittance-induced demand. Building workers reported that they found employment more easily thanks to the fact that some remittances were used for reconstruction and repairs, and so on.

As an additional example, the 'three-for-one' Mexican programme represents another way in which public savings can be mobilized along with remittances to finance small community projects. This type of public programme, which encourages and taps endogenous remittance behaviour, can be set up for normal times and/or after disasters. In the Mexican state of Zacatecas, the Federal and local government match every dollar donated to local projects by remitters, such as small infrastructure projects (water treatment, schools, roads, parks, etc.), which have strong externalities, benefitting also poorer non-remittance recipient households (Solimano 2003). This programme, which can be on a two-for-one or a three-for-one matching basis, has completed more than 400 projects in eight years in Zacatecas (Ellerman 2003). The total investment made by migrants on those projects amounted to some 4.5 million dollars by the early 2000s (World Bank 2002).

> The port [of Kobe] was severely damaged, and during the period in which it was being repaired and restored, shippers turned to other container ports in the region. When the Kobe port returned to capacity, which also entailed making a number of important post-earthquake improvements, there was still no particular reason for shippers to bring their business back to Kobe. The port, which had already been experiencing revenue declines before the earthquake, never regained its position (Chang 2001).
>
> (Tierney 2006: 278)

The case of Hurricane Katrina in 2005, with its massive flooding due to a levee failure, strongly affected New Orleans and the surrounding areas. Businesses from outside the disaster area significantly bypassed those in directly affected areas. A good number of the latter could not reopen at least in the short to medium term, which made it even more difficult for them to operate profitably after they restarted, as a good number of their customers had already switched to other sources or left the city (Chu 2007; Vigdor 2008).

Another study shows that there was an important spatial shift in its aftermath (Xiao and Nilawar 2012). This is an econometric study that attempts to assess business and economic demand shift from the core disaster area towards adjacent and beyond counties and states. In other words they tested, over the first two years, the situation of ever-increasing (spatial) circles from the core zone to more and more distant areas. It shows fading (positive) effects (demands, output, employment) until negligible ones the further away the assessed counties were. Their conclusion is that

> We found that the growth rates of employment and income of the core disaster area did not differ significantly from other places before Katrina. However, post-Katrina, parishes in the core disaster area fared significantly worse than other counties/parishes in the study area, while those in the edge area significantly better, even after controlling for pre-disaster differences in unemployment rate, educational level, and growth patterns.
>
> (Ibid.: 45)

They are aware that in the edges areas a good deal of new demands was created by emergency and reconstruction personnel. But it is also clear that after the recovery was over a good number of businesses did not reopen. This conclusion seems too confined to a disaster that was extremely homogeneous in its core area, which necessarily was going to create demand and supply migrations towards near non-affected areas. But out-migrations and demand-supply network shifts are a permanent feature of strong disasters (Scanlon 1988, 2007; Webb *et al.* 2000; Stoltman *et al.* 2007; Zhang *et al.* 2009).

Likewise, as shown in Chapter 5, in the case of the 2010 Chile earthquake, there apparently was a massive network shift between the disaster region and an important but only peripherally affected one (Valparaiso). A year after the disaster, this region was growing at an unprecedented rate of 7.5 per cent, as compared to the country's 5.2 per cent and a significantly lower rate for the disaster region. No doubt, Valparaiso took an important share of the output of the directly affected region.

In turn, the attack on the Twin Towers in 2001, although being a different type of disaster, shows similar patterns:

> Many businesses located near the Ground Zero reconstruction area are still being affected by the fact that tens of thousands of people who once needed the goods and services they offered are working elsewhere. When the Trade Towers and other structures were lost, many of these businesses, especially those dependent on local foot traffic, effectively lost their markets.
>
> (Tierney 2006: 283)

As expected, whatever the country business networks and levels, there will always be an important demand shift associated with reconstruction needs. That is, unaffected firms within and outside the disaster area will benefit with new demands that cannot be satisfied by both affected firms and the capacity of unaffected firms in the area. This will normally involve mostly firms producing construction goods, e.g. cement, bricks, metal structures, tools and the like. But this is also likely to benefit firms producing food and other basic stuff for both frustrated demand in the disaster area and new migrant labour associated with reconstruction. For example, in the case of Sri Lanka after the 2004 Asian tsunami, a study concluded:

> In aggregate, the [demand] shift will generally be inward. But for some sectors (e.g. construction materials), demand may shift outward ... many trading relationships are destroyed, either temporarily or permanently. Reforming relationships takes a varying degree of time, depending on the nature of the relationships in a given sector.
>
> (De Mel *et al.* 2008: 4)

It is to be noticed that businesses not directly affected by the disaster, but under difficulties in receiving required utility services (i.e. water, electricity, gas and the like) are normally shown to be affected only for a short while, from a few hours to a few days (Tierney *et al.* 1996). This might not be long enough for firms to lose their customary links. So we expect this effect to be short-lived and therefore less significant for network bypassing.

In the same vein, a study about small businesses in a number of US natural disasters by Alesch *et al.* (2001) concludes that, first, when businesses cannot supply consumers and/or other businesses, they will look elsewhere for such goods and, on the same token, if customers lose their means of purchase, because of unemployment, migration or rundown on savings, businesses that are not diversified will experience sale losses and financial constraints. This is the very basis for network shift and local bypassing, and its likely consequence is a high degree of failure especially in the case of small businesses.

Although it is rare that disaster studies deal with the issue of demand or network shifts between directly affected areas and unaffected ones, most mention such behaviour in passing. So the question is which characteristics of affected firms make such phenomena more likely. Or, conversely, which characteristics make a firm more resilient or otherwise to disasters. It is normally the less resilient ones that will be exposed to consumers switching to other suppliers and these other suppliers switching to these frustrated consumers.

Business characteristics and effect levels

A number of studies carried out mainly for the USA show that larger firms are better able to cope with disasters than smaller ones, but the latter might also reduce vulnerability and increase resilience under certain network conditions. So there are business features that may have a direct bearing on both initial vulnerability and the degree and effectiveness of resilience. These features are associated with geographical diversification, economic sector, economic diversification, intra-business network, hazard insurance, own savings, political influence and flexible management. This should be considered within the community traits, as communities that do have some preparedness and mitigation plans for potential disasters and have made some effort to reduce vulnerability levels by enforcing building codes, land use and other risk reducing features, present an environment more conducive and effective for recovery than would be otherwise. For example, preparedness to restore transportation systems to give priority to the movement of things and people for the sake of easing both emergency and reconstruction is of paramount importance (Miles and Chang 2003).

As regards the importance of networks, it seems that communities with strong vertical and horizontal networks as well as participation from affected people are in better shape to speed up community and business recovery (Rubin and Barbee 1985; Albala-Bertrand 1993; Berke and Beatley 1997; Nakagawa and Shaw 2004b). Therefore, it is to be noticed that even if businesses take pre-disaster measures to reduce vulnerability to hazards and increase preparedness in case of occurrence, the business interruption may be highly dependent on the characteristics of the surrounding community and networks. Other things being equal, there are some patterns that can be useful in understanding potential effects on businesses.

Larger firms seem to be associated with a higher ability to absorb and respond to direct disaster effects (Tierney 1997; Alesch 2005; Zhang *et al.* 2009). As regards direct (stock) effects, larger businesses by normally having more own finance and not least better access to credit are likely to be built in less risky locations and under better building codes and conditions, as demanded by insurers. Larger firms normally have insurance against hazards. This is likely to make them less vulnerable to direct effects. As regards indirect (flow) effects, larger firms are more likely to have branches in several geographical locations, often supplying regional and international markets, which make them more resilient to respond to changes in disaster-zone demand patterns and levels. In addition, if the branches in the zone are affected by failures to access input suppliers, whether because customary ones have been directly affected or because road infrastructures are not operational or else, then unaffected branches within or outside the disaster area can compensate for the fluctuation for as long as that persists. In addition, insurance payments, access to credit and own resources are likely to compensate for most of their direct losses. Insurance often covers also part of the period when production and sales are interrupted by a disaster. For all these reasons larger firms have as a rule been reported to withstand disasters significantly better than smaller ones (Alesch *et al.* 2001; Tierney 2006).

But there are also other factors that count to reduce or increase resilience, which may be features of both large and small firms. The sector more likely to be affected seems to be the wholesale and retail firms, but here again the smaller firms would be more likely to be affected, as this sector is highly competitive and less stable. This sector normally requires less capital to be set up, it is more mobile and may, as in many developing countries, be surrounded by informal sector activities that compete for a part of their markets. But they are normally more dependent on local markets, which may be the ones that are bound to be more upset after a disaster. Still, trade and services are normally the areas that recover faster. The output type is also another important consideration after disasters. Businesses that supply goods that are of elastic demand, especially non-essential goods, might suffer most as the consumer base changes their patterns of purchases in favour of essentials and basic goods, the more so if they are not large enough to have customer markets outside the disaster area (Alesch and Holly 1997; Webb *et al.* 2000, 2002; Alesch *et al.* 2001). Migration out of the disaster area can also affect business demand demographics, which may make it even more difficult for firms to regain their pre-disaster positions (Smith 1996; Smith and McCarty 1996; Girard and Peacock 1997; Alesch *et al.* 2001).

In addition, firms that produce or sell a diversified output are more able to cope with changed patterns of demand. And not least, firms that belong to an ongoing network, where they have developed customary patterns of trade and loyalties, are better able to recover than they would be otherwise, provided that the network itself is not down. If it is, then firms with more responsive and flexible management will look for the most appropriate network to link in the aftermath. Here ownership matters. It seems that firms that rent, rather than own their premises, are significantly more flexible to relocate in search of opportunities. Larger firms are, as said, more likely to be insured, but also more likely to have political and policy influence directly or via their associations, so they are likely to be served before in terms of reconstruction aid, credit, supplies and the like (Chang 2001; Tierney 2006; Zhang *et al.* 2009).

It is also well known that firms and individuals that have had experience with previous disasters are more likely to prepare for such eventualities by reducing the risks of location, output, demand shift, and so on. Larger firms are more prepared to do this, as they have more available resources, for example, by carrying some redundancy as a buffer against fluctuations (Tierney 2006; Fraccastoro 2008), and, as said, by contracting insurance against hazards.

How firms fail

We have described the main characteristics that a firm should normally have to be better able to cope with disasters, but we have not shown how especially small firms fail after disasters and why. Again, resorting to the same sources, there are a number of patterns that can be identified.

A study by Alesch *et al.* (2001) covers such features well. First, it seems that traditional precautions don't help businesses to survive after disasters. Structural precautions to protect premises and capital are necessary to reduce losses to life and property, but not sufficient to help businesses survive. The latter is related to how businesses are related to each other and their customer base, i.e. business and consumer networks, including non-economic community networks. Second, most business don't appear to fail immediately after the event. That is, the weakest firms are likely to fail right away, but for most of the others the survival and recovery will be a long trying struggle. They have to cope with a number of factors, especially demand shifts. That is, most losses do not occur right after the disaster, but during the recovery phase via business interruptions, fall in demand for their output and loss of business value, which will affect their capacity to access credit. Third, the pre-disaster conditions of the firm and the new economic climate will have a strong bearing on their capacity to survive. A study by Tierney (2006: 280) reports:

> Businesses are sensitive both to general economic trends and to the economic climate in particular business sectors. Disasters can exacerbate 'everyday' vulnerabilities, while pre-disaster economic health can cushion the impacts of extreme events. Eighteen months after the Northridge earthquake, for example, firms in industries that had been experiencing growth in the two-year period just before the earthquake were significantly less likely than firms in declining industries to report being worse off than before the disaster (Dahlhamer and Tierney 1998). In studies on the longer-term impacts of Hurricane Andrew and the Loma Prieta earthquake, business owners who considered the general economic climate to be positive for their firms were significantly more likely to report positive recovery outcomes.
>
> (Webb *et al.* 2002)

In addition, the managerial ability of firms is another important factor for recovery. Normally, business owners are greatly unprepared to face an abrupt change in business environment. So they may struggle for months, under the impression that the disaster is just a fluctuation and that things are going to get back as they were, before giving up. But in each disaster area it seems that on average even in the short term businesses do recover. But an average implies that some are better off and some worse off than before the disaster, and some have simply quit. Tierney (2006: 285) reports the results of a study on four different disasters in the USA as follows:

> These studies showed that even in the short-term (i.e., a year to 18 months after a disaster event) most businesses do at least return to pre-disaster levels of economic performance. For example, a little over a year after the Midwest floods and the Northridge earthquake, 12.2 per cent and 23.3 per cent of businesses, respectively, reported being worse off, and comparable numbers actually reported being better off. With respect to the longer term, 21 per cent of businesses in hard hit Santa Cruz County reported being worse off, but 37 per cent said they were better off than before the earthquake. Findings were roughly the same for businesses in South Dade County 6 years after Hurricane Andrew; while 34 per cent of businesses surveyed reported being worse off, 31 per cent were better off than before the hurricane.

And adds:

> However, despite urban legends indicating that a large proportion of businesses fail following disasters, that does not appear to be the case. Moreover, quitting business after a disaster may be a prudent choice for some business owners, rather than an indication of disaster induced failure.
>
> (Alesch *et al.* 2001)

In other words, a number of businesses that don't make it after the disaster may not have made it even without it. And probably, given some generous post-disaster funding from the US Small Business Administration (SBA), they may have failed a lot earlier than they did, which is the reason why pre-disaster business and economic trends are an important variable to consider so as not to attribute results to the wrong cause.

There is also some evidence that some types of response to back business are less appropriate than others. It has been put forward for many disasters in the USA that:

> The lack of a relationship between post-disaster aid and business recovery, which has been found consistently across a range of studies, is likely due to several factors. First, the types of aid that are available to businesses generally come in the form of loans, either from agencies like the Small Business Administration or from banks. This automatically leads to increased debt for the business owner. Second, even if aid is obtained, it typically covers only a portion of the losses businesses experience in disasters. Third, no amount of assistance can offset problems such as a loss of customers, disaster-induced declines in demand for goods and services, or losses associated with the disruption of local business ecologies. Nor can assistance reverse pre-disaster trends that affect business fortunes over the long term.
>
> (Tierney 2006: 192)

In addition, as shown in Chapter 3 and in Box 6.1 in this chapter, cash aid to affected households might be preferred to in-kind aid, let alone loans, as otherwise businesses may undergo additional falls in demand, making even more difficult both the recovery of the firms and that of the community. It is also known that a good deal of businesses, especially in developing countries, are mostly dependent on local markets with normally stable customer patterns. So these are likely to be more vulnerable and less resilient if their surroundings are affected by a disaster, even if they themselves are not badly affected directly (Nakagawa and Shaw 2004b; Srinivasan 2006; De Mel *et al.* 2008; Aldrich 2011).

What we would like to know

As shown above, most of the existing papers about firms under stress have useful contributions, but concentrate more on the firm itself (i.e. productivity, employment, aid and the like) than on its particular relation to the wider economic networking. For example, as shown above, there are studies on the role of business in relation to the public sector for disaster prevention (Warhurst 2006a, 2006b; Binder and Witte 2007), and about some general patterns of business response to disasters in the USA, from a useful sociological viewpoint (Webb *et al.* 2000; Tierney 2006), and a descriptive analysis of aid and recovery funding for firms in Sri Lanka after the 2004 tsunami (De Mel *et al.* 2008). There are of course good books and studies about normal businesses network types (Perry 1999; Kilduff and Tsai 2003).

We need more focused information about business networks, normal network shifting and network bypassing of both firms and households under stress. We suggest that in future every time a disaster strikes, the standard surveys about destruction and needs should be restructured and extended to include questions about key traits of networks, especially related to business behaviour. This will create a wealth of information about these issues, which could be policy exploited in the useful systemic directions we have been dealing with in this book. But to carry such studies would necessarily imply follow-up surveys of disaster affected firms over a longer term, which would require appropriate funding and not least commitment, which is more likely to be secured with the cooperation of international organizations, so that this can be made comparable across countries and be systematically achieved. The surveys should enquire about the above traits directly, first, at national levels and, then, be comparably collated at international levels. This effort would be policy useful and bound to help efficient recovery in a faster and less expensive way, helping in passing the development of networks and therefore development itself. For a general approach to this type of enquiry, see our Appendix.

What response policies can be appropriate

In light of the previous sections and chapters, responses that can be more appropriate can be partly derived from there, but local and national effects have to be carefully balanced. We know now that both customers and/or suppliers within the disaster zone can be frustrated by failure to satisfy their business, even if they themselves are not badly affected. They then will look for markets elsewhere, normally in the surrounding areas, but also beyond it including foreign markets. That is, there will be a demand shift to alternative connections and networks. We in addition know that full or partial destruction of business assets will impose a severe interruption to the firm in question, which may put it out of activity for good. These are precisely the firms that will be bypassed, both within the disaster zone and outside it, more permanently by other unaffected firms looking for new opportunities, especially but not only those associated with reconstruction. In other words, whether firms were unaffected or not in the first place, if they are still not operating after the rehabilitation of infrastructures took place, then it is highly likely that they will struggle to keep their viability.

We also know now that in-kind aid has to be very limited to avoid depressing local markets, and that cash aid, grants, low-interest loans and insurance payments to both firms and households play a significantly more systemic role in recovery. This should be understood in the context of local capabilities and policy encouragement and information. Assuming that there is awareness of the main patterns of demand and network shift, and that official authorities and foreign aid are prepared to tap them to speed up recovery, while securing a balance between the local and the national, then that should strengthen the counteraction of indirect flow effects and therefore reduce the reconstruction investment necessary to keep the economy as if there was no disaster. Revisiting the model we refer to in Chapter 4, we show here theoretically how this could happen.

Box 6.4 Insurance illustration

The December 2004 Indian Ocean earthquake leading to a massive tsunami affected the coastal regions of Indonesia, Sri Lanka, Thailand and India. In Sri Lanka, according to official estimates, some 35,000 people lost their lives and a further half a million people were directly affected from housing destruction or damage, leading to displacement. Damage to the capital stock was estimated at over US$1 billion and, if flow interruptions are added, at around US$1.5 billion, representing some 7 per cent of the country's GDP. The former however is always difficult to assess and normally overestimated and the latter is a misleading estimate from the viewpoint of the national macroeconomy, as shown in Chapter 1 and elsewhere.

One of the main features associated with recovery in developing countries is the lack of formal disaster insurance for both housing and firms. Contrariwise, in the case of the USA, while about 50 per cent of losses from Hurricane Andrew (Florida) and the Northridge earthquake (California) were covered by formal insurance, less than 15 per cent of the losses from the tsunami were covered by it, which were normally associated with large firms, which in turn are usually less affected than smaller firms (Ferguson 2006). Insurance for micro enterprises and housing was nearly absent. As regards small and medium firms, of 423 firms surveyed by De Mel *et al.* (2008), around 13 per cent had insurance coverage for any type of loss, and around two-thirds of those with some type of insurance reported some compensation for losses, which covered about one-quarter of the losses. In such circumstances, official and international aid and not least informal insurance from remittances by family and friends solidarity can create financial flows and funding for recovery. It is well known that the international aid was overgenerous on this occasion (around US$2 billion committed) and it is also to be noticed that remittances were estimated as some 90 per cent of total official losses (TEC 2007). Most of these flows went to residential capital and transportation, but covered only a proportion of household damage, which together with utilities are normally the most pressing recovery requirements after any disasters. Firms in general did not enjoy equal support, except in some localized high-employment and basic-need activities like fishing. However, 'while insurance payments are closely related to the insured entity's losses, aid payments may not reflect the actual losses suffered by business owners' (De Mel *et al.* 2008: 14). This is another reason to support insurance. Still, all these flows represented significantly more than the overestimated losses, but just as too little aid is a problem, too much of it is just as bad. For problems with the use and disbursements of this aid, see TEC (2007).

On the other hand, as reported by a Chilean newspaper, insurance following the 2010 Chile earthquake, as compared to the one in 1985, reads as follows:

> The earthquake and ensuing tsunami of February 2010 generated estimated losses of US$30 billion. This figure is 28 times larger than the 1985 earthquake. The Association of Insurers estimate that insurance will cover some 25 per cent of such losses for around US$7.5 billion. Such coverage will be 94 times larger than that of the 1985 earthquake, where insurers covered only 8 per cent of the losses, for around US$85m. On 30 November 2011, the Association reported that they have paid to 131,143 households of the 190,299 houses with reported losses, for US$1.3 billion, remaining only 188 cases to complete. As regards non-housing coverage, insurers have already paid US$4.4 billion, which gives a total disbursement of US$5.7 billion so far.
>
> (*La Tercera*, 26/12/2011)

Setting aside the fact that losses were highly overestimated (some 25 per cent of the US$30 billion was attributed to business interruptions; see Chapter 1), insurance has become more and more important over time (domestic and international, including re-insurers), covering a good proportion of total losses and releasing partly the public use of funds for bailouts for reconstruction via grants and easy loans. This is welcome on all the positive grounds presented earlier, as this is a systemic mechanism that acts endogenously to both increase prevention and mitigate effects. But it is also to be noticed that insurance premiums in general and especially those associated with mortgages rocketed in the aftermath of the 2010 earthquake, increasing by as much as 40 per cent over pre-disaster levels.
(Google: www.portalinmobiliario.com/diario/noticia.asp?NoticiaID=14230)

New income flows and network shifting

As been shown above, after disasters, income compensatory flows come from many quarters to address the plight of many actors and activities affected by them. Insurance payments from insurers to especially housing and firms; remittances from family and friends living abroad to especially households and small and micro enterprises; cash transfers from the government to especially households; grants and subsidized loans from the government to especially firms; public funding for reconstruction of public assets, especially infrastructures and service utilities. In addition, foreign aid in the form of bilateral and multilateral grants and subsidized loan as well as foreign and domestic charity flows channelled via NGOs will complement domestic sources of response. Charity sources normally reach both affected people and small projects such as agricultural terracing and irrigation, urban drinking water and hygiene, local marketing infrastructures and the like. In parallel with this, and from similar sources, there will be in-kind aid mostly to deal with early emergency and rehabilitation (ALNAP Papers various years; Albala-Bertrand 1993; Rodriguez *et al.* 2006).

A good deal of the above income flows will be fresh ones, i.e. without the disaster they would not have arisen. But others may be, as has been widely reported, shifting normal developing financial flows from standard items to disaster responses. This latter shift involves both public domestic funds (associated with the public budget) and foreign flows (overseas development assistance and other foreign aid). This type of aid is normally associated with long-term projects such as education and health, which may not create additional demand, except via differential income multipliers. That is, disaster response financing may have a greater short-term multiplying effect than say motorway development, let alone weapons and other warfare procurement purchases. Let's however assume that multipliers from this alternative usage is the same so they fully compensate for each other, i.e. one unit of income detracted from an existing project to a disaster item has the same total income impact. So, in static accounting, these flows are supposed to compensate for local destruction and reduced income flows, but not at the macroeconomic level as a whole, as the same amount that is now directed locally has been taken away from somewhere else.

Fresh flows however are a different kind of income injection. First, statically, they do add to income and hopefully demand, which dynamically may create a stimulus for the local and national economy that was not present before the disaster event. So they do at least help compensate the macroeconomy for the potential indirect losses. Second, fresh flows in association with post-disaster network shifting may more than compensate the macroeconomy. Let me explain this phenomenon.

Assume that a corner shop is destroyed by the disaster and that it has full disaster insurance cover for the losses to its capital stock. And also assume that consumer demand levels have not been affected. Customers will shift their demand to similar unaffected shops in or outside the disaster area. The latter will increase their sales and of course provisions to satisfy it, whether from the same wholesale suppliers as those that supplied the destroyed corner shop or otherwise. In other words, the expected loss of income from the destroyed corner shop has been shifted and compensated *endogenously* by means of existing market alternatives or networks. Then assuming that insurers do not renege on their contract, the destroyed corner shop will receive the insurance payment accordingly. Whether the owners rebuild their lost shop or change location or retire, the fact is that there is now an additional income that can come into the economy one way or the other. Even if after rebuilding, the corner shop does not become viable due to loss of its customer base, the fact is that there will be income spent on the economy on capital stock replacement. So although the capital stock has just been replaced with the insurance, the macroeconomic income would have been more than compensated for by the loss of the corner shop in virtue of the dynamics of network shifting, which is an endogenous behavioural reaction. The case is equally valid if the firm is unscathed, but insurance pays for business interruption due to infrastructure failures or to relocation of the customer base.

The same reasoning can be applied to remittances, cash transfers, grants, subsidised loans and the like as long as they represent fresh, rather than detracted, income. It is of course not straightforward to differentiate existing 'new' income from fresh income. But it should not be in doubt that a proportion of these income flows is actually new and fresh. This has implications for the macro model that we summarized in Chapter 4. That model simply showed that under realistic assumptions, there was no need to replace all the capital stock lost to a disaster to compensate the macroeconomy for potential losses of future income. A small proportion of it would suffice to secure such compensation. Implicitly in it, there were the effects of normal network shifting after disasters. However, if a degree of potential network shifts, associated with the substitution potential (SP) of the situation, is not exercised, but can actually be made to do so via stimulation from appropriate policy, then in the case of developing countries with a minimum of potential market networks and substitution, the compensatory replacement can be even smaller to achieve the same result. This will add a parameter to the model, which makes the response as having a larger impact than without it. Let us simply call this the degree of policy-induced substitution parameter or simply 'induced bypassing parameter'. So our equation 4.2 (Chapter 4), which represents the gain in the growth rate of GDP from reconstruction investment, becomes:

$$g_{Y2} = \beta m \Delta v \tag{6.1}$$

And equation (4.3), which represents the compensatory required investment, becomes:

$$\Delta v = d / \beta mc \tag{6.2}$$

Where β: induced bypassing parameter, g_{Y2}: growth rate of GDP, m: income multiplier, $\Delta v = I_R / Y$: variation in total investment-to-GDP ratio due solely to reconstruction investment and $c = \Delta K / \Delta Y$: incremental capital-output ratio, which is the inverse of the incremental productivity of capital. In other words, reconstruction investment would now have a larger impact on GDP (equation 6.1) and therefore a lower level of it would be required to compensate for potential losses of GDP from capital losses (equation 6.2). That is, if say 10 per cent of the total directly and indirectly affected businesses are induced to shift networks, other things being equal, then the parameter should take a value of 1.1 and should multiply the previous response value. That is, the effect of reconstruction investment would be 10 per cent stronger than without such shifts, and therefore the required reconstruction investment to keep the economy as if there were no disaster would be 91 per cent of that without such shifts. Or alternatively, the same reconstruction investment will speed up economic recovery.

The first implication of the above is that a country with better, or post-disaster-created, information about possible market pairing, i.e. alternative networking, let alone public funding and policy to stimulate such shifts, will have a higher degree of bypassing by initially frustrated market participants than it would be otherwise. The second implication is that in countries with poor business networks, an important role for the state after disasters is to create information and facilitate such demand and supply shifts following disasters. Frustrated customers (for final and intermediate input) will look for suppliers and supplies in alternative markets, while frustrated suppliers will look for customers in alternative markets. The two may coincide, making the exercise more efficient and prompt. The government can provide here a useful role as facilitator, as a kind of broker for information as well as infrastructure, organization and funding for the purpose, as partly shown in Chapter 3 and the boxes in this chapter.

But civil society can produce a good deal of the required information. The ubiquitous and widespread use of the Internet, its social networks and mobile phones have already been used by private individuals, as a naturally initiated crowdsourcing, to indicate to others where there were available supplies and/or consumers in the aftermath of disasters, e.g. the 2010 Chile earthquake. This is a welcome development, which should be strongly backed officially so that government and foreign response can also learn where and how much to supply first. This should hopefully be done in a balanced way, initially preferring the shift towards unscathed and/or operational businesses in the disaster area. Failing that, the link should be facilitated towards outward areas. This is what normally happens anyway, as we have shown above, but it could be more effective and efficient if the government and/or social networks can provide the information and both physically and financially facilitate the action.

Notice that the alternative to the above is not to facilitate the pairing between customers and producers or, worse, to prevent bypassing altogether. The only case in which this can be justified is if the disaster zone, especially its business base, can be brought back to effective functionality fast enough, without creating anti-systemic dependencies. If that is not available and bypassing is not encouraged, then the zone risks starting living off handouts, discouraging proper business and indirectly economic and social development. In addition, this may also prevent the dynamics of the more-than-compensatory network shifting vis-à-vis fresh income flows. So in most real cases, a balance has to be struck between preventing the rundown of the disaster zone by market desertion and encouraging national income recovery. Or at least securing some kind of market redress once the in-zone business recovery is well under way.

To summarize, if a firm loses its customers and is fully bypassed, then other things being equal macroeconomic income will be the same as before the disaster. All that has happened is a redistribution of income/output generation. In addition, if the negatively affected firm can manage to bring back the same customer base after reconstruction, then the macroeconomic income can be larger than before the disaster on account of reconstruction expenditure, assuming that this is done with fresh income flows. So in virtue of network shifting via demand and supply linking jumps, the macroeconomy will not be negatively affected and can be positively affected, when riding on fresh reconstruction recovery income flows. Of course, response investment multipliers might be stronger than investment multipliers from both detracted projects and from the impact effect itself, which is likely (Albala-Bertrand 2004/1993), making the positive effects of reconstruction investment and network shifting stronger on output and general GDP.

Notice that this implies that although flow interruptions can be heavy in the disaster zone, and more particularly for the directly affected private and public productive firms, the macroeconomy would be unlikely to endure significant fluctuations after disasters. The avoidance of serious discontinuities, by keeping the economic flows with little hindrance, is tantamount to a system with healthy endogeneity. In other words, this is a system in which functionality is not heavily affected, let alone broken, so societal resilience, both inherent and adaptive, or endogenous and exogenous, will help bring the system back to normality. This means that the economy and society have both flexible inbuilt societal processes and enough resources, both endogenous and exogenous, to recover from the setback. The contrary case would be what we defined as a catastrophe in Chapter 2, i.e. a system in which institutional processes are so strongly surpassed by the disaster effects that resources, even if available, can no longer be managed endogenously, so exogenous aid and resources cannot re-ignite the system engines, but only support the helpless victims. A situation like this is very unlikely to occur from natural disasters.

A desirable network context after disasters

If disasters don't appear to have a negative effect on macroeconomic functionality, then what are the specific reasons for such a result? A desirable systemic context for indirect effects not to have negative consequences can be presented as follows. In the case of an economy undergoing a disaster, (i) if each household and firm face a wide network of possible markets for both their demands and supplies (domestic and foreign), (ii) if each household and firm are reasonably informed about such network by the market and society themselves, but especially as part of the public response, (iii) if households' and firms' switching to any alternative market in the network is not particularly onerous, which again can be due to development, but especially to public support, and (iv) if some credit and/or cash support as well as remittances are readily available and properly channelled, which is again an important role for the public sector, then it would be less likely that indirect disaster effects can significantly spread over the economy. If in addition, public sector information and facilitation for new investment opportunities associated with reconstruction are prompt and expedite, including owner-based reconstruction, then there will be little support for the existence of important indirect effects in the medium term, let alone in the longer term.

Foreign response can support all these conditions with funding, information and technical advice, which may speed up the outweighing of indirect effects, let alone their counteraction. This means that firms (and households) within and outside the disaster zone, which are or could be affected, can resort to these networks to keep doing their business and activities. This would be a desirable response framework and therefore one that should be supported by public policy, which may translate into usefully used deficits, debt and the like, but the economy as a whole will be unlikely to undergo productive and functionality failings due to the disaster. Although by design or default public policy normally gives some support to the above requirements, this is nonetheless a fertile ground for *ex-ante* and *ex-post* well-designed policy.

Public and foreign policies should tally with the country's networking development. That is, given a level of disaster localization, in countries that enjoy a well-developed interconnectedness, network-focused policy incentives might be enough for functional recovery; as such, these incentives will endogenously operate via regular economic inter-linkages. Contrariwise, in countries with very underdeveloped linkages, the systemic role of public and foreign policy should be to help put together otherwise isolated activities and households by creating linkages, e.g. via marketing infrastructures, financial support and information. This may help develop domestic networking, making both the macroeconomy more reactive and helping more effectively the weakest social strata. Lastly, in the case of countries with an intermediate network development, i.e. too weak to prevent endogenously the wider spreading of localized shocks, the affected localities are likely to fragment, so public and foreign policy should primarily aim at reinforcing such weak initial linkages, whether physically or institutionally. This is also likely to increase local future resilience. If this can be done, then domestic and international resources will also be supporting development and therefore be better used and less wasteful.

Based upon a well-known proposition by Kuznets (Thirlwall 2011), the above tallies with a variation of it from the disaster literature that suggests an inverted-U curve between disaster vulnerability and development, in connection with sub-Saharan droughts (Benson and Clay 1998). That is, vulnerability might be lower in poorly and highly developed countries, but higher in intermediate ones. This is also likely to be the case in terms of network development. Within it, we would like to suggest a complementary curve to that one, i.e. an *equal (or iso)-macroresilience curve* (Figure 6.1). This would be negatively sloped, like an *iso-quant*, with disaster localization on one axis and societal networking on the other, so that the higher the localization (i.e. the more economically confined the direct effects), the less developed the networking required to achieve a given level of resilience (systemic capacity to counteract the indirect effects of a disaster), and therefore to secure stable societal functionality.

It can be seen that if public policy can help network shifts, then for each level of localization, there will be more effective networking, meaning that the iso-resilience curve would jump outwards. Seen the other way round, for each level of networking, public policy will make the disaster more localized and therefore economic and social recovery less difficult. Given that intermediate levels in the curve are supposedly weaker, then public policy to reinforce networks might be of paramount importance in some cases.

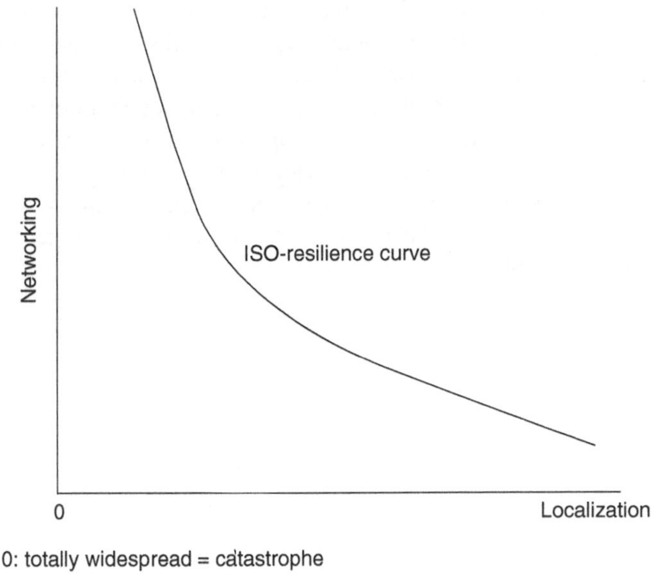

Figure 6.1 Iso-resilience curve.

Conclusion

Business networks are an essential part of community networks, but they have been scantily studied. Firms under disasters have been mostly studied for developed countries and normally more in terms of isolated units than in terms of their networked existence and dependencies with other firms, customers, the government and the community where they belong. Such studies show that size, sector, diversification, management and other characteristics do matter for both vulnerability to disasters and resilience to bring the firms back to stability and development. They also show that firms that fail do not do that right away, but after a struggle, and that those that were in precarious conditions before the disaster are likely to fail first after it. But that is normally compounded by the exogenous response, which may keep alive firms for longer than they would have survived otherwise, even without the disaster. More focused information and surveys about networked firms (and households as consumers) under disaster stress are required. Here is an important role for the government so that standard responses can be made more systemically consistent, especially via market networks.

Networks are a fundamental foundation of vulnerability reduction and enhanced resilience after disasters. Network shifts appear to be a normal reaction after disasters by both firms and people. We showed that in a macro context, a positive degree of substitution potential, which is actually exercised, whether stimulated by public policy or otherwise, is analytically bound to reduce the reconstruction investment required to keep the economy as if there were no disaster. This would make for a more efficient recovery of functionality and activity levels than it would have been otherwise. If this is so, then a role for public policy would be to tap such network shifting. This could be done intuitively, but it would be more useful if policy design relies upon actual and more detailed information about such network shifting behaviours and possibilities. We then suggest that standard post-disaster surveys should be enhanced with the aim of incorporating questions about such business network reactions, as we generally set up in our Appendix below.

7 Conclusions

The main rationale behind this work is that the social system is not an inert thing, but a living organism, which is endowed with systemic networks and reactive feedbacks that aim at self-preservation by keeping required balances and counteracting functionality losses in a sustainable fashion. Local disaster failures are then primarily tackled via inbuilt compensations, substitutions and circumventions, which are aimed at rehabilitating impaired productive and distributional functions by means of counterbalancing flows. These should be identified and tapped to help the design of public and international responses. In most cases, sudden disasters would not have serious consequences on the functionality of the macroeconomy, even if the directly affected locality was badly affected and still trying to recover a few years after the impact. The latter may be an indication of functionality bypassing, which responds to a permanent systemic tension between the local and the national, for which *ex-ante* and *ex-post* public response policy may play a systemic role to secure a minimal balance so that neither is the local economy exogenously sustained by public and foreign resources nor is the affected local economy fully insulated and bypassed by the national economy.

That is, two balances should be in the eye of public and foreign response policy: one between the local and the national and – a complementary one – between endogenous reactions and exogenous responses. The former should avoid that national insulation and bypassing sever local networks with the wider economy on a permanent basis, while the latter should avoid that exogenous public and foreign policy suffocates endogenous reactions in a systemically inconsistent way, which may force an unnecessary dependency by those units so affected.

We can all agree that disasters may have a serious negative effect on the directly affected localities and people, but this is not tantamount to concluding that they will have an equally serious effect on the national economy. Argumentations about negative disaster impacts on development can be entertained from seeming disaster response reallocations and substitutions of earmarked development projects and from increased deficit funding, but then if these make the system more resilient to future natural events, and in passing enhance economic linkages and strength functionality, then they are in themselves developmental.

Development is hardly a linear, harmonious and ever-enhancing journey, but a messy, complex, discontinuous and often brutal process.

The fact is that a disaster cannot have indirect flow effects on the wider economy if the potential for which is counteracted by the economy itself, i.e. a mix of inbuilt reactions and exogenous responses. And a disaster is highly unlikely to exhibit longer-term effects, let alone cumulative ones, if its potential indirect effects on the economy fade away in the short term. So the aim of this book is to show how societal networks, complemented with appropriate public response, especially at economic level, are likely to counteract potential indirect effects on the economy. Our main conclusions are as follows.

First, it is highly unlikely that quantitative methods will settle the issues about the importance of negative indirect effects on the economy in the medium to long run, let alone the issue of cumulative effects. Any quantitative study produces results that are assumption ridden. Assumptions on data sources enter assumptions on quantitative techniques, the results of which are then interpreted with assumption- and axiom (dogma)-dominated theoretical models. In the case of quantitative techniques applied to disasters, the assumptions cascading the numerical results are even more unreliable than in normal studies. Setting aside the poverty of data, on the one hand, black-box methods are not strong enough to capture sudden shocks like disasters, let alone if the shock fades away soon after the impact, as they misleadingly carry the first year effect forward. This in addition has the problem of securing a realistic interpretation, which more often than not is relegated to axiomatic theory with its plethora of convenient assumptions. On the other hand, simulation methods create models that already contain the interpretation of 'reality', normally, via mathematical features of standard economic theory, which is mounted on a bed of axioms and assumptions that depart from reality as a matter of both vested ideological interpretation and vested mathematical tractability fact. Not surprisingly their results are all over the place. They may even contribute to confusion and therefore misguided policy. So at best they should be taken with a good deal of scepticism and caution, which is not a reliable or useful way to understand disasters and policy design.

Second, given that disasters represent discontinuities and fast substitutions in a networked societal environment, typical of a living organism, then an argumentation founded in a general political economy framework may help advance knowledge and policy with more propriety. Partial quantitative studies can then be set within this framework to learn about these and other effects, as required. We then set up an analytical framework that contains our main approach. Within it, we introduced the concept of societal functionality and economic localization, showing that this is a key to understanding and analysing disaster effects in the context of socio-economic networks. Consequently, we introduced and contextualized our political economy approach by means of social and economic networks. This approach is essential to help assess the economic importance of longer-term and cumulative effects from disasters. We showed here the main difference between a local system that is network-isolated from a national set-up (a state of being) and one that is network-insulated by the national system (a societal response), showing that the latter is the one that matters in real societies. In this context, a conclusion from the literature is that, consistently with the preservation of society and therefore socio-economic institutions, individuals, households and business do not respond to disasters only to palliate physical adversity, but also to preserve both their livelihood and social status. This implies the preservation of community relationships, activities and dynamics within itself and with wider domestic linkages. This may help explain why organized endogenous reactions and responses by communities are so prominent in the aftermath of disasters, mostly acting with independence of external and exogenous responses and aid. Public policy, whether purposefully or otherwise, has normally acted on this area, but could act more consistently with systemic networks if they are brought to the fore when designing disaster response policies.

Third, as a general conclusion from our argumentation, we suggest that natural disaster effects are as a rule exogenous to the institutional workings of a system, which is the main reason why long-term, or for that matter cumulative, effects are unlikely to happen. Contrary to a complex emergency, or some technological disasters, it would not affect the institutional basis of a system's societal dynamics, but only the quality of such dynamics for a relatively short while, forcing some secondary structural change for as long as the physical set-up and conditions are not recovered and/or substituted. That is, institutional functionality will hardly be impaired, which is not the case in complex emergencies, which normally come from political conflict. Within this context, disasters may not only force reallocation of scarce public resources, but also unlock resources and conditions that were not available before the disasters, creating new business and policy opportunities associated both with disaster responses and longer-term development. In the overwhelming majority of natural disasters societal functionality is not impaired, except in the very short term. Systemic and exogenous responses depend on functionality recovery in a mutually reinforcing fashion. So the issue would mostly be about the speed and efficacy of functionality recovery, rather than on the fact of it.

Fourth, at an aggregate, macroeconomic and sectoral level, we showed why disasters are unlikely to have the medium- and long-term effects that are not only so commonly portrayed in the mass media, but also from more specialized quarters, and why the spectacularly photographed destruction of the early hours is likely to be counteracted, if not outweighed, at flow levels, in the short term. Here, we showed in the context of general networks and the concept of functionality why a disaster is unlikely to become a catastrophe, which was explicitly defined. We then showed via a macroeconomic argument and a simple model what was required to counteract the potential effects on GDP from capital stock losses to a disaster, concluding that the effort in terms of additional investment over normal investment-to-GDP was quite modest to secure it. We recalled some examples of major disasters that appear to confirm such a result, and many other examples are available in the literature. We then move from the single national aggregation towards sectoral disaggregation to show how the input–output economic interconnectedness or networking can help explain such an outcome. We differentiated these interrelationships into supra-networks, intra-networks and inter-networks, indicating that all of them interact with each other in an institutional or political economy context. We showed here how endogenous responses via buffer stocks, prices and network shifting can prevent negative disaster flow effects to spread over the economy, which associated with standard exogenous responses may render unwarranted the claim that indirect effects are important for the economy in the medium and the longer term, but also often in the short term. This emphasizes the importance of approaching response public policy in the context of networks.

Fifth, coupled with the argumentation via input–output networks, we called attention to the need to count with regional and sectoral statistics to anticipate the importance of large disasters on the economy via the concept of economic localization and its derived substitution potential. Interregional input–output tables, which are most useful in such cases, are rarely available for most countries, especially poorer ones. National account statistics, disaggregated regionally, are also useful and more available, but not everywhere. So we suggest that both development in general and disasters in particular would benefit with the production of such statistics in systematic ways. We analysed two cases of large disasters where some statistics were available for the task, the 2004 Indonesia tsunami and the 2010 Chile earthquake, and showed that it could have been anticipated, as it was from some sources, that it was highly unlikely that the disasters were to cause national negative economic effects of importance, especially in the medium, let alone the long, term. Both Indonesia and Chile more than substituted their potential negative flow effects over the first few months, ending up with a higher than expected GDP growth rate a year later. Not surprisingly either, neither case suffered important functionality losses and were growing strongly only a few months after the disaster. A good deal of this good result was due to exogenous domestic and foreign response, but the central role of endogenous market and non-market responses cannot be underestimated.

Sixth, endogenous reactions from businesses and communities are of paramount importance. The failure of exogenous responses, whether domestic or foreign, to tap them is bound to lead not only to short-term wastage and a catalogue of unnecessary insufficiencies, as shown in the case of the 2004 Asian tsunami, but also to long-term wasted opportunities for securing a recovery in terms of systemic consistency and functionality. We express the need that exogenous responses be in tune with the inbuilt reactions of people and markets, with a view of securing a systemically consistent recovery. In such context, we analytically presented the cases of cash transfers and in-kind aid, remittances and its infrastructure, shelter provision and migration, insurance and loans, and general systemic public policy. The aim was to show the importance of learning about people's reactions in disaster situations for public policy and in passing to show that networks and endogenous reactions are ubiquitous at all levels of societal action.

Seventh, after a disaster, there will be disaster unscathed market participants that cannot satisfy their needs, as they lost their regular sources, and there will also be directly affected participants that can no longer participate in the market, as they lost their means of participation. An important role for *ex-ante* and *ex-post* public response will be to facilitate the contact between frustrated economic participants and new or existing economic networks as well as speeding up the recovery of directly affected participants to prevent their market disenfranchising. Affected business and households will necessarily take the required initiative themselves to look for alternative markets and sources so as to come out from their predicament, but this can be facilitated and systemically orientated by public policy, supporting their endogenous reactions via information as well as incentives and disincentives associated with information, administrative links, specific funding and the like. Retaking our macro model of Chapter 4, we showed that in the presence of networks, if public policy can stimulate and speed up network shifting by affected economic participants, then recovery would be faster and more developmentally efficient, as the additional investment over normal investment-to-GDP to keep the economy as if there were no disaster is likely to be even smaller than it would be otherwise.

Eighth, the above should be done by paying attention to the balance between the local and the national while supporting market and non-market endogenous reactions. Network bypassing seems to be a normal state of affairs after disasters by both firms and people. Business networks are an essential part of community networks, but they have been scantily studied. Firms under disasters have been mostly studied for developed countries and normally more in terms of isolated units than in terms of their networked existence and mutual dependencies with other firms, customers, the government and the community where they belong. Such studies show that size, sector, diversification, management and other characteristics do matter for both vulnerability to disasters and resilience to bring the firms back to stability and development. They also show that firms that fail do not do that right away, but after a struggle, and that those that were in precarious conditions before the disaster are likely to fail first after it. But that is normally compounded by the exogenous response, which may keep alive firms for longer than they would have survived otherwise, even without the disaster. More focused information and surveys about networked firms (and households) under disaster stress are required. Here is an important role for the government so that standard responses can be made more systemically consistent, especially via market networks. To such an aim, we propose that the standard surveys that are carried out after disasters, by especially the government to assess damage and needs, which normally focus more on infrastructures and housing than on business, should be complemented with enquiries about networks and behaviour of affected businesses. This should be done with a common methodology, which means that an important role for international organizations comes to the fore, which should also usefully collate such surveys. We suggest how such surveys should be generally structured in the Appendix.

As a general conclusion, given a level of disaster localization, for countries that enjoy a well-developed networking, well-focused policy incentives might be enough for recovery. Contrariwise, when countries have very underdeveloped network linkages, the role of public policy should be to help put together otherwise isolated activities and households by creating linkages, e.g. via marketing infrastructures, pecuniary incentives, information and the like. This may help develop domestic and wider networking, making both the macroeconomy more reactive and help the weakest social strata more effectively. Lastly, in the case of intermediate network development, i.e. too weak to prevent endogenously the spreading of shocks, the affected localities may tend to fragment, so public and foreign policy should primarily aim at reinforcing such initial linkages, physically and/or institutionally.

Finally, we encapsulate in two sentences the main conclusions and thrust of this book. The main reason why disasters don't have longer, let alone cumulative effects, of note on the economy is because society is a living networked system with permanent functionality and feedbacks associated with inbuilt reactions from horizontal relationships as well as exogenous and endogenized routine responses from vertical linkages. After disasters, network shifting and reactions, by businesses and people, can in addition be systemically stimulated by public and foreign policy so that the recovery becomes faster, less costly and developmentally useful.

Appendix

Suggested surveys of networks after disasters

As indicated in the text, these types of surveys should be carried out by, or with the cooperation of, governments and multilateral international organizations, as they should be systematic, comparable and count with a minimum funding. That is, they should be applied every time, especially when there is a large disaster and be carried out with a common methodology, which allows for comparability across countries and disaster types, and not least they should count with a minimum commitment about both support and funding. This effort should help the recovery in question, both endogenously and exogenously, and gain useful information for both future disaster situations. If systematically carried out, these surveys should give information about countries with different development levels, and therefore networking development, which can then be analytically collated and properly used by international organizations, public policy and research.

At country level

Customarily, after each disaster, especially large ones, apart from human victimization, the government carries out a fast assessment of capital losses to especially infrastructures and housing, but a very scant one about affected private businesses. The latter assessment is often carried out by businesses associations themselves, like the standard national confederations of businesses and trade. Complementary to learning about businesses' conditions after a disaster, it is a missed opportunity not to carry out properly designed surveys to learn about businesses' vulnerability and resilience vis-à-vis existing and potential links and networks for both directly and indirectly affected firms and in passing households as customer bases. These types of surveys should be carried out on at least two occasions. First, immediately after the disaster as a general assessment, which should not imply a major additional cost, as it will be an extension of the standard assessment. Here appropriate university students can be invited and quickly trained for the purpose, among others. Second, they should be carried out for a key sample after the emergency is over and rehabilitation is mostly finished. This implies one or more follow-ups for this key sample from a few months to a few years after disaster day. This should cover firms and customers as follows:

1 Firms should be differentiated between directly affected, indirectly (and/or potentially) affected and not affected (but participating) in the recovery and reconstruction. This is where knowledge about existing business networks can be gained.
2 For the former two (directly and indirectly/potentially affected), in addition, there must be a distinction between firms that survived and those which did not (this is part of the role of the follow-ups). For the latter (not affected, but participating), there must be a control sampling of firms that were not affected and did not participate (this is to avoid attributing to the former something that can be common for all).
3 The sample should differentiate firms according to size (small, medium and large) by means of usual indicators, e.g. market share or market value or sales volume or number of employees or a mix of them all, and also according to sector, e.g. primary, secondary, tertiary and appropriate subdivisions within it.
4 For customers or households, *mutatis mutandis*, a similar effort would be required.
5 The follow-ups should be conducted via both interviews with the firms and households in the samples, and statistical analysis of hopefully disaggregated information at company level as well as information about public and foreign response, which should check the consistency of the answers coming from firms and households.
6 The survey should focus on the firm and the household (as customer) and look to answer key questions:
   - What happened to the normal links for input supply and final demand after the disaster?
   - What new input supply and final demand links, or sources and outlets for them, were created after the disaster?
   - What was the role played by foreign markets in terms of existing and new linkage?
   - What was the general role played by domestic markets, both within and outside the disaster zone?
   - Why did it happen that way?
   - What role did the public sector and foreign responses play in terms of funding and linkage support?
   - What was the situation of inventories, standard funding and savings during recovery?
   - What was the situation of management and labour during recovery?

That is, we are aiming to know how important the existing intra- and inter-networks and how determinant supra-networks were. In addition, as indicated above, appropriate control groups should be analysed to avoid attributing to the disaster features that were part of the economy anyway. If the latter was true, i.e. if effective supply and demand disaster-induced shifts were similar to those of the rest of the economy, then that would be another indication that a more sophisticated economy is in better *endogenous* conditions to absorb, if not outweigh, a local failure than it would have been otherwise.

A project like this might contribute to help answer whether indirect disaster effects on the macroeconomy are important in the medium term, let alone the long term. Even if there were no discernible functional effects at macro level, a good deal of indirect effects on industrial and household structure and dynamics, including financial implications, might be necessary for this to happen, i.e. this would represent a long-term effect in terms of structural and other institutional changes to secure stable functionality. That is, in the face of capital and other stock losses, for functionality to stay the same, some structural change will be required. The extent of it would depend much on development levels and the disaster interference with existing societal dynamics, including purposeful and incidental effects of the response.

This type of study would contribute to design public disaster policy *ex ante* and *ex post* to make more prompt and efficient the required disaster-induced structural change, giving priority to the national level of functionality without sacrificing the directly affected locality. This balanced priority seems necessary, because if the macroeconomy compensates or outweighs potential macroeconomic disaster effects on growth, employment, investment and other variables at macro level, then the required macro functionality, including resources and conditions, will be more available to help the directly affected communities than it would be otherwise. Of course, the latter would require political will and commitment.

At international level

On the basis of the surveys carried out by countries and supported by multilateral organizations, like the World Bank or the UNDP, at both international and academic levels, once the information has been properly collected and disseminated, this type of survey should help tackle some permanent issues. How important are long-term and cumulative effects on the macroeconomy and affected regions? How could an appropriate framework help improve response policy, improving recovery speed and reducing wastage? These studies should follow a similar structure as above, but in an international context. They should carry out assessments as follows:

- Multi-country studies for various disaster types and intensities, carried out generally immediately after the impact and with follow-ups between one and three years after the impact.
- Categorized into useful development levels, e.g. high, medium and low, and refinements.
- Using information on public and foreign response and funding and aggregate statistics about the disaster aftermath.

- Exploiting the information generated at country level about (i) firms' and households' networked reactions, including public support, (ii) differentiating between directly affected and indirectly affected, and between surviving firms and otherwise, (iii) differentiating by sector and size, (iv) analysing control sampling of fully unaffected firms and households, (v) differentiating between those that reacted to opportunities opened by severed supplies or demand, within and outside the disaster zone, and those that did not.

The above should help in learning about how important were the existing intra- and inter-networks and how determinant were supra-networks? As presented in Chapter 6, a desirable context for an efficient endogenously orientated disaster response toward networks would be if each household and firm:

- faced a wide network of possible markets for both their demands and supplies (domestic and foreign);
- were reasonably informed about it by the market itself, but especially as part of the public response;
- faced a not particularly onerous switching to any alternative market in the network, which again can be due to development, but especially by public support;
- had ready access to some credit and/or cash support;
- made sure that their transfer payments and remittances are properly (systemically) channelled, which can again be an important role for the public sector.

This desired context will not always be available, so public/foreign policy can target response in accordance to network development: stimulate (if well developed), reinforce (if weakly developed) and create (if absent). Then the information generated at country level can be analysed via cross-country panel assessments to help design policy systemically consistent for both the purpose of effective recovery and development itself.

In addition, as presented in Chapters 4 and 5, setting aside standard macro statistics, for an assessment of responses via networks, input–output tables, especially regional ones, when they are available in a timely fashion, is the most appropriate way to assess generally indirect potential disaster effects on the macroeconomy. From here, the estimation of appropriate substitution potential indexes (SP) and backward (Bw) and forward linkages (Fw) are likely to be the most useful predictors of potential indirect effects. So it would be also recommendable for statistical offices to produce regular interregional input–output tables.

Notes

1 The problem with quantitative studies

1 Proposing to conceptualize the measurement of capital losses by the discounted value of the services of the capital lost so as to avoid double counting, as the World Bank does strenuously in a report that acts also as a manual for policy makers (World Bank 2010: 57–60), is theoretically and empirically unwarranted. Such a way of measuring capital was fully debunked in the capital controversies and debates of the 1960s, as capital is not homogeneous, the interest/discount rate is not exogenous to capital and a real economy does not operate under perfect competition (Harcourt 1972; Kregel 1976; Cohen and Harcourt 2003). There is then little or nothing of double counting by calculating capital at the actual production cost or market price, as this value has little or nothing to do with the value of capital services. In addition, at an empirical level, setting aside the standard difficulty of picking a discount rate (e.g. for cost-benefit analysis), even if a homogeneous capital for a single firm could be calculated this way, then at macro level the same should be calculated for all the possible substitutions and networks shifts, which would not just be absurdly costly, but also close to impossible. A manual for policy makers, which is otherwise fair, should not introduce such inappropriate concepts if usefulness is to be maximized.

2 For example, the Chilean government did not ask for cooperation from the UN (particularly ECLAC) after its earthquake of February 2010, so ECLAC only produced an internal document based mostly upon mass media information (ECLAC 2010a, 2010b). The opposite happened in the case of the Haiti earthquake of January 2010.

3 To be sure, mathematics can *only* be considered neutral when it is kept at an abstract level, just as a gun can *only* be considered neutral when it is well kept in a drawer. The use of maths in social disciplines does require forcing fuzzy reality and aspects of it (e.g. individuals' behaviours, continuity, equilibrium, formal processes, capital, labor, etc.), which are ambiguous, heterogeneous, uncertain and changing, into clear-cut definitions, variables and functions. So, the only way to do this is by often forcing reality to behave in the service (and corset) of mathematics, rather than the other way round, by means of strong assumptions, whether they are stated or not.

4 The Great Recession, on the back of unproven mainstream academic theories that were ideologically proselytized and propagated by vested institutional actors via universities, research funding bodies, central banks, international institutions, employers' organizations, great financiers, politicians and their controlled or co-opted mass media should serve as a clear-cut cautionary reality check. So to paraphrase: 'beware of academic economists and powerful institutional actors bearing policy gifts'.

5 The Kuznets hypothesis proposes that income inequalities are lower for countries that are poor and those that are rich but high for those in the middle, i.e. fast GDP *per-capita* growth from underdeveloped settings will increase inequalities at first, but then it will reduce them, producing an inverted U or a hill. But this is not what is observed in reality

of single countries, nor in cross-sections when the large countries of Latin America are excluded, as it is the quality of development and not the fact of it that produces greater or fewer levels of inequality. For example, fast-growing South Korea has one of the lowest levels of inequality in the planet, while fast-growing Chile has one of the highest (World Bank Development Report 2012). The former developed via the so-called Asian model, while the latter via the so-called Washington Consensus model.

6 Take for example the case with the complacent and clearly wrong economic predictions that came just before the worst international economic crisis ever, i.e. the 2008 Great Recession. At the beginning of each year we normally have a collection of forecasters predicting the evolution of the economy over the year (see *The Economist* in January any year), which very rarely hit the right numbers when later checked with the actual ones for the year. Forecasters are so aware of this that after their first predictions they spend the rest of the year revising them! No wonder that economists have often been accused of not making predictions, but only excuses.

7 This is like saying that candidate A will win an election over candidate B by 0.1 percentage points of the votes *with a sampling error of 5 per cent*!

8 Take the case of Libya, which in his original paper had the strongest effect on his results. The fall in secondary enrolment has nothing to do with disaster presence, but with a 1980 policy that allows secondary students to move to vocational training (rather than dropping out), which by 2007 represented some 300,000 students (of a country of some six million people) (Otman and Karlberg 2007).

9 After I reviewed this paper calling attention to the Libyan case, he receptively removed it as an outlier together with four other cases. But not by observing the countries' policies, but 'through inspection of the residuals'. The problem therefore persists by neither having a vocational training variable nor investigating what was the actual domestic situation of the other countries for which the dropouts appear statistically significant and relatively large.

10 Just like trying to estimate potential output and the output gap, this is a cottage industry of speculation. In this paper, the author uses a Perpetual Inventory Method (PIM), which is based on gross capital formation series and a conventional depreciation to estimate capital stock levels had the disaster not happened. It would be generally acceptable to anticipate GDP levels via capital-output ratios, especially in the short- and medium-term. But if and only if capital idleness, capital and investment structure and labour patterns are controlled for, i.e. political situation, policy changes, international shocks and the like, which is not done here (see Albala-Bertrand 2007, 2010).

11 It would require another methodological study, yet again founded on a collection of strong assumptions, to assess which of these studies is the less statistically inaccurate, but then this belongs to the usage of econometrics in any case rather than disasters in particular.

12 There are also mathematical programming models, but these are less amenable as economy-wide simulations. They are more appropriate to engineering and efficient resource usage for rather simple empirical maximizing exercises than to the sectorally interactive macro effects from disasters (Dervis *et al.* 1982; Vaserstein 2003). Other types of studies are meant to be analytical rather than numerical, normally associated with two- or three-sector macroeconomic models. For example, Freeman *et al.* (2002) develop a variation of a two-gap macro model for some regions prone to floods and other localized disasters in some Latin American countries. This relies heavily upon fixed coefficients, an actuarial concept of losses and an inert conception of society, which are serious shortcomings. First, fixed coefficients would be a problem for any normal projection beyond three to five years, let alone in the case of a disaster shock. Second, the actuarial concept might be useful for isolated items, but certainly not for societal processes. And third, associated with the two previous points, the inert approach to society is even less tenable. So these may capture some elements of real disasters in the economy, but are insufficient for the task.

13 Of course, the imposition is already in the name of the technique: it is 'computable general equilibrium model', so equilibrium is assumed from the outset, as is the need to make computable such convergence to equilibrium. And this is the real problem with these models. The choice of processes, like production functions, expenditure systems, closure rules and the like, is done for their capacity to produce such convergence rather than their realism. That is to say mathematical tractability trumps realism, which is one of the reasons why CGE practitioners prefer neoclassical functions. The other reasons are argumentative ideological judgements. These are meant for the very long run, which would exclude sudden disaster as a matter of fact.

14 This is normally done by adjusting the model to a SAM by means of so-called calibration, i.e. forcing one or more residual variables or parameters to acquire quantitative values that are consistent with the SAM equilibrium. Notice also that the SAM contains a fixed parameter IO for intermediate requirements in its structure, which can be at odds with neoclassical functions.

15 CGE uses an indirect, non-probabilistic test called 'sensitivity analysis'. This seeks to assess the robustness of the model by varying certain key parameters and assessing how sensitive the model is to such perturbations. If from empirical and/or theoretical considerations an economy is supposed to be insensitive to such parameters and the CGE model is not, then the model would fail the test, and vice versa. So if within a range the model is insensitive to real expectations, then it will receive a seal of approval as a representative of the economy that it simulates. It can be seen that through such a method almost any model can be approved without representing 'reality', as all that is securing is model stability. The point is that such a type of robustness can be due to many factors that can have little or nothing to do with 'reality'. If both types of parameters are sensitive or otherwise, then what would the acceptable range be? This is a very unsatisfactory test for technical validation cum 'realism'.

16 Some authors have tried to give more realism to these models by being pluralistic to the type of economics behind the many sectors. For example, the agricultural sector is represented via neoclassical, well-behaved functions, while the industrial sector is approached via structuralist functions, which allow for unemployment and other inflexibilities. Imposing alternative closures rules, i.e. the equation that imposes the macro balance, which depends on the thought school behind the model, generate pretty different alternative results. This is why the neoclassical closure should be taken as a particular and not very realistic case (Dutt 1990; Thissen 1998). But by pluralizing the closing rules and functional behaviours, equilibrium convergence becomes extremely difficult, so ad hoc assumptions are introduced to force the system into compliance. Even if these models now have some features that are significantly more realistic than in standard neoclassical CGEs, this is still very much a tractable rather than realistic simulation model (Taylor 1990, 2011; Taylor and Arnim 2006).

17 CGEs are static or two or more stages 'dynamic'. Development is a messy, discontinuous and often unpredictable process, which a CGE cannot possibly capture. It only deals with some traits of an assumption-dominated system representing an ordered, continuous, predictable and tidy world.

18 Okuyama (2009) in a more disaggregated fashion and using data mostly from ECLAC, World Bank and regional banks data, rather than EM-DAT, attempts a similar exercise. But the procedure and conclusions bear similar insufficiencies as the one we report here.

19 Given that we have seen many absurd numbers about this comparison, I believe it seems necessary to clarify how this comparison should be made. The Richter scale is an open logarithmic scale on base 10, which means that each point in the scale represents ten times more energy released than the previous point. The Chile earthquake registered 8.8 degrees on that scale, while that of Haiti 7.0 degrees. This means that $\log x = 8.8$ in Chile implies that $x = 10^{8.8}$ and $\log y = 7.0$ in Haiti implies that $y = 10^7$, so $x/y = 10^{8.8}/10^7 = 630957344/10000000 = 63.09573$ or simply 63 times as much.

20 To take the case to an extreme, as substitutions are not allowed, then if a motorway is destroyed producers that use that road to deliver their intermediate inputs will not even consider using an alternative road, even if that road was only a few metres away from the affected one! More to the absurd, if the intermediate input that was delivered via this road was, say, bicycle seats, and this was the only road to deliver this item, then there will be as many less produced bicycles as undelivered seats. Seats cannot represent more than 5 per cent of the cost of a bicycle, but that does not mean that the bicycle production is to fall by 5 per cent. It will fall by 100 per cent!

21 Development is certainly more than growth of GDP (or income) *per capita*. It refers to low poverty levels and not least low income inequalities and other social disparities. Countries with relatively high income *per capita* can have deep inequalities (e.g. Chile) or pretty low levels of inequalities (e.g. South Korea), and so on. But income *per capita* is an indication of potential for development if constraining institutional structures can be overcome and political will is present for the task (Todaro 2003; Thirlwall 2011).

22 The well-focused bombing and destruction of logistic support lines in any war, e.g. of Japan and other combatant countries in the Second World War, aiming deliberately to upset utility networks, especially transport and electricity, had *mutatis mutandis* significantly less impact than the above hypothetical earthquakes. During the war, utilities were one way or another rehabilitated within days. Why can that not happen in peacetime?

2 A political economy framework: functionality, localization and networks

1 Once a disaster impact has occurred, three main types of effects ensue: direct (or stock) effects, indirect (or flow) effects and societal interfering (or institutional) effects. Direct effects have an impact on the quality and levels of human populations (injury and deaths) as well as on the quality and levels of physical and animal stocks (damage and destruction). In turn, indirect effects derive from the disarticulations caused by the direct effects, affecting the interrelations between physical structures and between people, which translate into failure of functioning flows of the economy, public activities, household conditions and the states of health and nutrition. For the economic system, direct effects mainly represent losses to the capital stock and labour, whereas indirect effects mainly represent losses to functioning flows, in terms of foregone production and income, savings and investment, productivity and efficiency and the like. In addition, there are some societal interfering effects from the impact and the response, which are bound to have some variable degree of intromission in normal society and economy, making the prevailing resources undergo some rationalization and redirection, affecting institutional patterns. In the case of natural disasters, this is mostly an incidental and short-lived effect of a disaster situation. For socially made disasters, like complex emergencies or technological hazards, the institutional effect is more all-embracing, as the triggering event, the proneness and vulnerability to breakdowns are themselves both institutionally based and due to institutional failure. Societal interference can be expressed in short-term changes in private savings and stocks, in shifting of supply and demand sources, in shifting of investment opportunities and credit sources, in public and trade deficits, in changes in inflation and relative prices, in changes in capital flows and remittances. But it can also be seen in terms of institutional changes, translating into fragmentation and politicization, technological changes and migration, corruption and speculation, and in the stimulation of less common long-term changes in economic and political structures (see Albala-Bertrand 1993).

2 See note 5 to Chapter 1.

3 This is also the case for technological disasters, but here the inducing phenomenon is also fully endogenous. This is associated with the institutional failure to master the

production, containment and use of risky technology. In turn, a socially/politically induced disaster impact, like riots, civil wars, wars and the like (i.e. 'complex humanitarian emergencies') is normally the result of a societal/institutional weakness that fails to accommodate competing identity groups. This is a fully endogenous phenomenon, inbuilt in social structure and dynamics. We generally exclude the latter two, as they have characteristics of their own, which are beyond this book (see Albala-Bertrand 2000a, 2000b).

4 These anticipatory (*ex-ante*) actions are costly technological and engineering measures that aim at inhibiting the event's primary energy or preventing its appearance, e.g. cloud seeding against droughts, pumping water into fault lines to control seismic stress, controlled triggering of landslides, destruction of pests at source to prevent their spreading, prediction techniques, etc. These actions are all fully exogenous, mostly experimental, and are unlikely to interfere with normal societal processes, as they are external to the standard functioning of society and the economy (Albala-Bertrand 1993; Kunreuther and Rose 2004: Vol. I, Part V).

5 These are exogenous anticipatory (*ex-ante*) engineering measures aimed at separating extreme events from vulnerable social settings so as to reduce the potential effects of their interaction, e.g. flood control dams, landslide retaining walls, flood bypass channels, embankments against floods, seawalls, tree lines against desertification, etc. These are costly endeavours, which may also affect the environment in not fully predictable ways, but they have proven to increase physical resilience, normally as part of the development process itself. So they are bound to create behaviour around confined areas, e.g. dams may rescue land for cultivation downstream, giving a sense of security and inviting people to work and live in floodplains, but they have failed on occasion with disastrous consequences (Burton *et al.* 1978; Goldsmith and Hilyard 1984; Albala-Bertrand 1993). We can also recall the failure of the levee in New Orleans in 2004, which created an unprecedented disaster in its wake. Preventive public policy has an important role by means of balancing the benefits of socio-economic activity with the potential costs of their possible failure. This requires a variety of assessment techniques that go well beyond cost-benefit analysis. The latter may not be fit for purpose via the often forced monetary values and rates of discount required for its analysis (Ackerman 2005; Zerbe and Bellas 2006).

6 These are anticipatory (*ex-ante*) sets of physical (engineering, technical) and societal (social, political, economic) actions and measures that seek to reduce the vulnerability of the main functions of the social system to disaster impacts, mitigating and hopefully preventing potential disaster effects on them. The two sets of measures are part and parcel of the ways in which the system operates, so measures on physical structure will normally impinge and be motivated by social structure and dynamics, and measures on the latter will have a bearing on physical structure, e.g. warning mechanisms and reactions, improvement of materials and design, technique change and absorption as well as insurance, emergency stockpiles, minimum entitlements, land use, remittances, etc. It must be then clear that public policy by means of its all-embracing supra-networks plays a fundamental role in facilitating these via physical and societal connections (Albala-Bertrand 1993).

7 This is an after-the-event (*ex-post*) compensatory or counteracting set of systemic actions and measures. Whether by design or incidentally, many measures that were introduced on the social system to tackle potential disasters unravel now to participate in the recovery from the impact, as such they are part of the endogenized response mechanisms. These responses aim at both containing the indirect (flow) effects from disarticulations and restoring the direct (stock) effects. Containment comprises all short-term emergency activities aimed at preventing further functioning deterioration from flows effects and at reinstating the framework for both functional recovery and longer-term reconstruction. In turn, restoration comprises all those responses aimed at bringing the system back to its original state by means of reconstruction activities. In

real situations, however, what the system seeks for itself is to re-establish its functional viability and output levels. This can and normally is achieved without full restoration, by means of substitutions, circumventions, priority shifts and other counteractions (Albala-Bertrand 1993).

8 For example, neoclassical macroeconomics with its methodologically unwarranted 'representative agent' rationalizes (i.e. 'explains') into its axiomatic theory almost any economic fact discovered by empirical researchers, but fails systematically to anticipate the existence of such facts. That largely departs from a proper scientific discipline (Keen 2011). How different from physics, which systematically anticipates the existence of facts that are later confirmed by empirical observation, e.g. the Higgs Boson. In a discussion paper, Sawyer (1995) wrote that the 'natural rate of unemployment', or its slightly more sophisticated cousin NAIRU (non-accelerating inflation rate of unemployment), was similar to black holes in physics. That is, a purely theoretical abstraction to help think about the world. He got it right about economics, but dead wrong about physics. Only a few years later, there was plenty of evidence about black holes, while economics is still debating whether NAIRU is a proper feature of reality! That is the difference between a proper science and a stream of economics that makes strenuous efforts to look like one.

9 The debate concerning the primacy of either *structure* or *agency* with regard to human behaviour has always been a central ontological issue in sociology, political science and the social disciplines. In this context, *agency* refers to the capacity of individuals to act independently and to make their own free choices, while structure refers to the patterned societal arrangements that enable or limit the choices and opportunities that individuals may have. The structure versus agency debate may therefore be understood as the tension between socialization and autonomy, which is part of the 'nature *versus* nurture' debate, i.e. the natural versus the social or institutional (see Giddens 2006).

10 Social capital is a sociological fuzzily defined concept, but for the same reason is hardly observable, let alone measurable. It has however made it into mainstream social disciplines, including economics, as a working general concept. Definitions vary, but somehow all include some common elements such as institutions, societal networks, organizations and the like. For example, Putnam *et al.* (1993: 78) defines it as 'features of social organization, such as trust, norms [or reciprocity], and networks [of civil engagement], that can improve the efficiency of society by facilitating coordinated actions'. The World Bank (2000: 32) defines it as 'the institutions, relationships, and norms that shape the quality and quantity of a society's social interactions'. In turn, Fukuyama (2002: 27) defines it as 'shared norms or values that promote social cooperation, instantiated in actual social relationships'. Whatever it can be, it is more a case of acknowledging its presence rather than establishing a workable measurement. Because of its blurred definitions, its lack of observable let alone measurement substance, its departure from the real societal issues of power and conflict, and the very fact that this is again something that has been present since the beginning of social theory, but greatly distorting such a theory, it has been strongly criticized as a useful concept (Fine 2008, 2010).

11 At this level, there could be the need to develop some targeted public exogenous reactions, associated with the requirements to avoid inward fragmentation toward primary groupings, including sectarian identity groups (e.g. religious, tribal or narrow political ones), so as to keep these relationships stable and effective for disaster recovery. So-called horizontal inequalities (Stewart 2008), e.g. between tribes, social groups and regions, which relate more closely to secondary relationships mediated by lopsided vertical relationships, are bound to come to the fore in disaster situations, if they are not the very cause of a politically induced disaster or complex emergency.

12 We use the term 'policy' in the sense of the exercise of the attributions of formal political power to achieve an aim. This is of course the most contentious area, as on

the one hand it musters most of the visible response resources, but on the other it may act as both distant and at cross-purposes with the local community. Policy-endogenized responses are different from ad hoc responses. The latter are typically responses that are planned and decided after the disaster impact, i.e. exogenous *ex-post* responses. They may come up to reinforce policy-endogenized responses, sometimes bypassing communities' own responses by considering them inert, helpless and confused (Rodriguez *et al.* 2006).

13 It is to be understood that not only ordinary individuals, but notably well-positioned ones are equally limited. For example, the US president cannot do whatever he would like, despite occupying one of the most powerful positions in the world. He is empowered by the presidential position, but he is institutionally constrained to act within its parameter, which is checked by a hopefully balanced legislature, a hopefully apolitical judicature, a hopefully independent press and hopefully democratic institutions. What is true for the president is *mutatis mutandis* even more true for ordinary individuals. Assuming that they are *individually* motivated, they cannot simply pick and choose without paying a social if not a legal price for doing so. Then the isolated individual motivation via axiomatic rationality holds little or no water. Apart from the fact that self-serving interest is just one of the many more important basic motivators, like passions, obsessions, emotions, most of social individuals' motivations are mounted on socialization via the conflict of socialized experience, participation and education, leading to ethical and moral preferences, political and ideological inclinations, sense of duty and belonging and the like. So a social being looks pretty different to the axiomatic *homo economicus*, i.e. the 'rational' maximizing individual of neoclassical economics.

14 Globalization is no unmitigated panacea. On the one hand, especially associated with unregulated capital flows, current globalization seems to engender bouts of instability and economic destruction, such as in Mexico 1994, South-East Asia 1997, Argentina 2001 and not least the Great Recession. And on the other, especially associated with fast trade integration, it seems to disenfranchise local communities, business and individuals at a faster pace than their ability to adapt, at least in the short and medium terms. The point is not to prevent this integration from happening, but to secure a smoother transition for those who are bound to be most affected. Not least important, international capital flows require definite and effective supervision and control, as their vagaries have produced significant havoc in otherwise stable economies. These are two important roles for foreign and public policy (Chang and Grabel 2004; Albala-Bertrand 2006a; Stiglitz 2006; Serra and Stiglitz 2008).

3 Networked reactions and public policy

1 Do not confuse endogenous with internal and exogenous with external, as internal actions can be exogenous and external actions endogenous. Endogenous and exogenous behaviours correspond to a *functional* categorization, while internal and external correspond to a *locational or geographic* categorization. That is why the use of the functional concept of *from below* and *from above*, for endogenous and exogenous, respectively, comes in handy to avoid confusion.

2 The flows recorded under unrequited transfers, in the balance of payment, would partly correspond to personal remittances. But unrequited transfers contain large amounts of bilateral and multilateral donations, which are different from purely personal (formal) remittances (e.g. IMF 2008). In addition, the breakdown is not always supplied by countries, and some countries do not report remittances, so estimates based on them are again tricky (Ratha *et al.* 2008).

3 The reason why poorer people are not prepared to innovate (e.g. use of dwarf seeds in agriculture) is not so much because they are traditionally impervious to change, but to the very real risk that innovation may go awry, when protection is not available. What

would be at stake would not just be a standard formal bankruptcy, but the precarious livelihood of innovators (Thirlwall 2011).

4 These views belong to Tom Corsellis, in interview with Joe Rowley on 4 September 2008 and can be found on the EWB-UK (Engineers without Borders-UK) webpage (www.ewb-uk.org/). Corsellis was at the time the project manager of the Camp Planning Project for EWB-UK and co-director of the Shelter Centre (an NGO with HQ in Switzerland that deals with shelter and housing in post-conflicts and disasters, and has a wealth of documentation about the issue). This project was originally scheduled to be completed by November 2008, but funding difficulties greatly delayed it.

5 We leave out political parties, not because they cannot play a useful role, as they often have, but because they are significantly more controversial than these other institutions, if only because of their short-term partisanship and need to recruit new members. Competition among political parties can create further conditions for societal fragmentation. This is less likely in the case of prominent religious institutions, in which proselytizing is a way of life, but not for the next election or the next rebellion, but for a longer perspective well beyond socio-political contingencies. Still, there have been reports of religious institutions being lopsided, if not sectarian, in the handling of aid, especially when these are associated with ruling class or caste political control.

4 The networked macroeconomy and disasters

1 Discontinuous trait of development normally happens when the capacity of societal absorption and tolerance to persistent stimuli is gradually over-reached, reaching a critical mass that produces a rather sudden qualitative (structural, institutional) change to re-accommodate the system. In extreme cases, this is the stuff of political revolutions, when both the existing institutional setting is not sufficiently flexible, becoming unable to accommodate increasing social tensions, and state repression is not enough to defuse the open challenge of a determined *avant-garde* that seeks major changes, which soon becomes popularly backed around a recruiting general concept, such as nationalism, democracy, freedom or the like. The current so-called Arab Spring is a good representative of this type, as was the dismembering of Yugoslavia after the collapse of the Soviet Union (Silber and Little 1996; Finlan 2004; Aswany 2011; Dabashi 2012). But this tension is a standard feature of socio-political life vis-à-vis the structure and dynamics of its economic base. This normally gives rise to political-ideological cleavages and conflict, which in democratic countries has the possibility of letting steam out via periodical changes of government that would normally engage in some smoothing policy adjustments. The result of this is what we would normally call development, i.e. a discontinuous, unequal and messy, if not vested and often ugly, process of addressing such tensions (Stiglitz 2002; Chang and Grabel 2004; Serra and Stiglitz 2008).

2 Notice that this short-term model is not meant to be static, but a variation in what we would like to call ad hoc dynamic, exogenously modifying the value of parameters or other traits and specifications, as the phenomenon studied is seen to change over time. That is, ad hoc solutions should not be relegated to a secondary place, as a disaster situation (impact and response) is more likely to represent behavioural discontinuities than smooth processes, even more so than in normal times. This model shows that disaster effects on capital stocks are heterogeneous, so initial average fixed parameters will not do for forecasting, and the response to disasters, whether endogenous or otherwise, is also likely to modify fixed parameters, at least in the short run. This also means that theoretical production functions, including so-called dynamic ones, will not do either. The institutional context of disasters and therefore of this model imposes strong qualitative changes that overrule any possibility of parameters stability in the short run. This is also the reason why standard dynamic economic models are unlikely to capture the short-term nature of these developments. So, based on solid evidence, our short-term model parameters are exogenously modified. In other words, development models

based upon standard axiomatic production functions are unlikely candidates for assessing this phenomenon, let alone differentials-based dynamic models, even in the long term. Economics is definitely not a hard science like physics. So attempts at capturing changing societal behavioural characteristics (parameters, functional forms, specifications and the like) with features endogenous to a mathematical model are at best academically interesting, but largely devoid of societal reality, and therefore not very useful for both understanding and policy design. In our opinion, the only way to capture such societal traits would be via an enlightened *adhocacy*. That is, one that responds to certain logical rules of exogenous incorporation into flexible models, based on both a proper political economy (institutional) framework and the observed reality. In other words, the mathematical model makes only sense within such specific context.

3 Immediately after the 2010 earthquake in Chile, private citizens set up an informal network of observers via the Internet, which grew very fast, to inform the population where exactly petrol stations and other basic-need shops were available by means of a street map of Santiago and other cities (*La Tercera*, 6/3/2010).

4 The main circumstances for a disaster impact to have strong indirect effects are: (1) high disaster loss, i.e. of capital stock or production or both; (2) high regional linkages between the disaster area and the rest of the economy, i.e. input linkages (high backward and/or forward linkages) and/or high income linkages; (3) high regional share (of the disaster area) in the overall economy, i.e. high input share and/or high income share; (4) high productivity of capital loss, i.e. high productive capacity per unit of capital loss; (5) weak inbuilt mechanisms, e.g. low levels of buffer stocks and credits, low levels of idle capacity and unemployment, weak potential of new suppliers, low levels of foreign trade, unresponsiveness to price adjustments, and lack of response initiative (inert system); and (6) highly elastic expectations downwards, i.e. any setback is considered as permanent, reinforcing downturns. For a disaster impact to have strong negative effects in the economy in the short to medium term, and probably in a longer term, the above conditions should hold simultaneously, which is highly improbable. As was put:

> If (2) holds, but not (3), the probable effect will be unimportant, even if (5) holds [the macroeconomy may bypass the local failure]. If (3) holds, but not (2), which is improbable except in enclaves [where it will be a systemically isolated productive failure, but may have financial repercussions], there could not be important wider transmissions, even if (1) holds. If (2) and (3) hold, it is unlikely that (5) holds, so wider effects cannot be significantly transmitted [the economy will endogenously tend to insulate itself for the local failure]. Lastly, if (1) and (2) or (1) and (3) hold, the external response assistance (domestic and foreign) will likely be larger, especially if the death toll is high [as it is well known].
>
> (Albala-Bertrand 1993: 129)

5 Regional disaggregation and two examples

1 Globalization can be and has been criticized on many grounds, but does play an important role in the development of countries' networking, at both domestic and foreign levels, playing in passing an important role in countries' resilience to natural disasters. Globalization is a societal process that widens and deepens the mutual interactions between the institutions and people of each country and the rest of the world. In particular, economic globalization refers to the institutions associated with the flows of traded goods and services, financial and direct capital, migrant labour and tourism, and economic information and ideas, within a global arena of cultural institutions and traits. In other words, globalization represents a fast extension of the traditional national and international networks that initially exist in a country. This extension has the particularity of affecting the traditional networks in both positive and negative ways, altering the patterns and structure of domestic networks as well

(Shaikh 2007; Stiglitz 2010). But it also diversifies macroeconomic linkages that can be of help in substituting for local failures in the case of disasters.

2 There are many good books and manuals about the use of both IO and IRIO tables, so we will not indulge in redundant appendixes about them (see Bulmer-Thomas 1982; Raa 2005; Oosterhaven and Stelder 2007; Resosudarmo and Nurdianto 2007; Eurostat 2008).

3 The IRIO tables, taken from Resosudarmo and Nurdianto (2007), were set up in terms of basic, not final, prices, which gives a more accurate picture of interrelations, although ratios in final prices do not differ significantly. On this basis, we carried all the matrix re-aggregations and calculations using the IRIOS software from Stelder *et al.* (2000).

4 The loss ratios normally reported are in terms of GDP (a flow variable) and not in terms of the capital (a stock variable) of the affected sectors, so there is no way to know the proportion that was actually affected, which must have been significantly lower than 100 per cent for Aceh's agriculture and fishing sectors, let alone for Sumatra as a whole.

5 After a long and highly repressive dictatorship that imposed an unfettered Washington Consensus model, i.e. unfettered free-market capitalism (1973–1990), the country has enjoyed democratic rule since then, which did not change the economic model, but only trimmed some of its excesses, resulting in a high reduction of the huge poverty levels inherited from the dictatorship, coupled with very high inequalities, inherited by the hardly changed economic model and its political custodians. From the viewpoint of GDP *per capita*, Chile is classified as an upper-middle income country (around US$16,000 in ppp), which made it into the OECD club a few years ago. It has relatively low levels of poverty with around 14 per cent of population under a poverty line (measured by a minimum basket of basic goods), but it has very high inequality levels (measured by the Gini coefficient and associated groupings). In 2009, it exhibited a Gini coefficient of 0.52, with the highest 20 per cent of population capturing 58 per cent of income, with the lowest 10 per cent capturing only 4 per cent of it, which makes its inequalities the 18th worse in the world (out of 176 countries) and, after taxes and transfers, the worse by far among OECD countries (World Bank 2011). The high inequalities, the unregulated and also the flimsily regulated systemic abuses from the free market, especially on education and health, have finally exploded into widespread unrest, challenging the current politico-economic system, which has opened a debate in a democratic fashion that may have important consequences for the way that power has been held and kept since democracy returned in 1990.

6 According to the Central Bank of Chile, the GDP growth rate was 6.1 per cent in 2010, but they changed the basis of calculation by using a new volume index, rather than the traditional constant price index, which is still used by INE (Banco Central 2012). Although we believe that the volume method might be more accurate, we will keep the Institute of National Statistics (INE 2011) measure, as it makes it comparable to national and regional series.

7 It actually grew by 3.4 per cent, although the most affected subsectors showed a fall of around 0.5 per cent, mostly due to the aquaculture of salmon, which was not affected by the disaster. In 2011, the manufacturing sector grew by 6.6 per cent (SOFOFA 2012).

8 It is to be noticed that this industry had been falling before and during the disaster year due to both the recession and a virus that affected aquaculture of salmon. Chile had become the main salmon exporter in the world, this industry representing the second most important export after copper (in which the country is the main export producer). The disaster and tsunami worsened an already bad situation in the directly affected areas.

9 Ten important firms of the wood and forestry sector, which represent some 52 per cent of total exports of this sector, belonged to the most affected region of Bío-Bío

(ECLAC 2010a, 2010b). Two main cellulose firms here were put out of activities for a couple of months, but started to recover afterwards (SOFOFA 2010, 2012).

10 These data come from the 2009 input–output tables for 111 sectors produced by the Central Bank of Chile (Banco Central 2012). The coefficient calculation for backward (Bw) and forward (Fw) linkages was done via the IRIOS software used for Indonesia (see note 3).

11 The normal sectoral substitution potential and the actual sectoral substitution potential of the directly affected capital, however, cannot be calculated. The former because no IRIO tables are available, while the latter because there are no available data for the actually affected capital in the many sectors of the disaster region, except for scattered and incomplete information. As indicated earlier, apart from estimation problems, general capital losses-to-GDP are not a good indicator for the purpose of assessing functionality.

References

Ackerman, F. (2005) 'Priceless Benefits, Costly Mistakes: What's Wrong With Cost-Benefit Analysis?' *Post-Autistic Economics Review*, 25, pp. 2–7.

Adams, L. and Winahyu, R. (2006) *Learning from Cash-based Responses to the Tsunami – Case Studies*, London: ODI.

Akita, T., Kurniawan, P.A. and Miyata, S. (2011) 'Structural Changes and Regional Income Inequality in Indonesia: A Bidimensional Decomposition Analysis', *Asian Economic Journal*, 25(1), pp. 55–77.

Alarcon, J., Heemst, J., Keuning, S., Ruijter, W. and Vos, R. (1990) *The Social Accounting Framework for Development*, Aldershot, UK: Avebury.

Albala-Bertrand, J.M. (1993) *The Political Economy of Large Natural Disasters*, Oxford: Clarendon Press.

Albala-Bertrand, J.M. (1999) 'Industrial Interdependence Change in Chile: 1960–1990: A Comparison with Taiwan and South Korea', *International Review of Applied Economics*, 13(2), pp. 161–92.

Albala-Bertrand, J.M. (2000a) 'Complex Emergencies versus Natural Disasters: An Analytical Comparison of Causes and Effects', *Oxford Development Studies*, 2, pp. 187–204.

Albala-Bertrand, J.M. (2000b) 'Responses to Complex Humanitarian Emergencies and Natural Disasters: An Analytical Comparison', *Third World Quarterly*, 2, pp. 215–27.

Albala-Bertrand, J.M. (2004/1993) 'Natural Disaster Situations and Growth: A Macroeconomic Model for Sudden Disaster Impacts', Selected for Critical Writings in Economics in H. Kunreuther and A. Rose (eds) (2004) *The Economics of Natural Hazards* (Volume II, pp. 453–70), Cheltenham, UK: Edward Elgar.

Albala-Bertrand, J.M. (2006a) 'Globalization and Localization: An Economic Approach', in H. Rodriguez, E. Quarantelli and R. Dynes, *Handbook of Disaster Research*, New York: Springer, pp. 147–67.

Albala-Bertrand, J.M. (2006b) 'Changes in Chile's Production Structure, 1986–1996: Output and Industrial Interdependence', *Cepal Review*, 88, pp. 159–72.

Albala-Bertrand, J.M. (2007) 'Relative Capital Shortage and Potential Output Constraint: A Gap Approach', *International Review of Applied Economics*, 21(2), pp. 321–52.

Albala-Bertrand, J.M. (2010) 'A Contribution to Estimate a Benchmark Capital Stock', *International Review of Applied Economics*, 24(6), pp. 633–64.

Albala-Bertrand, J.M. and Mamatzakis, E.C. (2004) 'The Impact of Infrastructures on the Productivity of the Chilean Economy', *Review of Development Economics*, 8(2), pp. 266–78.

Aldrich, D. (2011) 'The Externalities of Strong Social Capital: Post-Tsunami Recovery in Southeast India', *Journal of Civil Society*, 7(1), pp. 81–9.

Alesch, D.J. (2005) 'Complex Urban Systems and Extreme Events: Toward a Theory of Disaster Recovery', Peri Public Entity Risk Institute, University of Wisconsin–Green Bay, USA.

Alesch, D.J. and Holly, J.N. (1997) 'Small Business Failure, Survival, and Recovery: Lessons from the January 1994 Northridge Earthquake', in *Proceedings of the NEHRP Conference and Workshop on Research on the Northridge, California Earthquake of January 17, 1994* (pp. 48–55), Richmond, CA: California Universities for Research in Earthquake Engineering.

Alesch, D.J., Holly, J.N., Mittler, E. and Nagy, N. (2001) 'Organizations at Risk: What Happens when Small Businesses and Not-for-Profits Encounter Natural Disasters', *First Year Technical Report of the Small Organizations, Natural Hazards Project*, Center for Organizational Studies, University of Wisconsin– Green Bay. Fairfax, VA: Public Entity Risk Institute.

Alexander, R. (2006) 'Tsunami: Build Back Better: Mantra Aside, an Aid Gone Wrong Story? A Livelihood Sector Review', *Bangalore: Development Consultancy Group*, www.ideasint.org/Documents/Tsunami%20Aid.pdf.

ALNAP (2008) 'Responding to Earthquakes: Learning From Earthquake Relief and Recovery Operations', www.proventionconsortium.org www.alnap.org.

ALNAP (various years) *ALNAP Lesson Papers*, www.alnap.org/resources.aspx, accessed 22 August 2012.

Alvarez, R. and López, A.R. (2008) 'Trade Liberalization and Industry Dynamics: A Difference in Difference Approach', *Central Bank of Chile, Working Paper* No. 470.

Anderson, C.W., Santos, J. and Haimes, Y.Y. (2007) 'A Risk-based Input–Output Methodology for Measuring the Effects of the August 2003 Northeast Blackout', *Economic Systems Research*, 19(2), pp. 183–204.

Arias, D. and Covarrubias, K. (2006). 'Agricultural Insurance in Mesoamerica: An Opportunity for Deepening Rural Financial Markets', IDB, February.

Aschauer, D.A. (1989) 'Is Public Expenditure Productive?', *Journal of Monetary Economics*, 23, pp. 177–200.

Aswany, A.A. (2011) *On the State of Egypt: What Caused the Revolution*, Edinburgh: Canongate Books.

Auffret, P. (2003) 'High Consumption Volatility: The Impact of Natural Disasters', *World Bank, Working Paper* No. 2962.

Baez, J.E. and Santos, I.V. (2007) 'Children's Vulnerability to Weather Shocks: A Natural Disaster as a Natural Experiment', Mimeo, Syracuse University.

Bailey, S. (2008) 'Cash Transfers for Disaster Risk Reduction in Niger: A Feasibility Study', *Humanitarian Policy Group*, ODI.

Banco Central (2012) *Cuentas Nacionales 2008–2011*, Santiago: Banco Central de Chile.

Bank Dunia/World Bank (2005) 'Indonesia: Economic and Social Update', October, Jakarta: Bank Dunia.

Bank Dunia/World Bank (2007) 'Aceh Economic Update', November, Jakarta: Bank Dunia.

Barton, A. (1970) *Communities in Disaster. A Sociological Analysis of Collective Stress Situations*, Garden City, MI: Anchor Doubleday.

Beggs, J., Haines, V. and Hurlbert, J. (1996) 'Situational Contingencies Surrounding the Receipt of Informal Support', *Social Forces*, 75(1), pp. 201–22.

Below, R., Vos, F. and Guha-Sapir, D. (2010) 'Moving Towards Harmonization of Disaster Data: A Study of Six Countries', *CRED Working Paper* No. 272.

Benson, C. and Clay, E. (1998) 'The Impact of Drought on Sub-Saharan African Economies', *World Bank Technical Paper* No. 401.
Benson, C. and Clay, E. (2002). 'Bangladesh: Disaster and Public Finance', *Disaster Management Facility Working Paper Series* No. 3. Washington DC: World Bank.
Benson, C. and Clay, E. (2004) 'Understanding the Economic and Financial Impacts of Natural Disasters Disaster Risk', *World Bank Management Disaster Series* No. 4.
Bergmann, B. (2007) 'Needed: A New Empiricism', *The Economists' Voice*, 4(2).
Berke, P.R. and Beatley, T. (1997) *After the Hurricane: Linking Recovery to Sustainable Development in the Caribbean*, Baltimore, MD: The Johns Hopkins University Press.
Binder, A. and Witte, J.M. (2007) 'Business Engagement in Humanitarian Relief: Key Trends and Policy Implications', *Humanitarian Policy Group (HPG) Background Paper*, London: ODI.
Blanco, E.A., Fengler, W. and Ihsan, A. (2008) 'The Impact of the Tsunami and the Reconstruction Effort on Aceh's Economy', *World Bank*, Draft.
Bottomore, T.B. and Nisbet, R.A. (1979) *A History of Sociological Analysis*, New York: Heinemann Press.
Briguglio, L. (2004) 'Economic Vulnerability and Resilience: Concepts and Measurements', Malta: Commonwealth Secretariat and the University of Malta, University Gozo Centre.
Browne, M.J. and Hoyt, R.E. (2000) 'The Demand for Flood Insurance: Empirical Evidence', *Journal of Risk and Uncertainty*, 20(3), pp. 291–306.
Bruneau, M., Chang, S.E., Eguchi, R., Lee, G., O'Rourke, T., Reinhorn, A., Shinozuka, M., Tierney, K., Wallace, W. and von Winterfelt, D. (2003) 'A Framework to Quantitatively Assess and Enhance Seismic Resilience of Communities', *Earthquake Spectra*, 19, pp. 733–52.
Bulmer-Thomas, V. (1982) *Input-Output Analysis in Developing Countries*, New York: John Wiley.
Burton, I., Kates, R.W. and White, G.F. (1978) *The Environment as Hazard*, Oxford: Oxford University Press.
Carter, M.R. (2007) 'Poverty Traps and Natural Disasters in Ethiopia and Honduras', *World Development*, 35(5), pp. 835–56.
Cassidy, J. (2009) *How Markets Fall: The Logic of Economic Calamities*, London: Allen Lane.
Causton, A. and Saunders, G. (2006) 'Response to Shelter Needs in Post-Earthquake Pakistan: A Self-Help Approach', *Humanitarian Exchange*.
Cavallo, E. and Noy, I. (2010) 'The Economics of Natural Disasters: A Survey2', *IDB Working Paper* No. 124. Washington DC: Inter-American Development Bank.
Cavallo, E., Galiani, S., Noy, I. and Pantano, J. (2010) 'Catastrophic Natural Disasters and Economic Growth', Washington DC: Inter-American Development Bank.
CEPAL (2000) 'Informe De La Reunión de Expertos Sobre Remesas en México: Propuestas Para Su Optimización', LC/MEX/L.452 (SEM.115/2).
Chang, H.J. (2002) *Kicking Away the Ladder – Development Strategy in Historical Perspective*, London: Anthem Press.
Chang, H.J. and Grabel, I. (2004) *Reclaiming Development*, London: Zed Books.
Chang, S.E. (2001) 'Structural Change in Urban Economies: Recovery and Long–term Impacts in the 1995 Kobe Earthquake', *The Kokumin Keizai Zasshi Journal of Economics and Business Administration*, 183, pp. 47–66.
Charvériat, C. (2000) 'Natural Disasters in Latin America and the Caribbean: An Overview of Risk', *Inter-American Development Bank, Working Paper* No. 434.

Chu, K. (2007) 'Smaller Businesses Struggle to Recover from Katrina', *USA Today* www.usatoday.com/money/smallbusiness/2007–08–28-katrina-finances_N.htm, accessed 16 February 2010.

Ciaschini, M. (ed.) (1988) *Input-Output Analysis: Current Developments*, London: Chapman and Hall.

Clay, E., Barrow, C., Benson, C., Dempster, J., Kokelaar, P., Pillai, N. and Seaman, J. (1999) *An Evaluation of HMG's Response to the Montserrat Volcanic Emergency*, 2 vols, Evaluation Report EV635. London: DFID.

Clay, E., Bohn, L., Blanco de Armas, E., Kabambe, S. and Tchale, H. (2003) 'Malawi and Southern Africa: Climatic Variability and Economic Performance', *World Bank Disaster Management Facility*, Working Paper Series, No. 7.

Cohen, A.J. and Harcourt, G.C. (2003) 'Whatever Happened to the Cambridge Capital Theory Controversies?', *Journal of Economic Perspectives*, 17(1), pp. 199–214.

CORFO (2011) 'Programas de Reconstrucción', Gobierno de Chile, Ministerio de Economía.

Cosgrave, J. (2007) *Synthesis Report: Expanded Summary. Joint Evaluation of the International Response to the Indian Ocean Tsunami.* London: Tsunami Evaluation Coalition (TEC).

Crowe, A. (2012) *Disasters 2.0: The Application of Social Media Systems for Modern Emergency Management*, Boca Raton, FL: CRC Press.

Cuaresma, J.C. (2009) 'Natural Disasters and Human Capital Accumulation', World Bank, GFFDRR, *Policy Research Working Paper* No. 4862.

Cuaresma, J.C., Hlouskova, J. and Obersteiner, M. (2008) 'Natural Disasters as Creative Destruction?: Evidence from Developing Countries', *Economic Inquiry*, 46(2), pp. 214–26.

Cuny, F.C. (1983) *Disaster and Development*, Oxford: Oxford University Press.

Dabashi. H. (2012) *The Arab Spring: The End of Postcolonialism*, London: Zed Books.

Dahlhamer, J.M. and Tierney, K.J. (1998) 'Rebounding from Disruptive Events: Business Recovery Following the Northridge Earthquake', *Sociological Spectrum*, 18, pp. 121–41.

Davis, I. (1978) *Shelter After Disasters*, Oxford: Oxford Polytechnic Press.

Dawkins, R. (ed.) (2008) *The Oxford Book of Modern Science Writing*, Oxford: Oxford University Press.

De Mel, S., McKenzie, D. and Woodruff, C. (2008) 'Enterprise Recovery Following Natural Disasters', University of Peradeniya, World Bank and University of California, San Diego.

Dervis, K., Melo, J. and Robinson, S. (1982) *General Equilibrium Models for Development Policy*, Cambridge: Cambridge University Press.

Deshingkar, P. and Aheeyar, M.M.M. (2006) 'Remittances in Crisis: Sri Lanka after the Tsunami', *HPG Background Paper*, London: ODI.

Di John, J. (2008) 'Conceptualising the Causes and Consequences of Failed States: A Critical Review of the Literature', *SOAS Working Paper* No. 25.

Donaghy, K.P., Nazmiye Balta-Ozkan, N. and Hewings, G. (2007) 'Modeling Unexpected Events in Temporally Disaggregated Econometric Input–Output Models of Regional Economies', *Economic Systems Research*, 19(2), pp. 125–45.

Donovan, C., McGlinchy, M., Staatz, J. and Tschirley, D. (2005) 'Desk Review: Emergency Needs Assessment and the Impact of Food Aid on Local Markets', *World Food Programme*, Emergency Needs Assessment Branch.

Dornbusch, R., Fischer, S. and Startz, R. (2008) *Macroeconomics*, International Edition, Tenth Edition, Boston: McGraw-Hill.

Dutt, A.K. (1990) *Growth, Distribution and Uneven Development*, Cambridge: Cambridge University Press.
Dynes, R.R. (1970) *Organized Behavior in Disaster*, Lexington, MA: Heath Lexington Books.
Earthquake Emergency Recovery Project (2006) *Livelihood Support Cash Grant: Operational Manual*, Washington DC: World Bank.
ECLAC (2003) *Handbook for Estimating the Socio-economic and Environmental Effects of Disasters*, Chile: CEPAL.
ECLAC (2010a) *Terremoto en Chile. Una Primera Mirada al 10 de Marzo de 2010*, Santiago: Naciones Unidas, CEPAL.
ECLAC (2010b) *The Chilean Earthquake of 27 February 2010. An Overview*, Santiago: United Nations Publication, CEPAL.
Ellerman, D. (2003) 'Policy Research on Migration and Development', *World Bank Policy Research Working Paper* No. 3117.
EM-DAT website: www.emdat.be/source-entry, accessed 6 June 2012.
Eurostat (2008) *Eurostat Manual of Supply, Use and Input–Output Tables*, Luxembourg: Office for Official Publications of the European Communities.
Fagen, P. (2006) 'Remittances in Crises: A Haiti Case Study', *HPG Background Paper*, London: ODI.
Ferguson, R. (2006) 'Insurance Solutions for Emerging Markets', paper prepared for London Economic Forum, December 2006.
Ferreira, J., Dias, J. and Lopes, J.C. (2007) 'Complexity as Interdependence in Input–output Systems', *Environment and Planning*, 39, pp. 1770–82.
Ferris, E. (2008) 'Natural Disaster- and Conflict-Induced Displacement: Similarities, Differences and Inter-Connections', www.brookings.edu/speeches/2008/0327_displacement_ferris.aspx?emc=lm&m=214900&l=31&v=658612, accessed 23 November 2009.
Fideus, M. and Widyasanti, A.D. (2010) 'Indonesian Interprovincial Trade: What Can Be Revealed from a Gravity Modeling?', www.unescap.org/tid/artnet/mtg/gravity10_weds3.pdf.
Fine, B. (2008) 'Social Capital in Wonderland: The World Bank behind the Looking Glass', *Progress in Development Studies*, 8(3), pp. 261–9.
Fine, B. (2010) *Theories of Social Capital: Researchers Behaving Badly*, London: Pluto Press.
Finlan, A. (2004) *The Collapse of Yugoslavia 1991–1999*, London: Osprey Publishing.
Flint, M. and Goyder, H. (2006) *Funding the Tsunami Response*, London: Tsunami Evaluation Committee.
Fomby, T., Ikeda, Y. and Loayza, N. (2009) 'The Growth Aftermath of Natural Disasters', *Policy Research Working Paper* No. 5002, Washington DC: World Bank.
Fraccastoro, K.A. (2008) 'Entrepreneurial Recovery from Natural Disaster: A Consideration of Influential Factors', *Journal of Business & Economics Research*, 6(12).
Freedman, D.A. (2005) 'Statistical Models for Causation', University of California at Berkeley, Technical Report No. 651.
Freeman, P.K., Martin, L.A., Mechler, R. and Warner, K. (2002) 'Catastrophe and Development: Integrating Natural Catastrophes into Developing Planning', *Disaster Risk Management Working Papers Series* No. 4. Washington DC: World Bank.
Fukuyama, F. (2002) 'Social Capital and Development: The Coming Agenda', *SAIS Review*, XXII(8).
Galleguillos Jara, J.P. (2010) 'Informe de la Comisión Especial Investigadora del Estado

de la Institucionalidad en Relación a Su Capacidad de Respuesta Frente a Desastres Naturales', Septiembre, Comision de la Camara de Diputados de Chile.

Geipel, R. (1982) *Disaster and Reconstruction*, London: Allen & Unwin.

Giarini, O. (ed.) (1984) *The Geneva Papers on Risk and Insurance*, Geneva: The Geneva Association.

Giddens, A. (2006) *Sociology*, Fifth Edition, Cambridge: Polity Press.

Girard, C. and Peacock, W. (1997) 'Ethnicity and Segregation: Post-hurricane Relocation', in W. Peacock, B. Morrow and H. Gladwin (eds) *Hurricane Andrew: Ethnicity, Gender, and the Sociology of Disaster*, New York: Routledge, pp. 191–205.

Gobierno de Chile (2010) *Plan de Reconstrucción. Terremoto y Maremoto del 27 de Febrero de 2010*, Santiago: Gobierno.

Goldsmith, E. and Hilyard, N. (1984) 'The Social and Environmental Effects of Large Dams', Wadebridge Ecological Centre, Wadebridge, Cornwall.

Gordon, P., Richardson, H.W. and Davis, B. (1997) 'Transport-related Impacts of the Northridge Earthquake', *Journal of Transportation and Statistics*, 1, pp. 21–36.

Government of Pakistan (2006) 'Pakistan: Government Distributed Rs45 Billion in Quake-Hit Areas So Far', Islamabad: Government Publication.

Goyal, S. (2007) *Connections*, New Jersey: Princeton University Press.

Greenaway, D., Leybourne, S.J., Reed, G.V. and Whalley, J. (1993) *Applied General Equilibrium Modelling: Applications, Limitations and Future Development*, London: HMSO.

Guha-Sapir, D. and Below, R. (2002) *The Quality and Accuracy of Disaster Data. A Comparative Analyses of Three Global Data Sets*, WHO, Centre for Research on the Epidemiology of Disasters, University of Louvain, School of Medicine, Brussels, Belgium.

Hammond, L. (2008) 'Strategies of Invisibilization: How Ethiopia's Resettlement Programme Hides the Poorest of the Poor', *Journal of Refugee Studies*, 21(4), pp. 517–36.

Hanneman, R.A. and Riddle, M. (2005) *Introduction to Social Network Methods*, Riverside, CA: University of California, Riverside (published in digital form at http://faculty.ucr.edu/~hanneman/, accessed 9 September 2010).

Harcourt, G.C. (1972) *Some Cambridge Controversies in the Theory of Capital*, Cambridge: Cambridge University Press.

Hare, A.P. and Hare, J.R. (1997) *J. L. Moreno*, London: Sage Publications.

Harvey, P. (2007) 'Cash-Based Responses in Emergencies', London: ODI, HPG Report 24.

Harvey, P. and Lind, J. (2005) 'Dependency and Humanitarian Relief: A Critical Analysis', London: ODI, HPG Report 19.

Hausman, D.M. (1992) *The Inexact and Separate Science of Economics*, Cambridge: Cambridge University Press.

Heger, M., Julca, A. and Paddison, O. (2008) 'Analysing the Impact of Natural Hazards in Small Economies: The Caribbean Case', UNU/WIDER Research Paper 25.

Hendry, F.D. (2000) *Econometrics: Alchemy or Science?*, Oxford: Oxford University Press.

Hernández-Coss, R. and Bun, C.E. (2007) 'The UK–Nigeria Remittance Corridor Challenges of Embracing Formal Transfer Systems in a Dual Financial Environment', Washington DC: World Bank.

Hirschleifer, J. (1987) *Economic Behavior in Adversity*, Chicago: University of Chicago Press.

Hobsbawm, E. (1997) *On History*, New York: The New Press.

Hochrainer, S. (2009) 'Assessing the Macroeconomic Impacts of Natural Disasters – Are There Any?, *World Bank Policy Research Working Paper* No. 4968. Washington DC: The World Bank.
Hofmann, C.-A. (2005) *Cash Transfer Programmes in Afghanistan: A Review of Current Policy and Practice*, London: ODI, HPG.
Horwich, G. (2000) 'Economic Lessons of the Kobe Earthquake', *Economic Development and Cultural Change*, 48(3), pp. 521–42.
Hoskins, A. (2006) *Markets and Emergency Needs Assessments: Cairo Workshop*, World Food Programme: Emergency Needs Assessment Branch.
IMF (2005) 'Preliminary Assessment of the Macroeconomic Impact of The Tsunami Disaster on Affected Countries, and of Associated Financing Needs', Prepared by the IMF in Cooperation with the World Bank, 4 February. Washington DC: IMF.
IMF (2008) *World Economic Outlook*, Washington DC: IMF.
INACER (various years) *Indicador de Actividad Regional*, Santiago: Instituto National de Estadistícas.
Indonesia Relief (2005) '7 Trucks of Expired Tsunami Food Aid Destroyed', *Tsunami Relief New*, Banda Aceh: Indonesia Relief, www.indonesia-relief.org/mod2d7b-2.html, 20 December 2011.
INE (various years) *Análisis de Coyuntura*, Santiago: Instituto National de Estadistícas.
INE (various years) *Informe Económico Regional*, Santiago: Instituto National de Estadistícas.
Ingram, J.C., Franco, G., Rumbaitis-del Rio, C. and Khazai, B. (2006) 'Post-Disaster Recovery Dilemmas: Challenges in Balancing Short-Term and Long-Term Needs for Vulnerability Reduction', *Environmental Science and Policy*, 9, pp. 607–13.
Jackson, M.O. (2008) *Social and Economic Networks*, New Jersey: Princeton University Press.
Jacobsen, K. (2005) *The Economic Life of Refugees*, Bloomfield, CT: Kumarian Press.
Jaramillo, C. (2007) 'Natural Disasters and Growth: Evidence Using a Wide Panel of Countries', CEDE, Document Cede 2007–14.
Keen, S. (2011) *Debunking Economics: The Naked Emperor Dethroned?* Second Edition, London: Zed Books.
Keipi, K. and Tyson, J. (2002) 'Planning and Financial Protection to Survive Disasters', *IDB Sustainable Development Department Technical Papers Series*.
Kendra, M.J. and Wachtendorf, T. (2006) 'Community Innovation and Disasters', in H. Rodriguez, E. Quarantelli and R. Dynes, *Handbook of Disaster Research*, New York: Springer, pp. 316–34.
Kennedy, P. (2008) *A Guide to Econometrics*, Sixth Edition, Oxford: Blackwell Publishing.
Khan, F. (2006) 'The Response to the Earthquake in Pakistan: The View from the Federal Relief Commission', *Humanitarian Exchange*, 34.
Kilduff, M. and Tsai, W. (2003) *Social Networks and Organizations*, London: Sage Publications.
Kirman, A. (1992) 'Whom or What Does the Representative Individual Represent?' *The Journal of Economic Perspectives*, 6(2), pp. 117–36.
Kirman, A. (2010) 'The Economic Crisis Is a Crisis for Economic Theory', *CESifo Economic Studies*, 56(4), pp. 498–535.
Kirman, A. (2011) *Complex Economics: Individual and Collective Rationality*, The Graz Schumpeter Lectures, London: Routledge.
Kregel, J.A. (1976) *Theory of Capital, London:* The Macmillan Press.

Krugman, P. (2008) *The Return of Depression Economics and the Crisis of 2008*, London: Penguin.

Kunreuther, H. (1996) 'Mitigating Disaster Losses Through Insurance', *Journal of Risk and Uncertainty*, 12, pp. 171–87.

Kunreuther, H. and Pauly, M. (2004) 'Neglecting Disaster: Why Don't People Insure Against Large Losses?', *Journal of Risk and Uncertainty*, 28, pp. 5–21.

Kunreuther, H. and Rose, A. (eds) (2004) *The Economics of Natural Hazards*, Cheltenham, UK: Edward Elgar.

Kuznets, S. (1955) 'Economic Growth and Income Inequality', *American Economic Review*, 45(1).

Lateef, N.V. (1982) *Crisis in the Sahel: A Case Study in Development Cooperation*, Boulder, CO: Westview Press.

Leontief, W.W. (1953) *Studies in the Structure of the American Economy*, New York: Oxford University Press.

Levi-Strauss, C. (1963) *Structural Anthropology*, New York: Basic Books.

Ligon, E., Thomas, J.P. and Worrall, T. (2002) 'Informal Insurance Arrangements with Limited Commitment: Theory and Evidence from Village Economies', *The Review of Economic Studies*, 69(1), pp. 209–44.

Loayza, N., Olaberría E., Rigolini, J. and Christiansen, L. (2009) 'Natural Disasters and Growth: Going Beyond the Averages', *World Bank Policy Research Working Paper* No. 4980.

Lukes, S. (ed.) (1982) *Durkheim: The Rules of Sociological Method*, New York: The Free Press.

Marx, K. (1976) *Capital: A Critique of Political Economy*, London: Pelican.

McClelland, J.S. (1996) *A History of Western Political Thought*, London: Routledge.

Miamidian, E., Arnold, M., Burritt, K. and Jacquand, M. (2005) 'Surviving Disasters and Supporting Recovery: A Guidebook for Microfinance Institutions', World Bank, *Disaster Risk Management Working Paper Series* No. 10.

Miles, S.B. and Chang, S.E. (2003) *Urban Disaster Recovery: A Framework and Simulation Model*, Multidisciplinary Center for Earthquake Engineering Research, Technical Report No. MCEER-03–0005, Buffalo, NY.

Mileti, D. (1999) *Disasters by Design: A Reassessment of Natural Hazards in the United States*, Washington DC: Joseph Henry Press.

Miller, D.L. and Paulson, A. (2007) 'Risk Taking and the Quality of Informal Insurance: Gambling and Remittances in Thailand', Working Paper Series, WP-07–01, Federal Reserve Bank of Chicago.

Minski, H. (2008) *Stabilizing an Unstable Economy*, New York: McGraw-Hill.

Mitra-Khan, B.H. (2008) 'Debunking the Myths of Computable General Equilibrium Models', New York: Schwartz Center for Economic Policy Analysis, New School for Social Research.

Morris, S.S. and Wodon, Q. (2003) 'The Allocation of Natural Disaster Relief Funds: Hurricane Mitch in Honduras', *World Development*, 31(7), pp. 1279–89.

Murlidharan, T.L. and Shah, H.C. (2003) 'Economic Consequences of Catastrophes Triggered by Natural Hazards, *Blume*, Report: 143.

Nafziger, W. and Auvinen, Y. (2002) 'Economic Development, Inequality, War, and State Violence', *World Development*, 30(2).

Nafziger, E.W., Stewart, F. and Väyrynen, R. (eds) (2000) *War, Hunger, and Displacement: Volumes I and II*, Oxford: Oxford University Press.

Nakagawa, Y. and Shaw, R. (2004a) 'Social Capital and Disaster Recovery: A Comparative

Case Study of Kobe and Gujarat Earthquake', *13th World Conference on Earthquake Engineering*, Vancouver, BC, Canada, Paper No. 771.

Nakagawa, Y. and Shaw, R. (2004b) 'Social Capital: A Missing Link to Disaster Recovery', *International Journal of Mass Emergencies and Disasters*, 22(1), pp. 5–34.

Noy, I. (2009) 'The Macroeconomic Consequences of Disaster', *Journal of Development Economics*, 88(2), pp. 221–31.

Noy, I. and Nualsri, A. (2007) 'What Do Exogenous Shocks Tell us About Growth Theories?' *University of Hawaii Working Paper* No. 07-28.

Okuyama. Y. (ed.) (2007) 'Special Issue: Economic Modelling for Disaster Impact', *Economic Systems Research*, 19(2).

Okuyama, Y. (2009) 'Critical Review of Methodologies on Disaster Impact Estimation, Background Paper for Assessment on the Economics of Disaster Risk Reduction', The Global Facility for Disaster Reduction and Recovery (GFDRR), World Bank.

Okuyama, Y. and Sahin, S. (2009) 'Impact Estimation of Disasters: A Global Aggregate for 1960 to 2007', *World Bank Policy Research Working Paper* No. 4963.

Okuyama, Y., Hewings, G.J.D. and Sonis, M. (2004) 'Measuring Economic Impacts of Disasters: Interregional Input–Output Analysis Using Sequential Interindustry Model', in Y. Okuyama and S.E. Chang (eds) *Modeling Spatial and Economic Impacts of Disasters*, New York: Springer, pp. 77–101.

Oosterhaven, J. and Stelder, D. (2007) 'Regional and Interregional IO Analysis', The Netherlands: Department of Economics and Econometrics, Faculty of Economics and Business, University of Groningen.

Otman, W. and Kalberg, E. (2007) *The Libyan Economy*, New York: Springer.

Oxfam (2005) 'A Place to Stay, A Place to Live. Challenges In Providing Shelter in India, Indonesia And Sri Lanka, After The Tsunami', *Oxfam Briefing Note*, December.

Oxfam (2006) 'The Tsunami Two Years On: Land Rights in Aceh', *Oxfam Briefing Note*, November.

Özerdem, A. and Jacoby, T. (2006) *Disaster Management and Civil Society: Earthquake Relief in Japan, Turkey and India*, New Delhi: I.B. Tauris.

Pantoja, E. (2002) 'Microfinance and Disaster Risk Management. Experiences and Lessons Learned', World Bank: ProVention Consortium.

Peacock, W.G., Dash, N. and Zhang, Y. (2006) 'Shelter and Housing Recovery Following Disaster', in H. Rodriguez, E. Quarantelli and R. Dynes (eds), *The Handbook of Disaster Research*, New York: Springer, pp. 258–74.

Perrings, C. (2001) 'Resilience and Sustainability', in H. Folmer, H. Landis Gabel, S. Gerking and A. Rose (eds) *Frontiers of Environmental Economics*, Cheltenham, UK: Edward Elgar, pp. 319–41.

Perry, M. (1999) *Small Firms and Network Economies*, London: Routledge.

Prince, S.H. (1920) 'Catastrophe and Social Change', *Studies in History, Economics and Public Law*, 1(94).

Putnam, R. (2000) *Bowling Alone: The Collapse and Revival of American Community*, New York: Simon & Schuster.

Putnam, R.D., Leonardi, R. and Nanetti, R.Y. (1993) *Making Democracy Work: Civic Traditions in Modern Italy*, New Jersey: Princeton University Press.

Pyrenne, E. (1958) *A History of Europe From the End of the Roman World in the West to the Beginnings of the Western States*, New York: Doubleday.

Quarantelli, E.L. (ed.) (1978) *Disaster Theory and Research*, London: Sage Publications.

Raa, T.T. (2005) *The Economics of Input-Output Analysis*, Cambridge: Cambridge University Press.

Raddatz, C. (2009) 'The Wrath of God: Macroeconomic Costs of Natural Disasters', The World Bank, Development Research Group, *Macroeconomics and Growth Team, Policy Research Working Paper* No. 5039.

Raschky, P.A. (2008) 'Institutions and the Losses from Natural Disasters', *Natural Hazards and Earth System Sciences*, 8, pp. 627–34.

Rasmussen, T.N. (2004) 'Macroeconomic Implications of Natural Disasters in the Caribbean', *IMF Working Paper* No. 224.

Ratha, D. (2005) 'Workers Remittances: An Important and Stable Source of External Development Finance', in S.M. Maimbo and D. Ratha (eds), *Remittances: Development Impact and Future Prospects*, Washington DC: World Bank.

Ratha, D., Mohapatra, S. and Xu, Z. (2008) 'Outlook For Remittance Flows 2008–10: Growth Expected to Moderate Significantly, But Flows to Remain Resilient', *Migration and Development Brief* 8, World Bank, Washington DC. November.

Resosudarmo, B.P. and Nurdianto, D.A. (2007) *Fundamentals of an Input-Output Analysis with an Application to the 2005 Indonesian Inter-Regional Input-Output Table*, Indonesia: CSIRO.

Rodriguez, H., Quarantelli, E. and Dynes, R.R. (2006) *Handbook of Disaster Research*, New York: Springer.

Rose, A. and Liao, S. (2005) 'Modeling Regional Economic Resilience to Disaster: A Computable General Equilibrium Analysis of Water Service Disruptions', *Journal of Regional Science*, 45(1), pp. 75–112.

Rowley, K. (2008) 'The Role of Community Rebuilding Plan in the Hurricane Recovery', GulfGov Reports, Rockefeller Institute of Government, Retrieved from www.rockinst.org/disaster_recovery/.

Rubin, C. and Barbee, D. (1985) 'Disaster Recovery and Hazard Mitigation: Bridging the Intergovernmental Gap', in Emergency Management: A Challenge for Public Administration, *Public Administration Review*, 45, pp. 57–63.

Russell, B. (1991) *History of Western Philosophy*, London: Routledge.

Saldaña-Zorrilla, S.O. (2006) *Reducing Economic Vulnerability in Mexico: Natural Disasters, Foreign Trade and Agriculture*, Doctoral thesis, WU Vienna University of Economics and Business.

Saleh, N. (2010) *An Anatomy of the Financial Crisis: Blowing Tumbleweed*, London: Anthem Press.

Santos, I. (2008) 'How Do Households Manage the Effects of Natural Disasters? Empirical Evidence from Central America', Bruegel, Draft.

Savage, K. and Harvey, P. (eds) (2007) 'Remittances During Crises: Implications for humanitarian Response', London: ODI, HPG Report 25.

Savage, K. and Suleri, A. (2006) 'Remittances in Crises: A Case Study from Pakistan', *HPG Background Paper*, London: ODI.

Savage, K. and Umar, E. (2006) 'Independent Evaluation of Oxfam GB Malawi's Cash-Transfer Programme', London: ODI, HPG Report 22.

Save the Children (2005) *Rapid Livelihoods Assessment Report: The Impact of the Earthquake on Livelihoods in Muzaffarabad & Bagh Districts Azad Jammu & Kashmir Pakistan*, Save the Children.

Save the Children USA (2006) 'Update on Housing Reconstruction in Aceh, Indonesia', Save the Children.

Sawyer, M. (1995) 'New Keynesian Macroeconomics: A Critique of its Contribution', University of Leeds, School of Business and Economic Studies, *Discussion Paper Series* No. E95/12.

Scanlon, T.J. (1988) 'Winners and Losers: Some Thoughts About The Political Economy of Disasters', *International Journal of Mass Emergencies and Disasters*, 6(1), pp. 47–63.

Scanlon, T.J. (2007) 'A Perspective on North American Natural Disasters', in J.P. Stoltman, J. Lidstone and L.M. Dechano (eds) *International Perspectives on Natural Disasters: Occurrence, Mitigation, and Consequences*, The Netherlands: Kluwer Academic Publications, pp. 323–40.

Schubert, B. (2006) 'A Capital Based Income Generation Scheme for Tsunami Affected Households in Trincomalee District, Sri Lanka', ODI Feasibility Study for Save the Children.

Schwarze, R. and Wagner, G. (2007) 'The Political Economy of Natural Disaster Insurance: Lessons from the Failure of a Proposed Compulsory Insurance Scheme in Germany', *European Environment*, 17(6), pp. 403–15.

Serafini, A. (2001) *The Epic History of Biology*, London: Perseus Books Group.

Serra, N. and Stiglitz, J.E. (eds) (2008) *The Washington Consensus Reconsidered*, Oxford: Oxford University Press.

Shaikh, A. (2007) *Globalization and the Myths of Free Trade: History, Theory and Empirical Evidence*, New York: Routledge.

Shoven, J.B. and Whalley, J. (1992) *Applying General Equilibrium*, Cambridge: Cambridge University Press.

Silber, L. and Little, A. (1996) *The Death of Yugoslavia*, London: Penguin.

Silva Malig, M. (2011) Seremi de Economia. Region de Valparaiso, Hemeroteca, www.mauriciosilvamalig.cl/, accessed 10 July 2012.

Simmel, G. (1971) *On Individuality and Social Forms*, Chicago: University of Chicago Press.

Skidmore, M. and Toya, H. (2002) 'Do Natural Disasters Promote Long-run Growth?', *Economic Inquiry*, 40(4), pp. 664–87.

Skoufias, E. (2003) 'Economic Crises and Natural Disasters: Coping Strategies and Policy Implications', *World Development*, 31(7), pp. 1087–102.

Slater, R. and Mphale, M. (2008) 'Cash Transfers, Gender and Generational Relations: Evidence from a Pilot Project in Lesotho', London: ODI, HPG.

Smith, S.K. (1996) 'Demography of Disaster: Population Estimates after Hurricane Andrew', *Population Research and Policy Review*, 15, pp. 459–47.

Smith, S.K. and McCarty, C. (1996) 'Demographic Effects of Environmental Disasters: A Case Study of Hurricane Andrew', *Demography*, 33, pp. 265–75.

SOFOFA (2010) 'Evolución de los Principales Sectores Industriales Post Terremoto', Septiembre, Minuta, Departamento de Estudios.

SOFOFA (2012) *Informe Estadístico Mensual, Junio*, Santiago: SOFOFA.

Solimano, A. (2003) 'Remittances by Emigrants: Issues and Evidence', *Santiago: CEPAL, Serie Macroeconomía del Desarrollo*, No. 26.

Sorokin, P.A. (1942) *Man and Society in Calamity*, New York: Dutton.

Srinivasan, K. (2006) 'The State and Civil Society in Disaster Response Post-Tsunami Experiences in Tamil Nadu', *Journal of Social Work in Disability and Rehabilitation*, 5(3/4), pp. 57–80.

Stark, O. (1993) *The Migration of Labor*, Cambridge, MA: Blackwell.

Stelder, T.M., Oosterhaven, J. and Eding, G.J. (2000) *Interregional Input-Output Software. IRIOS 1.0 Manual*, The Netherlands: University of Groningen.

Stewart, F. (ed.) (2008) *Horizontal Inequalities and Conflict: Understanding Group Violence in Multiethnic Societies*, Basingstoke, UK: Palgrave Macmillan.

Stiglitz, J.E. (2002) *Globalisation and its Discontents*, London: Allen Lane–Penguin.

Stiglitz, J.E. (2006) *Making Globalization Work*, London: Blackwell.

Stiglitz, J.E. (2010) *Freefall: Free Markets and the Sinking of the Global Economy*, London: Allen Lane–Penguin.

Stoltman, J.P., Lidstone, J. and Dechano, L.M. (eds) (2007) *International Perspectives on Natural Disasters: Occurrence, Mitigation, and Consequences*, The Netherlands: Kluwer Academic Publications.

Szreter, S. and Woolcock, M. (2004) 'Health by Association? Social Capital, Social Theory, and the Political Economy of Public Health', *International Journal of Epidemiology*, 33(4), pp. 650–67.

Tata Institute of Social Sciences (2005) *The State and Civil Society in Disaster Response: An Analysis of Tamil Nadu Tsunami Experience*, Mumbai: Tata Institute.

Tata Institute of Social Sciences (2007) *Case Study Follow-ups 2 Years after the Tsunami*, Mumbai: Tata Institute.

Taylor, L. (1983) *Structuralist Macroeconomics*, New York: Basic Books.

Taylor, L. (ed.) (1990) *Socially Relevant Policy Analysis: Structuralist Computable General Equilibrium Models for the Developing World*, Cambridge, MA: MIT Press.

Taylor, L. (1994) 'Gap Models', *Journal of Development Economics*, 45, pp. 17–34.

Taylor, L. (2004) *Reconstructing Macroeconomics: Structuralist Proposals and Critiques of the Mainstream*, Cambridge, MA: Harvard University Press.

Taylor, L. (2011) 'CGE Applications in Development Economics', *SCEPA Working Paper* 2011–1.

Taylor, L. and Arnim, R. (2006) *Modelling the Impact of Trade Liberalisation: A Critique of Computable General Equilibrium Models*, Oxford: Oxfam International.

TEC (2006) *Tsunami Evaluation Coalition: Consolidated Lessons and Recommendations from the TEC Synthesis Report and TEC Thematic Evaluations*, London: Tsunami Evaluation Committee.

TEC (2007) *Tsunami Evaluation Coalition: Consolidated Lessons and Recommendations from the TEC Synthesis Report and TEC Thematic Evaluations*, London: Tsunami Evaluation Committee.

Telford, J. and Cosgrave, J. (2006) *Joint Evaluation of the International Response to the Indian Ocean Tsunami: Synthesis Report*, London: Tsunami Evaluation Coalition (TEC).

Theil, H. (1971) *Principles of Econometrics*, New York: John Wiley.

Thirlwall, A.P. (2011) *Economics of Development*, Ninth Edition, New York: Palgrave McMillan.

Thissen, M. (1998) 'A Classification of Empirical CGE Modelling', University of Groningen, *SOM Research Report* No. 99C01.

Thomas, J. (1992) *Informal Economic Activity*, London: LSE.

Tierney, K.J. (1997) 'Business Impacts of the Northridge Earthquake', *Journal of Contingencies and Crisis Management*, 5(2), pp. 87–97.

Tierney, K.J. (2006) 'Businesses and Disasters: Vulnerability, Impacts, and Recovery', in H. Rodriguez, E. Quarantelli and R. Dynes (eds) *Handbook of Disaster Research*, New York: Springer, pp. 275–96.

Tierney, K.J., Nigg, J.M. and Dahlhamer, J.M. (1996) 'The Impact of the 1993 Midwest Floods: Business Vulnerability and Disruption in Des Moines', in R.T. Sylves and W.L. Waugh, Jr. (eds), *Disaster Management in the US and Canada: The Politics, Policymaking, Administration and Analysis of Emergency Management*, Springfield, IL: Charles C. Thomas. pp. 214–33.

Todaro, M. (2003) *Economic Development in the Third World*, Eighth Edition, London: Longman.

Todaro, M.P. and Smith, C.S. (2006) *Economic Development*, Ninth Edition, London: Pearson Education.

Townsend, R. (1994) 'Risk and Insurance in Village India', *Econometrica*, 62, pp. 539–92.

Tschoegl, L., Below, R. and Guha-Sapir, D. (2006) 'An Analytical Review of Selected Data Sets on Natural Disasters and Impacts', Bangkok: UNDP/CRED (Workshop on Improving Compilation of Reliable Data on Disaster Occurrence and Impact).

Tsuchiya, S., Tatano, H. and Okada, N. (2007) 'Economic Loss Assessment due to Railroad and Highway Disruptions', *Economic Systems Research*, 19(2), pp. 147–62.

UK Remittance Working Group/DFID (2005) 'UK Remittance Market', www.dfid. gov. uk/pubs/files/uk-remittances-report.pdf, accessed 9 July 2012.

UNDP (2011) *Human Development Report*, New York: UNDP.

Varshney, A. (2001) 'Ethnic Conflict and Civil Society: India and Beyond', *World Politics*, 53(3), pp. 362–98.

Vaserstein, L.N. (2003) *Introduction to Linear Programming*, New Jersey: Prentice Hall.

Vigdor, J. (2008) 'The Economic Aftermath of Hurricane Katrina', *Journal of Economic Perspectives*, 22, pp. 135–38.

Walras, L. (2003/1954) *Elements of Pure Economics*, London: Routledge.

Warhurst, A. (2006a) 'Disaster Prevention: A Role for Business?' World Bank, ProVention Consortium.

Warhurst, A. (2006b) 'Logistics Companies and Asian Tsunami Relief', *Ethical Corporation Magazine*.

Wasserman, S. and Faust, K. (2009) *Social Network Analysis*, Cambridge: Cambridge University Press.

Webb, G.R., Tierney, K.J. and Dahlhamer, J.M. (2000) 'Businesses and Disasters: Empirical Patterns and Unanswered Questions', *Natural Hazards Review*, 1, 83–90.

Webb, G.R., Tierney, K.J. and Dahlhamer, J.M. (2002) 'Predicting Long-term Business Recovery from Disaster: A Comparison of the Loma Prieta Earthquake and Hurricane Andrew', *Environmental Hazards*, 4, 45–58.

Werker, E. (2007) 'Refugee Camp Economies', *Journal of Refugee Studies*, 20(3), pp. 461–80.

Wetterberg, A. (2004) *Crisis, Social Ties, and Household Welfare: Testing Social Capital Theory with Evidence from Indonesia*, Washington DC: World Bank.

WFP (2006) *Overview of the SENAC Project: Strengthening Emergency Needs Assessment Capacity*, Rome: World Food Program.

WFP-ODI (2005) *The Effects of Food Aid on Household Migration Patterns and Implications for Emergency Food Security Assessments*, London: ODI.

White, G.F. (ed.) (1974) *Natural Hazards: Local, National, Global*, Oxford: Oxford University Press.

Wooldridge, J.M. (2010) *Econometrics Analysis of Cross Section and Panel Data*, Second Edition, Cambridge, MA: MIT Press.

World Bank (2000) 'What is Social Capital?' from www.worldbank.org/poverty, accessed 15 April 2012.

World Bank (2001) 'Honduras: Poverty Diagnostic 2000', Report No. 20531-HO, Washington DC: World Bank.

World Bank (2002) *Migrants Capital for Small-Scale Infrastructure and Small Enterprise Development in Mexico*, Washington DC: World Bank.

World Bank (2006) *Global Economic Prospects: Economic Implications of Remittances and Migration*, Washington DC: World Bank.

World Bank (2007) *Aceh Public Expenditure Analysis, Spending for Reconstruction and Poverty Reduction*, Washington DC: World Bank.

World Bank (2009) *Aceh Growth Diagnostic*, Washington DC: World Bank.

World Bank (2010) *Natural Hazards, Un-Natural Disasters: The Economics of Effective Prevention*, Washington DC: World Bank and the UN.

World Bank (2011) *World Bank Development Report*, Washington DC: World Bank.

World Bank (2012) *World Bank Development Report*, Washington DC: World Bank.

World Bank-ADB-UN (2005) *Maldives Tsunami: Impact and Recovery*, Maldives: Joint Needs Assessment by World Bank-ADB-UN System.

World Conference on Disaster Reduction (2005) 'Hyogo Framework for Action 2005–2015: International Strategy for Disaster Reduction. Building the Resilience of Nations and Communities to Disasters', Kobe: www.unisdr.org/wcdr, accessed 3 December 2012.

Xiao, Yu and Nilawar, U. (2012) 'Winners and Losers: Analyzing Spatial Economic Demand Shift after Disasters', *Disasters*. Forthcoming.

Yamano, N., Kajitani, Y. and Shumuta, Y. (2007) 'Modeling the Regional Economic Loss of Natural Disasters: The Search for Economic Hotspots', *Economic Systems Research*, 19(2), pp. 163–81.

Zaman, A. (2010) 'Causal Relations via Econometrics', *International Econometrics Review*, 2(1), pp. 36–56.

Zaman, A. (2012) 'Methodological Mistakes and Econometric Consequences', *International Econometric Review*, 4(2), pp. 99–122.

Zerbe, R.O. and Bellas, A.S. (2006) *A Primer for Cost-Benefit Analysis*, Cheltenham, UK: Edward Elgar.

Zhang, Y., Lindell, M.K. and Prater, C.S. (2009) 'Vulnerability of Community Businesses to Environmental Disasters', *Disasters*, 33(1), pp. 38–57.

Index